WITHOUT WINGS THE WAY IS STEEP
THE AUTOBIOGRAPHY OF SYBIL SHEARER

Volume I
Within This Thicket
2006

FORTHCOMING

Volume II
The Midwest Inheritance

Volume III
Title not assigned

WITHIN THIS THICKET

WITHOUT WINGS
THE WAY IS STEEP

THE AUTOBIOGRAPHY OF SYBIL SHEARER

VOLUME I
WITHIN THIS THICKET

Morrison-Shearer Foundation
Northbrook, Illinois

Library of Congress Control Number: 2005932307

ISBN-10: 0-9769353-1-7
ISBN-13: 978-0-9769353-1-5

The paper in this book meets the guidelines
for permanence and durability of the Committee on Publication
Guidelines for Book Longevity of the Council on Library Resources.

Contents

Foreword

One of the great joys of this year has been reading the manuscript *Without Wings the Way Is Steep*.

This autobiography is written with the unique flair and wisdom of a creative spirit who went her own way, developing into one of the innovators of the 20th century. It is a compelling story, one of a butterfly solo dancer struggling to emerge from a chrysalis universe into the uncertain freedom of creativity. The book contains Shearer's letters; the responses to her are lost, which is the obverse of the usual pattern. They express a profound sense of "being different" and of being awakened from a slumber while at Skidmore College.

It is a lively account of the era of Martha Graham and Louis Horst, of Bennington and Perry-Mansfield, of the Neighborhood Playhouse and of Doris Humphrey, Agnes de Mille and John Martin. These letters are expressions of intense needs and of instincts, of Love and Will balanced in harmony, with a germ of innate confidence and a combination of the terror of appearing on stage together with the joy of dancing. There is, too, the description of times of injury, touring, and apprenticeship, periods common to all emerging artists.

For audience members or artists, Sybil Shearer articulates thoughts and observations which readers are only beginning to reach. Probably, readers who are younger than seniors in college will not grasp the depth of artistic growth being described. For a reader who is in the "dance community," as a creator, performer or observer, thoughts like this one will reverberate: "I certainly hope you can love me without being possessive, because my love for the dance, which is so great, will be a constant annoyance to you if you cannot." The "nets" of ballet and marriage were "surface forms" which Sybil Shearer was not ready to face. Her book is timely for today's society, especially teachers, and it is essential reading for young performers or for anyone who ever was one.

The Morrison-Shearer Foundation was a partnership of two artists, in fact two women, photographer Helen Morrison and dancer Sybil Shearer, supporting the tradition of the solo concert artist. The introduction to the autobiography should be read by every artist, as it pertains to the discipline necessary to art.

Madeleine M. Nichols
Curator, Dance Collection
The New York Public Library for the Performing Arts
September 29, 1997

Acknowledgments

All of these letters were written by me in books before sending them, so they have been in my possession for many years; a few letters included here were sent to me. However, I want to thank all these people in my past—most of whom, perhaps all of whom, are deceased—for their friendship and help.

As for those in the present I particularly wish to thank Masao Yoshimasu, trustee of the Morrison-Shearer Foundation and Museum, for the enormous job of reading my handwriting and placing these letters into the computer.

James Cunningham, another of our trustees, has been invaluable in helping with all kinds of computer problems and purchases. Mary Sue Wheeler, also a trustee, and Bob Knight helped to transfer us from an old IBM to a new Macintosh. All of these people have been wonderful friends to me. I could never have brought my past to light without their help.

I am especially grateful to Marjorie Spock for reading the first draft of this book and letting me see my life through her eyes; to Tain Balfour who was my second reader; to Margery J. Turner who gave me excellent advice on editing and publishing; and to Carol Doty who spurred me to write about myself in the first place and has encouraged me to write more.

Introduction

Those of us who need an audience have to make one. But what is the reason one needs an audience? It seems to me either you have discovered something that you enthusiastically want to share, or you feel it important to share because you think it might be beneficial for people to experience, whether they recognize its worth or not. Or, on the other hand, you need to be comforted or admired by the attention of others. The performer knows both of these emotions, and in either category it is a matter of the degree of intensity or of maturity as to which will have the most lasting effect on the evolution of the earth, and the development of mankind.

The duality of giving and holding back on the part of the artist is difficult to understand because it is exaggerated beyond everyday life in both directions. The artist is characterized as being the most selfish and at the same time the most selfless person, depending on the sympathy and understanding of the audience—the audience being one person or the public at large. The truly selfless person has to be conscious of this duality and learn to regulate his life according to his capabilities, so that *through* his consciousness he is able to grow.

During my life I feel I have held back more than I have given, but when I have given I have done so completely. A performance for me was a complete emptying out, and after each one I had to have time to recuperate. I needed to withdraw between performances in order that I would have the full amount to give the next time. Since my medium was basically physical, taking the complete use of my body, and since giving a performance was also a spiritual act, taking the full use of my unseen powers, I was actually afraid—and for my immediate state of development in this life probably rightly so—afraid of giving myself completely to one other person. Right or wrong this was my life and, according to the written word of professionals and nonprofessionals alike, many experienced the power that this way of life gave me.

As the manager Harry Zelzer said when asked, why doesn't she perform more often? "I don't know, I don't know, but she filled the Arie Crown Theatre at 20 below zero." It is interesting that so far I have not been emptied out by life. This balance of emptying out and filling up again has stood me in good stead so that I not only still feel like giving, but actually can give, to the world in general and certain individuals in particular.

Reincarnation has always made sense to me because reincarnation seemed to be what happened after every emptying. The next day after a performance I invariably felt the seed of the new beginning. Often a new dance or a new performance would start to germinate. Death then seemed only an illusion; renewal was the actuality. This new life I felt could be not only a new dance, but a new self as well. Since this new self grows stronger after each virtual death, it is logical that this phenomenon has been happening on a larger scale throughout the ages and will continue into the distant future—a force of renewal that physical cataclysms have no power to stop.

I feel that finding this balance after so much intense swinging back and forth in my youth is my contribution not just to my own life but to the whole of human evolution, even though this contribution is mostly hidden from view. By voicing this now through all these words expended in the past, I hope this residue of my life may somehow contribute to and benefit a larger audience than I was able to reach through my art as a dancer.

This swinging back and forth from selflessness to selfishness to selflessness, and so on, is the process of growth and decay, and it seems as though the artist is the prime public example of this process.

What I found particularly interesting when I reread my letters is that I wrote to so many different people and that all those who were older, and most of them were, wanted to help me. Their letters do not exist for the most part; either they never existed or they are lost. But my ecstasies and anguishes, thoughts, opinions, philosophies and experiences fill pages, and reach out to people who were then caught up in my need to create and to express myself. What I remember about these people is not just how they looked and felt as individuals, but the underlying urge they had to help my desires and talents to blossom, each in his or her own way. They made a colorful pattern of humanness from which I could learn. Perhaps no one else needed them as much as I did. There was a bond between us. No matter what their thoughts might have been as far as the dance was concerned, they were nevertheless sympathetic to my intensities.

I remember when Doris Humphrey said to me, "What would you say if a student asked you if she had talent?" My answer was, "If she had to ask, she probably didn't have any." I was, of course, convinced that I *did* have talent. My question always was—and I was usually asking myself—how can I best *develop* my talent? I was pleased that so many people were interested to help. And, in a sense, I also thought that I was helping them. Although I was a soloist and a loner by nature, I was also instinctively strong in my feelings about connections, sympathies, cooperation, and love. This was a conscious ideal as well. Every nuance of feeling, positive or negative, was examined with magnifying intensity. Through the years I have discovered love and will to be even more powerful forces than I thought they were then. But now they are balanced by harmony.

When I was in high school my second-year English teacher was Miss Irene B. Quiri. I thought she was awful. She wore high-laced shoes at least 25 years after they were out of fashion. I wondered where she ever found them. She also wore a pince-nez. We thought the "B" in her name stood for Boss because she was also the drama coach and had a commanding voice. All my critical faculties bristled at the very thought of her.

Then one night I had a dream in which she confronted me, and said, "You don't like me." It was shockingly real, and the next day in class there she was wearing the same dress she wore in the dream—a maroon wool jersey with maroon flowers embroidered all over it, and a white stand-up collar and cuffs. I suddenly saw her in a different light. The high shoes and the pince-nez, the dress, her olive skin, and her black hair pulled tightly down over her ears with a bun in the back didn't seem so terrible. She was certainly different; perhaps you might call her an original. But more than that she had the courage to wear those shoes!

I started to watch her. Perhaps she was someone from another realm placed in our school for a reason.

I decided to try out for the speaking contest. Although I was terrified by the idea, I was not about to fail, and besides I wanted to impress her. So I chose a very dramatic old Victorian poem called, "Lord Ullen's Daughter," in which the daughter of a Scottish lord was escaping across the river with her lover from another clan, her irate father in pursuit.

It was a success. Everyone was impressed, especially because I hardly ever opened my mouth even to answer questions in class—any class. I was the observer building up material for later, I suppose. So I won the audition, but came in second in the contest; I was only a sophomore. However, next there was a play, and I had a chance to watch Irene B. Quiri at work with a group. My admiration increased. She had talent, something I had, too. I wanted the world to know about her.

Earlier I had learned to compost, and now I wanted to plant the seed. I wrote to Sir James Barrie, the author of *Peter Pan*, and asked him to write a play for us. That I thought would surely launch Miss Quiri into the big world, and as I was going there anyway she too would be able to leave this little high school in Upper New York State. Barrie never replied.

Later Miss Quiri told me that I had so upset her, telling her about her duty to humanity and the arts, that she sought advice and was told to stay where she was. So she sank back in relief, and ended her life in the same place years later.

But for me this was not the end. It was the beginning of a life of composting and planting for myself and for others: students, audiences, friends old and young, most of whose gardens did not flourish like mine. Perhaps seeds will come up in later incarnations. I am quite confident that the desire and will I have shown in this lifetime developed over millennia. I feel it is important to ask questions and to act on the answers. But so often I gave answers without being asked. My frustrations were being able to see talents that were not ready to blossom, and my gift, the ability to appreciate and admire what did bloom both in myself and others.

This chronicle of my life consists mostly of letters because I needed an audience. Just writing a journal never interested me.

First let me say, dance was my medium right from the beginning, although any kind of creativity and imagination from mud pies on up interested me. At age two or three when Mama would play the piano, I loved to dance around the living room, always conscious of unseen forces that I called fairies. In the nearby wooded garden of a neighbor, I said to my little friend, "Watch me fly," and I sailed over a large steppingstone. Running home to tell Mama the news, I pulled out my doll trunk, one-fifth the size of the stone, but I couldn't fly over it. This put me in two worlds forever afterward. As I had instinctively flown, I instinctively knew I would have to physically work to do so again.

At age four I was taken to dancing school—ballroom dancing—girls and boys all dressed up. For the first nine lessons I was too shy to participate. Then on a threat from Mama that we would not return for the second term if I did not join the others, I finally stepped into the group on the tenth lesson. I remember the feeling of terror that later recurred with every performance for the rest of my life, and the feeling of joy when I actually began to dance.

When I was age ten or eleven Mama took me to see Anna Pavlova. I was simply carried away! After the performance I ran up to an usher and said, "Where is she? I want to see her." He said, "Stage door, around the block, Miss, at the back of the theatre." I ran with the aid of what seemed like a tailwind, Mama panting behind. I had to wait, and then Pavlova came out. She was tiny, almost as small as I. We looked at each other. She signed my program. I had fallen in love with her, with the dance, with the theatre.

That same season we went to Toronto, and my Uncle Frank bought seats for her performance there. I wrote reminding Pavlova that we had met in New York, and said, "If you will look at me I shall wave." At the last curtain call she did look, and waving back I called out, "Mama, she sees me, she sees me!" The power of that encounter with the future will never be forgotten by me. A few years later, a freshman in college, I wrote to myself, January 23, 1931:

Tonight is one of sorrow. Pavlova is dead! One of my highest ideals is gone, and the earth is robbed of its greatest dancer, the most wonderful, in fact, that it is possible to have. I loved her, I still love her!

I saw her in flesh and blood, I saw her dance! Her smile still haunts me, dazzling me, as she looked at Row J where I sat in Massey Hall in Toronto. I can hardly realize that my opportunity to meet her has passed. It really passed when I neglected to write to her when I was in London. But it has gone, and it is just another terrible lesson to me. The main point is, however, that she died young when she was still able to dance. Surely, that is for the best, because how could that fairy ever bear to be old and decrepit? I am glad, but I am inexpressibly sorry.

As a sophomore the following year, May 19, 1932, I wrote to myself again:

The dancer should meet his audience through an outside force. The dancer does not belong to the audience, nor the audience to him; they both, however, belong to the spirit of the dance, or they would not both be in the same building. The great spirit stands aloof and absorbs and delivers emotions.

A year later as a junior, February 22, 1933, I expressed my philosophy of life to a hometown friend:

My Dear Jean,

Your greeting has just arrived and I thank you for your thoughtfulness, but whatever made you think it is my birthday I am at a loss to know.

As far as I know the only exact date set for my birthday is a minus May first and a plus April 30. However, do not mistake me, I do not mean I was born April 31 for there is no such date. I mean that point outside of space and time at which one is happiest not with life but at life.

I should hate to limit myself to any time of the year, for I cannot think of a single time at which I started to be born, or anytime at all when I am not still being born.

My stone is the amethyst, my flower the pink, my color rose, all more or less alike as you see, but not limited to seasons, for the eternal idea always remains the same.

Therefore, in truth, if you wish to celebrate my birthday, you will have to send me greetings, not only every day of the year, but every hour, every minute, every second, and I should hate to put anyone to such trouble. The only other alternative I can think of is no card at all. But do not, Jean, think that I cannot appreciate your friendship. I am glad you thought of me; I often think of you, but as to thinking of my birthday that is one of the peculiar conventions of life which I have never been able to understand.

Forgive me, Jean, if you do not like this letter for I shall very shortly write you some news to make up for it.

Six months later, just before my senior year, August 20, 1933, I wrote, again to myself:

My Dear Unknown,

I hate a day like this in late summer when memories crowd into my line of thought and make a few years seem like an eternity. I am sad and dissatisfied, but not more so than you. Or perhaps you have taken on new life and are working with spirit. Sunday, though, is a bad day to think on and remain happy.

If you are like Byron you won't have many regrets. For your sake I hope you are. Yet Byron was a brute, and for my sake I hope you are not.

Today we spun over country roads leaving whirls of yellow dust behind us. The shadows on the trees were jagged, so that only some sun struck the leaves on the outskirts of the woods. The houses looked deserted, and the few farmers that sat on benches seemed lazy because it was Sunday.

Autumn whispered in my ear as we sped along, and made my chest feel heavy. Summer almost gone, and autumn here again.

So many memories come when seasons change. In the dead of winter or the middle days of summer, one forgets in the present. Memories are dear things; I should hate to lose them, but they make me feel so old.

Isn't it strange how much I love you, and yet do not know you? It is your *idea* that I love. It shall always be mine, though you never will.

I was an English major with a special interest in the eighteenth century. Everyone wrote letters then. I wondered who saved them. My letters were written in notebooks, copied out by hand, and sent to friends—no doubt with an eye to the future, which is now 2002.

1

Then, in my senior year, I began thinking about the future.

March 14, 1934
Skidmore College

Dear Mrs. Miles,
[Grace Miles, my dancing teacher.]

Your letter in February came at a very opportune moment. I was home at the time to see the Monte Carlo Ballet perform in Rochester.

They did three very good numbers *Le Beau Danube*, *Les Sylphides* and *Concurrence*. One of my friends here at college is a good friend of the conductor, and she gave me a letter of introduction to take backstage.

Dorati introduced me to Massine and I was quite thrilled. But my memory of the night is not altogether a pleasant one, for Massine told me that I was too old to be a dancer, and that the life of a dancer was from 14 to 26. I was annoyed at his "all for business attitude" for he seemed to imply that at 26 a dancer was through because the constant work had broken her spirit (if she had any). The life of a dancer, to him, was not one of creation but of constant practice.

Again I was disappointed in the ballet as a whole, this time

1

not with the technique, that was excellent, but with the art itself. It seems to me that the technician is to the real dancer as the research writer is to the poet. There was only one dancer that had any trace of a soul and she was Tamara Toumanova, a child of 16, who will in all probability be through before she is 26 for she has a poor figure. With the Jooss Ballet I found the same fault, though I was not as disappointed because I did not expect as much. The first and last parts of the *Green Table*, however, were superior to anything I saw in the Monte Carlo Ballet.

I have heard that the latter is thinking of making its headquarters in New York instead of London. When I have my ballet, however, (for ballet I shall have as I prefer that to any other art form in the dance because it is narrative and at the same time gives opportunity for lyrical expression) I shall chase Massine back to Europe and only allow him friendly visits.

A week or two ago I was introduced to another dancer, Hanya Holm of the German school. She is a real artist and is wonderfully alive. My drama professor, who is a great friend of hers, tells me that she dances the way she smiles; consequently, I am dying to see her dance.

If you have time I would love to hear from you.

Most sincerely,
SLS

Ballet Russe de Monte Carlo was a great disappointment to me, quite apart from the fact that Massine literally tossed me aside. I had expected to be carried away by the magic of at least one dancer. Also, the choreography seemed empty and pointless, nothing I would want to do myself.

I had been thinking that this would be what for so long I had dreamed of doing. And, of course, I did not like anything about

Massine. It was not until many years later that I saw him as a character dancer and a choreographer of romantic proportions. But none of it appealed to me.

So where was the dance? I went back to school and for the first time in my life I did not sleep all night. I tried to sort things out. I knew I was going to be a dancer. I had made up my mind, and besides it was in me. By morning I had covered every thought I had ever had about dance.

Three years earlier I had written, "The passion that has so long possessed me of being different, of never really copying, of being independent, and first, has mounted so high that tonight, at least, it insists on my believing that such emotions of mine were not intended to be expressed by any of the present existing arts, but could only be revealed to the world in a new form of art, a new language of expression. As I have taken so long to grow up already, I believe that it will take three times as long a time for me to organize my emotions, and proceed as a creator in a new field."

So it was a new field of dance and theatre that I wanted. As soon as the library was open, I was there looking at every book on the subject. Among them was John Martin's *The Modern Dance*, and the phrase that caught my eye was, "The modern dance is not a technique, it is a point of view."

So this was the answer. I wanted to be a discoverer. My medium was movement. Even acting was action. As I thought through many phases, it all went together—dance as technique, dance as acting, dance as poetry, dance as painting and design, dance as music and rhythm, dance as life, as soul, as spirit. This was the life I wanted no matter how long it took. But for the moment I kept most of this to myself. I felt I needed more experience, and more contact with experienced artists. Fortunately, I was a late bloomer; so I concentrated on the subject at hand, which was drama.

When it came time to start producing *A Dollar* by David Pinsky, the play I had chosen for my drama workshop class under Miss Champlin, I held auditions. I put notices on bulletin boards of all dormitories. No one came. It was my first realization that if you want something to happen, you have to stir people's imagination—or serve food.

I was a little shocked that there was no interest in what interested me so much. Then I saw that it was much better this way. I could look over the whole campus and choose my actors for the parts. Everyone would be surprised and pleased to be chosen, and no one would be disappointed in being turned down. In fact, it was ideal. As I spotted each one in the dining hall, at convocation, or walking on campus, I would go up to her and say, "I am directing a fascinating play, and you would be perfect in the part I have in mind for you."

Not one of my chosen characters had ever thought of acting, and yet they all said "yes" when I explained what had to be done and how exciting it would be. Much to their surprise and pleasure, they could all act. Each person was perfectly cast, and they gave their hearts to it. Just before the performance I sent the following letter to my leading actor. I had become a director.

April 10, 1934
Skidmore College

Dear Comedian,

Remember, that although you are not actually a clown, you must make the word *clown* mean something. It means a direct contrast with the rest of the downhearted company. You are gay, funny, impetuous and fair-minded. Let the audience see all this the first minute you enter. In fact, and I think you can easily see it, there would be no play without the comedian. He is the one with a sense of humor among six without.

Do not be afraid to use your whole body. Listen to what the others are saying and act accordingly. I do not mean that you must act naturalistically, rather expressionistically, that is you must *express* the mood that the author has set for his play. You must set the tempo for the other actors. Do not rush your lines but make them vital. Pick up your cues quickly. Think ahead to your next speech and be prepared for it physically as well as mentally.

Read the play over to see if you can discover the way in which the author wishes it to be expressed. Then go over your lines keeping in mind what I have said. Be easy in your movements but meaningful and, above all, remember that you are the vital point in the play.

Most sincerely,
Sybil Louise Shearer

Then suddenly I found myself as critic, but fortunately decided to keep this to myself. I wrote the following letter, which I did not send.

April 23, 1934
Skidmore College

Dear Miss Champlin,

I was surprised and disappointed tonight to find that you do not like Draper as Rosalind. You say she does not have enough dignity. Do you really feel that it is impossible for her to acquire this? Think of her diction, her compelling voice, and her magnetism of personality and appearance. Ricky has none of these. She is nothing but Ricky wrinkling her brow and talking fast and being sentimental. I may be unfair, but I have seen her act three or four heroine parts and in every one, her own personality protruded so as to keep the audience from seeing the true character and allowing them to see her only. I saw Ricky play the part of Sir Wm. Gower from behind the scenes, and would you believe it, despite the heavy makeup, the shakiness of her limbs and the wheezy voice of Sir Wm., I saw Ricky smiling to herself at the idea of being Sir Wm. The audience was too far away to see it but I could, and I knew that she was not sincerely playing her part, because she could not forget herself.

If only I felt that my judgment were as sound as my feeling on this subject, it would be much easier to tell you this, but I know that although you do not agree with me, you do not mind hearing my opinion.

As ever, yours most sincerely,
Sybil Louise Shearer

May 5, 1934
Skidmore College

Dear Barbara,
[Barbara Brown, a young actress who visited her aunt, our next-door neighbor.]

What do you suppose? We are presenting *As You Like It* for our spring production. I am playing Jacques. I note what you say about the Shakespearean verse. It certainly is interesting to make it intelligible to the audience by putting new emphasis on the words. They lend themselves so beautifully to interpretation that it seems as though the real Shakespearean actors must have spoken realistically and not in that swooping tone of voice that always accompanies a production of *Macbeth* and others of the poetic masterpieces.

filled with pink pills to be taken with a *full* glass of water eight times a day.

This time he examined my heart and said, "You have a heart murmur, and should take it easy physically; only do horseback riding for exercise; take one step at a time going up stairs; never run or walk fast." This was bad news. It meant no dancing until this condition cleared up. So I had to stay in college and obey orders.

I made up my mind that it *would* clear up, so I was completely obedient. For two summers I rode Dorothy every morning. She was a sluggish beast who did not want to carry me around any more than I wanted to be carried. She only picked up speed on the way home, like the stagehands in my later life who only showed vitality when overtime started. I longed to be on a bicycle that I could leave at the bottom of a hill as I ran to the top to see the view. The only plus in this experience was my beautiful yellow and green linen outfit—jacket and jodhpurs—that my mother supplied to make me look authentic as Dorothy and I trotted out and back each morning. It was such an exhausting experience that I slept most of the rest of the day.

However, at spring break in my senior year, the doctor said after examining me, "It's a miracle! You are perfectly healthy again." Of course, both he and my father thought the extra two years of college would straighten out my fantasy of becoming a dancer. Since that did not happen, they had to be satisfied with a B.A. degree.

After graduation I started my correspondence with Miss Champlin.

June 14, 1934
Newark, NY

Dear Miss Champlin,

I have tried for ages to write to you, but too many things have happened. At first I felt so positively ill all the weekend that you left, that I did not have a heart for anything for several days. In fact I believe I still feel the effects of that one sleepless night, for there were only one or two people of whom I can think who did not irritate me. By the end of the week the two very stupid girls across the hall from me, Bobby and Eunice, annoyed me so that every time I saw them I felt like throwing myself face down on the floor and kicking for all I was worth. Dot Beaver, when I told her about it, said that she preferred to kick their shins, and I suppose looking at it from the point of view of amount accomplished, it would be more practical. But instead of doing anything, I just became more and more disagreeable inside until there was scarcely a soul whose shins I would not have kicked gladly, including Miss Upton's, whose sophomore English papers I was put under pressure to correct on Wednesday morning after my exams were over. I wished at that time that I had a dozen more exams to do instead of papers, for I was then nothing but contrariness.

Thursday, however, saw me a more revived spirit, and Friday a group of us went to the Riverwood and then to the Worden to celebrate. It was a gay evening and everyone but myself had a hangover. Having taken your suggestion, I escaped; I suppose because of the quantities of pretzels that I consumed while the others giggled.

The weekend was the grand finale and, contrary to my idea of a commencement, was exciting rather than dull. I could not help comparing that last week to a trip abroad—everyone together who would never be together again, the seasickness the first several days, then the revival and finally the entertainment.

Sunday we went to Bennington, and, what do you suppose! We met Miss Hill and Miss Shelly [founders of Bennington School of the Dance] who happened to be there for the weekend. They were very charming, and we sat and talked for quite a while in one of Bennington's very luxurious living rooms. They are such enthusiastic people, just the kind I like.

Please write and tell me what you are doing and what you are planning, and when you write, wish me good luck for I am a little frightened. I was sorry not to say goodbye to you that Sunday. I believe it put me out more than anything.

With much love,
Sybil L.S.

July 3, 1934
Newark, NY

Dear Miss Champlin,

Just a word to let you know that I am joyous again, for I am now spending my days ecstatically flinging my arms and legs about and my evenings quietly aching. I lost five pounds during play rehearsals that I never gained back, but Mrs. Miles prefers me the way I am, for she says my legs are much more shapely now.

But I have not told you how much I enjoyed your letter. Thank you so much for the advice. I shall do everything I can to follow it, for I know everything will be much smoother if I do. I really am much too excited about Bennington. The very thought that everyone there will be interested in dancing too quite thrills me.

My best love,
Sybil

P.S. I am very glad you feel as you do about good-byes for truly it is my fondest wish that your friendship should belong to the present and the future and not alone the past as will be true of other Skidmore relations.

2

And so my life in dance begins—Bennington, 1934. Starting my new book of letters, I wrote first to myself.

Last night out in the storm I was inside of a painting. Everything was colored; the yellow trees, the purple sky on one side. The purple trees and yellow sky on the other melted always from grays to blues and then to rose and back to yellow so easily and gradually that it made the enormous flashes of purple and red lightning stand out in contrast to the quietness of the constant changes. Then, today, Martha Graham arrived. She came just as the warm haze of the afternoon was smoldering everyone, and, like the burning lightning, she made the scene alive with interest. Some who knew her rushed to greet her, and Louis Horst sprang into action as well as his bulk would allow and hurried down the path to see the genius, (which everyone agrees on to be a fact) to give her a kiss, and take her hand.

Practice at five o'clock was disturbed several times when Miss Schönberg ran to the balcony to see what was going on below. Laughing with her soft accent she explained to us that it was only Martha Graham who could make her so excited.

Miss Schönberg is delightful. She has a long nose, slightly tilted upward, a narrow girlish smile, a pale freckled face and long brown crinkly hair which she does in two braided knots at the back or in one band wound about her head. She is rather large and well shaped, and quite freckled. Her gradual departure from an interesting reserve is making her a far more interesting person to me, and I dearly hope to become friends with her before too long.

I have discovered today that it is not the same thing to be a solo dancer and a creative dancer any more than it is the same to be a concert pianist and a composer. They both acquire the same fame perhaps, but how much more desirable to be creative! Everyone has told me that I have something the other dancers around me have not, and I imagined it could only be creative talent. I find I was mistaken about my confusion of these two talents, but I have yet to discover my further possibilities and not lose hope. Hope and work only will do it.

Many classes were held on the lawn in front of the commons building. It was a marvelously spacious stretch of grass with an unobstructed view of the Green Mountains. Word filtered through the school that the natives thought this was a nudist colony due to information from a low flying aeroplane observing us in our skin colored two-piece leotards leaping around on the open sward.

Movements mainly featured stretches, strong thighs, and falls. Those who were most proficient in these activities were most revered. Chest on the floor between outstretched legs was a must, and when I found I could do this with ease it gave me great hope for the future. Strong thighs as preparation for falls were also important.

At one point, all of us were in a huge circle holding hands in a class conducted by Martha Graham. We were leaning straight back from the knees to the top of the head. Suddenly, I wondered if I were doing what I should be and looked up to see what was going on, and immediately Graham pointed at me from across the room and said, "You! You are going to get away with murder with that head!" I snapped back quickly wondering if this were a reprimand or a compliment. Anyway, I didn't like it. I was mortified.

There were all kinds of students from many backgrounds and all ages, but the majority were teachers with previous knowledge of the "modern dance." John Martin's book was my main foothold, but I enthusiastically boned up on all the necessary reading, every bit of which seemed magical.

The place was lovely, the dormitories and studios and the dining room, especially Sunday morning breakfast with kippered herring.

July 19, 1934
Bennington School of Dance

Dear Miss Champlin,

You wanted my first impressions of Bennington, but they are so far away now, almost a week and a half, that I feel very settled. The first week of dancing, however, was marvelous and I went at everything with such gusto. I thought I was the most happy person on earth for the first little while, but Martha Graham's technique has somewhat dimmed my enthusiasm. It is almost like trying to learn ballet in one week. It seems quite futile and a little boring to do the same thing every day.

Miss Graham treats us as though we were morons. She talks baby talk to us, and I hate to be told that I look like an "anxious female" when I stick my chin out because another part of my anatomy hurts, and when I am not in the least sentimental about self-expression. She takes for granted that we have all spent every previous moment before meeting her in the soft flowing movements of calling to the skies or tossing the balloon of our self-expression. I am trying to be just to her because of your advice, but it is very hard to see everyone sticking out chins in admiration of Miss Graham's genius and remain unaware of my own reactions.

I met Fanny Aronson the first day, and I like her very much, but I do not know her well enough yet to talk to her or to draw her story out. In fact I have a feeling that I do not have the power to draw anyone out despite the fact that I am intensely interested in them. I was talking to Fanny this evening in her room, and then we went for a walk in the long dark grass behind the college. She feels that Bennington is anything but loose, and that Perry-Mansfield was much more sociable and creative in its atmosphere. Certainly it is very difficult for me to become acquainted with the older people who are interesting because they are satisfied with their own group. Those who welcome you with a sickening smile are the most forlorn and devitalized gym teachers who are here not only to learn the latest methods in the dance, but also to watch others rather than create themselves.

Miss Schönberg is a particularly delightful person, but one with whom it is most difficult to become acquainted because of her reserve; though with the older people she has a most hilarious good time. I have made no attempt to know her, but this next week Graham will be gone and I hope most of the great desire to play up to her among the elite and the administration will be gone as well. Miss S. seems to think she is particularly wonderful. Doris Humphrey will not create such adoration, I know, because Louis Horst and his devotion to Martha are an enormous influence on the community.

I know that as far as technique and advancement are concerned, I have done as well as anyone (because of my adaptable body) but I have become rather involved mentally as to whether I have any creative ability. And we are all terribly worried about Mr. Horst's class Movement & Music. If I could only come to know the worthwhile people! I feel so insignificant! The only way to get over that is to make my work noticeable, for I am afraid my personality is lacking in the demanded exuberance. Marion Shang of Barnard and Marian

16

Knighton of Sarah Lawrence are the two most popular people on campus and they are both at least 30 or 35.

July 21, 1934
Bennington School of Dance

Dear Miss Champlin,

Your letter arrived yesterday, and I was so glad to hear from you. No, I have not yet read *Nijinsky*, though someone gave me the money to buy it for graduation.

Last night I saw an entirely different Martha Graham and, you will be glad to know, a more pleasing one. She gave her recital and I can assure you—she is a genius. I have absolutely never seen anything so moving. She did her great and famous *Dithyrambic*. The one which moved me the most, however, was the first of her frenetic rhythms, *Wonder*. She is such an entirely different person in action than she is on the classroom floor. Her designs were perfect and her movement superb. I cannot imagine anyone dancing with more life and vitality! She is just what I have been imagining as perfect for the past several years, and anyone who wishes to be as splendid as she is will have to approach dancing from another side, for I am sure that she has gone the limit in her style.

I still have no desire to study with her, for I am afraid of her dogmatism, though I would like to be proficient in her technique. It is so all-embracing, and she used the same basis as ballet.

Her costumes were marvelous in color and in shape. She makes all her own, and 15 minutes before the curtain opened she was sewing the last stitches into her newest creation.

The lighting in *Lamentation* was very interesting. There were three medium spots, one from each side and one from directly above. They cut three streams of light across the black velvet curtains, focusing themselves on the dancer wrapped in a light purple jersey, which was a long rectangular piece of tubing that encircled her entire body including her head. Her movements were all within this cloth, and she was seated upon a box.

But for fear that you will never arrive at the end of this letter as it is, I feel it is time to stop.

Fanny wants to be remembered to you.

With very much love,
Sybil L.S.

Although my first look at Graham's *Lamentation* was impressive, it was my second that I remember most vividly. I was taken by a large, energetic young man to a Graham performance at the Needle Trades High School my first winter in New York. His name was Bill Blood. I probably saw him on other occasions, but this evening was memorable. We sat three quarters of the way back in an auditorium crowded to the periphery with silent adoring fans. When *Lamentation* started, Bill, who was large to the point of towering above the audience even when seated, stretched farther and leaned forward incredulously, and then in a huge booming voice said, "Oh, I see those are her knees!" We laughed all the way back to his apartment, put on skates and rolled all the way up Park Avenue at midnight, and across 85th street to the Three Arts Club, still laughing.

July 30, 1934
Bennington School of Dance

Dear Barbara,

Before I left home your aunt Edith told me that you were in a summer stock company. I was so thrilled that I wanted to congratulate you immediately, but my rushed plans prevented it until now. Please write and tell me what plays you are putting on and all about the company, etc. I am most anxious to hear.

I shall surely be in New York this fall, perhaps around the first of October. So I shall see you. It is a dreadful job trying to decide where to live and what to do exactly. I have pretty well decided to be a dancer, however, and am thinking of applying for a scholarship at the Neighborhood Playhouse where Martha Graham and Louis Horst teach. If you know anything about it, I would love to have you tell me.

Doris Humphrey is here at Bennington this week and is a very good teacher. I would like to get into her understudy group and eventually into the group, as they seem to have the faculty of making a little money whereas Martha Graham's group is as poor as possible.

Have you ever seen Graham dance? I did for the first time this summer and I find she is marvelous, really a genius. I ushered at her recital. It was unbearably hot and all her costumes are woolen, but despite discomfort on both sides, the audience was captivated by the dancer.

Quite a crowd came over from Putney, a summer theatre near here, and we had seats in the middle reserved for them. One very eccentric little man tried to leave his little round beret on one of the front seats to save it for himself. When I told him that he must sit in his own seat, he looked like a disconsolate boy with his lower lip sticking out. He came to me at every intermission and begged to sit in the front row (all seats were taken). I told him he could sit on the floor, because he said he just had to see (he lisped) Miss Graham's comedy interpretations. Later I saw him usurp someone else's seat, but I decided to let him alone because he was sitting so straight and looking so intent.

It is just grand to be here for six weeks doing nothing but dance and listening to music.

Most sincerely,
Sybil L. Shearer

Barbara Brown was one of the first persons I contacted when I arrived in New York. She was an attractive blond, a real New Yorker living in a real house with her parents, and she was also a real actress on the stage although she was hardly any older than I.

I was invited to a party. The guests were all young professional actors and actresses with or without jobs. Their sophistication, however, was immense—cigarettes, wine, in-jokes, and cynicism galore about everyone in the theatre and the theatre itself. They were the last word in criticism. I felt like Katherine Hepburn in *Morning Glory*. Suddenly, I was angry. This was not the way it was supposed to be. I drew myself up, went to my hostess, thanked her for asking me, and said, "I have to leave now." As I went down the steps I said to myself, "These people are the dregs." It never occurred to me that the "real theatre" might be infested with copies. This was surely the riffraff with whom I would never have anything to do!

July 31, 1934
Bennington School of Dance

Dear Miss Champlin,

Here it is the fourth week already and Hanya will be here on Sunday. You must come while she is here!

Everything has been going well for me. I am taking a tonic steadily to keep up the strenuous work. But the time has flown so that I feel as though I have accomplished nothing. I believe that I have received the most benefit from Louis Horst's class. It is a constant creating of dances, which is agony in itself but great joy at the same time.

I had a long talk with Louis yesterday. I began by asking him about the Neighborhood Playhouse. We agreed that it was far better to be successful artistically than successful financially (so I guess I shall have to be contented with poverty all my life).

Louis is a very nice person, for he said if I did not like New York I could go back home and teach. I said vehemently, "Never!" and he smiled. Now we always smile when we see each other. I am going to do a rigadoon tomorrow and I am just praying that he will see something good in it.

With much love & remember me to your mother.
Sybil L.S.

August 7, 1934
Bennington School of Dance

Dear Miss Champlin,

Your splendid letter arrived yesterday morning, and I have been in very high spirits ever since. In fact I cut all my morning classes and went out into my favorite field to create a dance called *Enthusiasm*. Flock by flock the cows, horses and sheep came from their different pastures and looked over the fence at me. The cows were the most impressed, because they find it so hard to move quickly (the dance was a failure for Louis was in a bad temper and said it was animation not enthusiasm, so I am trying a different approach for tomorrow).

You asked if I was convinced of the virtues of the modern dance. I can frankly say—not until yesterday. In fact I wrote and mailed a letter to the School of American Ballet over the weekend.

As to going to Skidmore, I can think of nothing more inspiring than being near you. But as long as dancing remains in the hands of the physical eds I have no chance. If, however, it should become part of the dramatic major there would be room for expansion and real work. Of course, my aim has always been dancing rather than teaching, but I am beginning to realize more and more that one needs nourishment in

order to dance, and that just dancing does not earn nourishment. I have a positive horror, however, of getting into a rut
the way Miss Hill has. She cannot do any technique but her
own, and that can be summed up in side pulls and suspen-
sions. I would want to keep working and creating continually
and your suggestion sounds splendid. I am really very thrilled
to think that you want me.

As to Humphrey, I have almost forgotten her. She is so put
in the shade by Hanya, and to think that last week I wrote to
my friends that I had hopes of entering her understudy
group! I don't know yet whether I am jumping at conclusions
or whether this existing sensation of having found something
new will extend into my real aim.

My best love to you,
Sybil L.S.

P.S. I also found out about sentimentality, which has bothered
me enormously. It is a kind of self-expression without form. It
is all right in itself and in the private life of an individual, but
not all right in public because it is formless and artless. This is
what Louis and all the modern dancers have been trying to
tell us when they used the word *distortion* as a means to art.
SLS

So Bennington concluded with the week under Hanya (lots of glid-
ing, running, leaping, bouncing, and no sitting on the floor stretching, no distorted movement). She was a happy person, and I was
happy. The profile I wrote years later for *Ballet Review* starts with
that first summer. (See Addendum I.)

3

Dear Dorothy,

[Dorothy Beaver, classmate at Skidmore, poet, writer, clairvoyant.]

Perhaps you will be surprised to hear that I have developed a profound respect for the modern movement in every art. Before this, all my life has been lived in the past. I do not regret it in the least, of course, but I am so glad that I have at last started on the real thing, and that the preparation of a conservative frame of mind is over. It is wonderful being a member of a new movement of whose value I am thoroughly convinced.

We had a lecture on modern poetry one evening at Bennington, and I was shocked to find out how little I knew of the moderns. I had been considering Sara Teasdale and Edna Millay moderns, but I find a new group who claim that real poetry should be read aloud in order to be appreciated because it is more akin to music than to the other types of literature. Some of T. S. Eliot's poems were read aloud, and I must admit they were exciting and illuminating. A very queer man by the name of Lincoln Gillespie came into our midst for a few days, and talked in what might be termed a simplified form, for he ran two words together whenever he could to make a more pointed meaning. The simplest example I can think of is the word *slanguage*. Another word he used was *muroidery* for mural decoration and embroidery. He claimed to be a follower of Gertrude Stein, but the fact that he was cross-eyed made many people think he was slightly daft, but perhaps they would have thought so anyway. I enjoyed his harangues despite the fact that I could not understand what he was saying much of the time.

John Martin advises all dancers to see as many art exhibitions as possible and to hear as many concerts. I am looking forward to finding out just what is new in art, for I am convinced that someone must have discovered something great since Cezanne, and that discoveries are going on continuously. The modern dance is certainly progressive. But one art remains the same, and that is the art of acting. There will certainly be a change soon, for all the other arts demand what they call creativeness in preference to imitation. Acting seems to be the only imitative art left.

Do you think that there will be such a thing as the creative actress of the future? In the dance, we have done away with music as a necessity and a leaning post, and merely use it as background. Do you think that soon the actor will say, "Let us do away with the play, let us create our own play." It seems perfectly possible to me, that is, if the cast consisted of creative people. They could decide on their plot and characters and build their own play out of that. Of course, there would have to be a director to start things going and to keep them together, but I really believe it is possible. Therefore, if I can I shall train myself with the future in view, and if it never comes I shall still be able to go on the old way.

My real aim however is an American ballet of modern dancing. It is the only way to reach the public and still remain an art. It is of necessity dramatic and at the same time, and above all, dancing.

I am so excited! If you think unreasonably so, please calm me down.

Much love and write soon,
Sybil

August 29, 1934
Newark, NY

Dear Helen,

[Helen Priest, a friend from Bennington, later in Graham's company, and still later an authority on Labanotation.]

Yes, it is terribly hard to practice faithfully every day and to compose as well. I have however made up one dance called *Anxiety*. It goes perfectly with Scriabin's Opus 11 No. 10.

Louis would probably dislike *Anxiety*, but my dancing teacher thought it gave quite a feeling of anxiety as well as some suspense. I had a long talk with her on modern dance and although she thinks me a paragon of intelligence, she does not agree with me, and in many cases does not understand my point of view.

My parents have decided (with my consent) to send me to the Three Arts Club until Christmas. At least it is very reasonable, $12 a week for room and board, except weekday lunches, and every convenience imaginable. Why don't you write there? The address is 340 W. 85th Street.

S.L.S.

September 29, 1934
Jamaica, Long Island

Dear Miss Champlin,

Papa thinks I have talent in acting and he says I must study that; he is not so keen on dancing, so our first visit was to Leo Nadon of the Academy of Allied Arts, which gives scholarships for the Actor's Workshop.

He was very businesslike as well as sympathetic and favorably impressed by both of my parents. He was pleased when my father said I was interested in dancing and immediately told how the whole field of dancing was opening in the theatrical world under Doris Humphrey and Charles Weidman (also of the Academy of Allied Arts). I signed for a full scholarship, told him I was a college graduate, etc. etc. Mama mentioned *A Dollar* [the play by David Pinsky that I had directed in college] and at each new thing his face lit up a little more. We left after having had a conversation of at least three quarters of an hour. I could see that both my parents were extremely satisfied with Mr. Nadon and his proposition.

Next we went to Ouspenskaya and found Miss Deitz very satisfactory. The next day however, Papa went back to Mr. Nadon and asked him just what kind of a chance I had to win the scholarship at the Actor's Workshop and he said I had a very small chance as there were only four scholarships and there were already quite a few applicants from theatrical families who had been brought up in the atmosphere and had even been on the stage. But he said I could get a part scholarship, and if I showed any talent at all he would practically guarantee me one. If I do not get one, however, I shall continue with Ouspenskaya for it has been settled I guess that I take dancing from Weidman & Humphrey.

I could go on forever as to my ambitions and ideals for the dance but it would be useless now and boring. I almost feel bilious with so much reflection.

But whatever direction it is I am still in the theatre and the dance and it will be thrilling for that reason alone. And certainly something will happen if I keep up my ideals and my desire to work.

My very best love to you and do write soon. I shall be waiting your letter.

Sybil

My address is: Three Arts Club
340 West 85th Street

Dear Janet,

[Janet Bardusch, best friend in college.]

Well, at last I am in New York. Now you must come in and
see me. I am at present taking from Ouspenskaya and she is
marvelous! On the first day I met a stunning girl who had
just graduated from Vassar. We arranged to go to see
Dodsworth together. Mme. Ouspenskaya has a part in that you
know.

Today we had an examination one by one. She asked each
person to recite four lines from memory, then she said "repeat" several times. She made up situations and we had to say
the same lines in those situations. Then it was necessary to
walk around the room, to describe a letter S at the same time
spelling Ouspenskaya backwards. Then she asked questions
as to what parts we dreamed of playing, where we had been to
school, etc. etc. But the sad part is she did not get to me, and
she may change the exam next time so I am trembling about
it.

I wish you could be here. It is only $25 a month for three
two-hour lessons a week—Mon, Wed & Fri from 10 to 12. At
the end of class we pretended we were children of 12 or 14
years on a picnic. It was a pile of fun. There is only one boy in
the class, but he seems to be very nice.

[This one boy was so interesting—thin, small, with a rather
large head and pointed features, soft silky red hair, and a kind of
transparency throughout his white body, which was a little misshapen as though his bones were soft. He seemed to be the only
artist there among a crowd of irregulars, for although he was

seriously remote he also gave off a warmth which drew you to him. I think his name was Bill Hansen.

Several years later I saw him again, on the stage, playing Mr. Lundi in *Brigadoon*, a perfect part for him in a perfect setting, and I wondered if anyone else in our class saw him and remembered.]

One poor girl broke down and wept because Mme criticized her posture and said one of her shoulders was higher than the other. When Mme asked her if she had ever taken dancing she broke into tears and said she was a dancer. We all felt very uncomfortable, but the next person up was the Jean Harlow type with plenty of self-confidence and brilliant red hair. She said she was 19 and had just graduated from Cornell and that Shakespeare had no interest for her.

I am also studying dancing with Doris Humphrey and Charles Weidman. I am the only beginner in the professional group and, who knows, I might be in a show this year, but that is wild imagining.

I could not get in the Club so I am living a couple of doors away (in a Stanford White house). But I eat and get my mail at the Club. Be sure to call me up if you are in town.

October 15, 1934
Three Arts Club

Dear Papa,

Your letter arrived this afternoon and I was glad to hear from you.

Yes, I started today at the Academy of Allied Arts with Mr. Irvine. I know you think a lot of Mr. Nadon and what he has to offer, but I hope at the same time you will listen to my point of view. I do not want to oppose you for I know you have my welfare and advancement in mind, but I must tell you that I am a little skeptical of what the Actor's Workshop can give me.

In the first place there are only 13 people in the school, each one of whom is trying for a scholarship. I am inclined to think that it is the scholarship and not the good teacher that is the drawing card. In the second place I do not find Mr. Irvine very inspiring. He is distinctly of the old school—Walter Hampden type. The people who endorse the school are Jessie Bonstell who is dead, Walter Hampden, who is almost dead and Katherine Cornell who has endorsed practically every school in New York. In the third place their prospectus, in my mind, overrates them, for if you remember they advertise John Martin. Mr. Nadon told me in your presence, vaguely I admit, that John Martin gave lectures on the dance and drama there. Mr. Martin told me himself that three years ago he was approached about giving classes there and he said he required a certain number of students and a certain amount of money before he could undertake it. They put his name on the catalogue and he has never taught a single class there.

In the fourth place Mr. Irvine keeps talking about being professional but I know nothing of his professional connections whereas I do know that Mme Ouspenskaya has a splendid reputation as a teacher and is herself on the Broadway stage.

In the fifth place Mr. Irvine mentioned that it would take quite a bit of scouting around to get judges for the final try-outs on Friday and Saturday. Just imagine! He has not collected the judges yet!

In the sixth place our first project is the play *The Whole Town's Talking*. It was the senior class play when I was in eighth grade. It has no literary standing at all, and it is to my mind merely of high school caliber. Mr. Irvine may think it a good beginning but I confess I prefer something which requires real character work and real acting.

The last thing is that I have signed a petition saying that if I win the scholarship I will take the whole course. I am going to find out if this also includes partial scholarships. If it does I am going right back to Ouspenskaya on Wednesday, for whichever way you look at it I am losing money, $10 at O's and $5 at the Academy, but money aside, I would much rather lose Irvine's lessons than O's for she is far superior.

Please do not think me headstrong. Surely you can see that I have thought it all out quite completely. I must admit that they put up a good front in the form of Mr. Nadon. You must realize that I, as well as you, am looking out for myself and feel that I am doing right to go back to O. I am in New York only for a year and I feel that if you can possibly afford it I should get the best instruction while I can. Of course, there is no school that is perfect, but all Mme O's associates are as good as herself and several months of voice would not cost too much more.

As to the Humphrey & Weidman lessons, I have talked with quite a few people who know them, have studied with them, and even been in the group and I find that it is very improbable that Miss Humphrey would choose anyone from her class for the group before six months' training at least! Mr. Nadon is a little too encouraging. I shall probably not have to worry about extra dance work, much as I might want it, for some time.

Above all let me ask you to read over my reasons several times before you judge me too severely and, please, do not repeat them to Mr. Nadon. Surely what knowledge you have of human psychology would show you that he would not understand and it would only make hard feeling for my dancing classes. You can tell him I insisted on going back to O. because I was headstrong if you like, and he will probably see the real reason for himself. This knowledge is only for you to account for my actions. Remember, I have seen the inside and you only the outside. I go again tomorrow and that decides whether I stay the week or not.

The only word that really describes what I have experienced so far at Mr. Irvine's school is *dingy*.

You asked me what I thought of Nadon. I think he himself as far as I know is a nice person, but I think he promises too much and makes everything appear far rosier than it is in actuality.

October 27, 1934
Three Arts Club

Dear Miss Champlin,

Well, I have suddenly acquired a roommate [Helen (Gail) Savory]. She is 26 and a member of Doris Humphrey's dance group. I met her at the Three Arts Club about two weeks ago when her sincerity and seriousness of purpose attracted me immediately. She is very much alive and has a sense of humor all of which good points remind me of you.

Then there is another thing of which I must inform you. Doris Humphrey is starting a demonstration group from her advanced classes. She has asked me to try out, so I now go down to her studio to practice three nights a week, which of course I like very, very much. She has been awfully nice to me, which I appreciate for there is nothing I hate worse than being ignored when criticism is being given. Doris is a very cold personality, supposedly, but I find her quite pleasing and feel it really thrilling to be directed by the creator herself. It has to me all the glamour of the Russian ballet in *Nijinsky*, for Doris is certainly a great person and a milestone in the history of the dance.

In my first class at the Academy, Miss Humphrey recognized me from the summer in Bennington and seemed pleased that at least one student arrived at her door. But she might not have recognized me if I had not gone up to her after class at Bennington and asked, "Is what you are doing ballet, modern style?" This, of course, is what I thought would be perfect. Miss Humphrey, however, answered with emphasis, "This is not ballet at all!"

So I had the clue. It was not wise to do spins and arabesques before class as some of the students did, thinking to make an impression. It was the wrong impression. I was careful to follow directions only.

Nov. 3, 1934

We read *Six Lessons in Acting* by Boleslavsky for O., and in class she demonstrates to us how to develop the five senses. We had the sense of touch first. The exercise we used was an interesting one. Each person separately would go to all the members of the class and feel with the fingertips each dress or suit on the knee. Then she would leave the room. The class changed seats and the experimenter would be led in and with closed eyes, by touching each knee, would be able to tell who the person was (if she had a good sense of touch).

Yesterday we all took lollypops to class and with closed eyes tasted them, trying to tell which was which. It is surprising how much alike lollypops can be. We also had the sense of smell when each person had to sit in the middle of the room and recall an assigned smell. Mine was bacon, which sounds very easy, but as I volunteered to be the first person up, I found it very difficult to really and truly smell it. After about two minutes of imaginary sniffing and actual dilating of nostrils, which seems to bring the best results, I looked helplessly at O. She said, "Do you smell it?" I shook my head. "Why do you stop then?" she said.

I wish I could dance for you, Champie, not because I could show you anything great, but because I want to express the love and gratitude I feel toward you for having awakened me so many times from that slumber, which like a grey mist, is always ready to envelop me. Before I met you, I was unaware that of all the swarming human beings around me, the greater part were dead. Now I am beginning to distinguish the living by the outward glow and the inward vibration which shows me they feel life deeply. You are so fortunate to be alive! You suffer more than the dead, I know, but how much greater is your joy!

My love to you,
Sybil

Nov. 15, 1934
Three Arts Club

Dear Janet,

Thank you for your invitation for Thanksgiving. I have oodles to tell you. Of course, you know I have a roommate. She is one of the nicest girls in the world but we are now parting company and she is going down to 8th St., and I expect to move into the Club either tomorrow or the next day. This is how it all happened. After the apartment episode into the middle of which you marched three weeks ago, I received a telephone call from my father saying that they would consider the studio apartment if first my mother could come down and look it over and meet the girls. Then under our very noses two Spanish dancers up and took the studio. Helen left the Club and we started rooming together at Mrs. MacDonald's (the Stanford White apartment house two doors from the Club). Then because it had always been Helen's idea to have an apartment where we could dance, we started hunting again, this time for the two of us. We found one, beautiful, and just what we wanted. I called Mama and she, in a state of excitement at the call when she had been expecting a letter, told me to go ahead and do as I pleased and she would come down the weekend to look it over. A half an hour after the call I received two telegrams saying to "wait letter," and "stop thinking of moving," signed, "*J. P. Shearer.*" Without "waiting letter" I called up home, and then began the battle. We both tried to talk at once (Papa and I) and we did not hear the girl say, "Three minutes up." The result was Mama came down over the weekend and the apartment idea has faded into the dust for a year at least.

Then I had to go and strain both knees, which has more or less incapacitated me for the present. I think I shall really be glad to be settled in the Club without any more worries, despite the fact that I wanted to be as independent as possible this year. I suppose I shall have to wait until I am earning my own bread and butter like you.

Remember me to your father and mother, and thank her for me.

Much love,
Sybil

My knee trouble was Charles's fault. He was a great one for "choreographing the knees in." That meant, not plies but running on the knees, dropping to the knees and other strenuous things that my knees had not experienced up to that time and as I always did everything at top energy out of a desire for perfection as well as an ease of movement, these necessary repetitions took their toll. With two swollen members of my body, I needed a doctor who would understand this strange calamity.

I went to Miss Dietz at the drama school for suggestions. While we were talking, in came Madame and when she heard the story she was simply furious to think a serious drama student would overdo physically; she immediately recommended their teacher of movement for actors instead of dance. When I said, "But, Madame,

I am taking acting to help with my dancing, not the other way around," she was so hurt that I was sorry I had said it.

But I did go to her teacher, Alice Pratt, and it was much more sane than modern dance. Her exercises, given in a large room filled with pillows and portieres stood me in good stead for years. I decided to say nothing to Charles or Doris, but got back on the floor as soon as possible for fear I would be replaced.

November 18, 1934
Three Arts Club

Dearest Miss Champlin,

The moon in New York is just like another streetlight! Are you having anyone visit you next weekend? You are very busy I know, but I would like to come Saturday and see the play and go back Sunday. But it is really you I shall come to see, so if you will be too occupied or have someone visiting you, I shall come another time. May I stay with you? I shall not look at train times till I hear from you (just a note you know). Loads of love and good luck in your last week of rehearsals,

Sybil

Nov. 20, 1934
Three Arts Club

Dearest Miss Champlin,

False alarm! I cannot come on Saturday and if it were for any other reason than the one it is I think I should come anyway. But the exciting good luck of being chosen for Doris Humphrey's demonstration group by that lady herself prevents my visit, as she is giving a demonstration both Friday (at the New School for Social Research) and Saturday (in the grand ballroom of the Waldorf Astoria).

I am awfully disappointed at not being able to go to Skidmore, but I am just hoping that you will be able to come to New York Thanksgiving. Try to make it and stay at the Club. I have not seen *Within the Gates* or *Distaff Side* both of which you will probably want to see.

Sybil

P.S. Your note arrived this morning and I feel dreadfully— before this I thought perhaps you couldn't have me anyway.

December 3, 1934
Three Arts Club

Dear Uncle Arthur,

We were all very upset about Aunty Sybil's death last June, and I was again very sad to hear about Theo through Uncle Bernard's last letter. Coming to England will never be the same again. I can hardly believe that it is nine years since I saw you.

But I did not write this letter to make you sad, rather to send you Christmas cheer and to tell you what we are all doing now.

We are still living in Newark, and I have at last graduated from college. I am still studying, however. I want to become a dancer and am studying acting to supplement it. Perhaps you remember how much I loved dancing when you knew me. It is the same now, and I work very hard, practicing every day.

My father wanted me to study painting and drawing but my heart has always been in the theatre. I am living alone in New York and find it very stimulating. The people in the city are interesting and intelligent.

We so often hear that in New York life is so quick and full

of bustle that there is no time to think. I find it quite different, for despite the fact that the subways speed along at what appears to be a great rate, it actually takes more than half an hour to go seven miles. At home we hop into the car and make it in ten minutes.

Walking in New York is a delight for there are so many sights to see and people to look at. The different speeds that the mechanical and living moving things travel at is ever a source of diversion to me; the different rhythms and heaviness and lightness of everything around; the tallness of the buildings and the smallness of the people and their pets running at their sides makes me wish to create a dance out of it all, but of course I am quite inadequate as yet. Someday, however, it may come to pass.

I hope you will be able to read my writing as it has changed a great deal since the last letter I wrote you.

I wish you a very happy Christmas and a splendid New Year. All my love and remember me to everyone.

Sybil Louise

Uncle Arthur was a fairy book character. He was beautiful, with white silky hair past his ears and a white silky moustache. He had a transparent quality as though he might disappear as he walked down the path into the woods that surrounded his cottage in a retirement village.

He might have been a poet because his little house was filled with books, all very neat. I felt that the fairies brought out his paper and pens for him when he needed them and put them back when he had guests.

I first laid eyes on him at teatime in the vicarage of my uncle in Lambeth, London. There he was, eating thin bread and butter, lifting his cup with my Aunt Sybil. I was immediately enchanted.

But all of England enchanted me—the vicarage itself, the Bishop of Southwarck's palace where I went to tea with my aunt and my mother, the lovely country house in Sheen with its conservatory and its gardens, and the pictures in gold frames from floor to ceiling, the streets of London with all the door stoops whitewashed every morning, the children in uniforms, the Victorian "Bonnets" walking each with a lady servant seven paces behind, the downs in the country, the seaside resorts with the broad walks, antique jewelry and traveling players, and my Uncle Theo who played the piano for Pavlova when she practiced.

I was a little girl in a storybook, with long curls and a sailor hat that said "United States of America" on the band, and everyone looked at me. It was my first big performance. It lasted four months, and it was magical.

December 11, 1934
Three Arts Club

Dearest Miss Champlin,

It was so good to receive your congratulations and I have been wanting to thank you. However, things have been happening thick and fast for the last few weeks. I have been in four demonstrations—three for Miss Humphrey and one for Mr. Weidman. This week Thursday we start working on her new compositions with the concert group. We are really starting to act as the understudy group for the first time.

During my one week of vacation I want to try to create a dance, and then present it to Miss Humphrey for criticism. But there are so many things that I want to do that I find myself just jumping up and down in place without accomplishing a thing.

I am really discouraged about acting. I have not once hit a

real mood or shown any feeling since the first of October. I find it very difficult to cooperate with the other players. And Mme. accuses all of us of giving individual performances. It is so terribly difficult to develop the five senses and the observation and the effective memory. I am just in a fog. If I could only do something good just once perhaps, I could get new hope. This Friday I am preparing a short scene with a girl older than myself who has quite a bit of intelligence, and it is really the first time that I have felt I could actually accomplish something. If I could only show one moment of real feeling perhaps Ouspenskaya would open up and take an interest in me. [Ouspenskaya probably lost interest in me when she found it was dance, not acting, that I wanted.] If she does not, I am lost for I don't know why it is, but I have never in my life been able to accomplish anything worthwhile unless I could contact the person with whom or for whom I was working. I have often thought that I ought to invent some being to whom I might look, so that I would not need to depend on others so much, but as yet I have not done so.

All morning I have been sitting for my portrait, which I am giving my parents for Christmas. One of the girls at the Club does beautiful watercolors and I think mine has turned out very well. It flatters me a little, of course, but that is good for one's grandchildren.

I have a piano in my room that I can't play, but I have become so attached to it that I pay for it rather than let them take it out. I am teaching myself Scriabin and the Moonlight Sonata, and I practice singing on it.

My very best love to you,
Sybil

P.S. Kitty Kennedy (still wearing her hair like a middle-aged librarian) is studying acting with Louise Elliot.

December 16, 1934
Three Arts Club

Dear Patty,

[Patty Comstock, high school friend.]

I love it in New York and I am looking forward to seeing you here in January. I understand that you have seen Mary Wigman. I envy you. It is one of my greatest desires. I became acquainted with her technique this last summer at Bennington. I shall ask you all about the concert when I see you.

As you can see by my address I am staying at the Three Arts Club. Last night I was awakened by the most awful clatter of shouting and laughing. After several annoying bursts of clamor I stuck my head out of the door and asked what was the matter and was informed through screams of laughter that one of the girls had found a man under her bed and that the police had just taken him away! No one will ever know the absolute truth of the situation as this morning it was necessary to talk over the details in whispers, while the authorities were announcing in loud tones that it was just a practical joke and we need not fear for the future. I knew I need never fear, for under my bed there are nothing but boxes.

Later it was rumored that the grandson of the president of the Club, Mrs. John Henry Hammond, had climbed in the window on a dare from a friend after a riotous party. The actuality was that the Club was swarming with policemen peeking under beds for more intruders.

Dear Miss Champlin,

Life has been a whirl of excitement since I arrived back in New York. The first thing I found on my arrival was that during my visit home tryouts had been held for the group, and five members of the understudy group had been chosen to join the group and go on tour with them. This of course left me out. All the girls in the city were called to come to the tryouts, but I was too far away.

However, my first reaction to the news was great joy because it shows that things are moving. Every girl who was chosen has worked with Miss Humphrey from one to three years just hoping something would happen. Things are really looking up now. In order not to be left behind too much I decided to go to all the rehearsals for the concert, and to really fulfill the duties of an understudy by learning all the dances. One of the group was ill so Miss Humphrey asked me to take her place. For a while there was some talk of my taking her place on tour, but she revived. However, Miss Humphrey told me last night that if anything happened on the road, she would send for me. It was a great reward for my work all week to hear her say that, for now I know she appreciates my interest. I have indeed come to know and like Miss Humphrey more than ever before during these rehearsals. She is a marvelous person and a genius as well. She and her dancing are like the best and most difficult music; you cannot appreciate her until you know her and you cannot know her without experiencing her again and again.

Last night was the first concert of the tour at the McMillian Theatre at Columbia. The group pieces were marvelous, especially the *Dionysiaques*, a ritualistic bacchanal in which Miss Humphrey is the one being sacrificed for the good of the many. She showed greater feeling in this dance than in any other.

There is one thing wrong, I feel, with the group dancers, and that is something that can be remedied with time. It is that they are so concerned with the movements (which are very difficult) that they neglect the dramatic meaning of the movements in particular, though they grasp the meaning as a whole. I do not think that they are feeling the dance down to their fingertips.

I just found out that one of the girls in the group, Katherine Manning, is a Skidmore graduate ('26) and that she gave a recital with another member of the group my freshman year. I remember it very well as it was the first modern dancing I had seen. I was not too favorably impressed, probably because I was prejudiced.

I went to the Wigman studio the other day and asked them when Hanya was dancing at Skidmore. She said the 20th of Feb., which is in the middle of the week and very inconvenient, but I would just love to go to see her and especially to see you. I guess I shall have to wait until nearer that time to decide.

Do write to me soon, I am so happy to hear from you.

My best love,
Sybil

The reason five members of the understudy group were chosen to join the company at that time was that Doris and Charles had put dancers from the concert group into Broadway shows with the idea that they could earn a living dancing, contribute a portion of their weekly salaries to the concert company for its upkeep, and re-join when they were needed for Sunday night performances at the Guild Theatre or when the company went on tour.

Some of the dancers did rejoin for the tour, but five did not want to give up their jobs, so there were openings for understudies.

Those who did rejoin were Letitia Ide, Jose Limon, Katherine Litz, Katherine Manning, George Bockman, Kenneth Bostock, and Cleo Atheneos. Earnestine Henoch had married the director of the show she was in, and the others I never met.

The five new members were Beatrice Seckler, Edith Orcutt, Joan Levy, Miriam Krakovsky, and Mildred Tanner. But there were other members who were not in shows who continued to work on a daily basis.

4

Feb. 4, 1935
Three Arts Club

Dear Miss de Mille,

Last evening I saw your recital at the Guild, and I was so very pleased with it that after thinking about it all day I finally cannot resist writing to congratulate you on your splendid dance *Witch Spell*. Although I have never seen you dance before I could not help feeling that this composition represents a very exciting point in your development as a dancer, which if left unexpressed would leave an enormous gap in your life. It was an absolute necessity, and is therefore very vital and alive.

Next in order I liked *Hymn*, the *Ballet Class*, *Dance Of Death* and *'49*. The only one on the program that I did not like was *Ouled Nail*. It was like a bottle of liquid—all right if held upright, but it was constantly being tipped over, allowing the liquid to spill out. The movements of *Nocturne* were to me too natural for a dance, but it was very sincere and for that reason I liked it.

Your *Ballet Class* was wonderful, if only ballet dancers could have your life and reality they would be worth watching. I saw Patricia Bowman in the afternoon and could not help realizing what a perfect blank she is.

I have never seen such variety on one program, and the way you adjusted yourself to the problem of connecting with your audience directly and then again finding that outside focus point to which both the dancer and the audience must look for connection was done perfectly.

I hope you will not think me forward in taking the liberty to criticize you, as I am still only a student of the dance. But I have attended most of the dance recitals during the fall and winter and I am convinced that you are one of the most interesting and most moving dancers in New York.

Most sincerely yours,
Sybil L. Shearer

P.S. We have heard that you danced at the Club several years ago, and the dancers here think it would be splendid if you could come again. I am going to speak to Mrs. Markloff when she comes home from her vacation. SLS

Miss de Mille's answer:

February 7, 1935

Dear Miss Shearer,

Thank you so much for your extraordinarily intelligent criticism. You may be only a student of the dance, but your point of view is mature and professional. I am sure you have performed many times before, and have learned much from audiences. If you dance as thoughtfully and clearly as you write, you are someone certainly to hope to see.

You are right. *The Witch Spell* represents an absolute break in my progress as a composer. It is the first dance in which I feel I have begun to assimilate emotion in gesture, to force dramatic action thru pattern. There is no less acting than in the earlier composed mime scenes, and there is no less or more dancing, but they are now one. It will be my job to work for closer and more integrated union. *Dance of Death*, my latest work, is a continuation of this development and an even greater departure from customary patterns because the emotion is more complex and the gesture more stylized.

Hymn is nearly always liked by musicians and disliked by non-musicians. The pattern is so fragile it takes a trained mind to follow it. *The Ouled* is important only as an accent on a program, and because it whips up the audience's attention. I'm ashamed to say it's rather fun doing it; the reaction of surprise is always so sharp.

Thank you again for taking the pains to write. And be sure to let me know where I may see your work.

Sincerely,
Agnes George de Mille

February 9, 1935
Three Arts Club

Dear Miss de Mille,

It is really impossible for me to tell you how pleased I was to receive your letter, and to hear from you that I was right about *Witch Spell*. I was also very interested to hear about *Hymn*. I am not a musician and, indeed, my musical education has been very neglected so that I was unable to follow it intellectually. But it was a very moving dance even without following the musical pattern. The *Dance Of Death* is splendid, and I am anxious to see it again for, although I understood what you were doing, I feel that it is one of those works, like good music and good poetry, which has to be experienced more than once to be really appreciated.

I am very happy to think that you wish to see me dance. I certainly hope to some day. But now I am really not at all clear about what I am doing. I just know my dreams for the future. In the meantime, it is necessary to learn about music, acting, and most important about dancing. My mind knows a great deal about the last two but my soul—how inexperienced it is! I need so much help, yet I know that most of the work depends on me alone.

Miss de Mille, may I call on you? I want so much to talk with you, for I am very interested in what you are doing. But I have had the exciting good fortune to be asked by Miss Humphrey, with whom I have been studying since October, to dance with the group in the opera at Philadelphia. Therefore, we should be rehearsing every day this week and next week we perform. If, however, I might call after that, I would feel very honored. Thank you so much for your letter.

Most sincerely,
Sybil L. Shearer

February 23, 1935
St. James Hotel
Philadelphia, Pa.

Dear Miss Champlin,

I thought of you several times on February 20 because I knew that Hanya was at Skidmore. I wanted so much to see her dance, but it was impossible.

Now I must explain to you why I am in Philadelphia. One of the girls in the group, my former roommate, has dropped out and Miss Humphrey asked me to come to Philadelphia to dance in her place in the opera *Iphigenia* and to understudy what I was not in. I was very thrilled of course. We rehearsed for a week in New York and then for a week here, and gave our first performance yesterday afternoon; we give another tonight, and the last one on Tuesday evening. I am now debating as to whether or not I should return to New York for Sunday or Monday.

It has been a grand experience, for Norman Bel-Geddes

designed the set and the costumes and he and his wife, whom he calls Miss Wait, have been here supervising. Bel-Geddes is a very amiable sort of a person with a great capacity for swearing. During one rehearsal he would stop everything at various intervals to fix the lights and Mr. Smallens, the conductor, who also is very temperamental, would scream out, "What's the most important thing in this opera anyway, the singing or the lighting?" The first dress rehearsal lasted from 7:30 to 12:30 and members of the cast and the ballet reminisced back to *Lysistrata* days when Mr. Bel-Geddes kept them there from 8:00 in the evening to 8:00 in the morning with a half an hour out at 5:00 for a bite to eat.

The set is quite effective and it is all painted with a blue watercolor so that our feet and legs and hands are in a constant state of blueness.

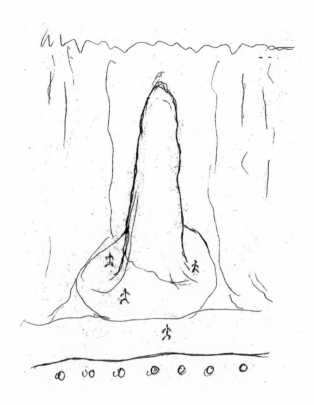

This is something of the idea of the design. It is in the center of a huge stage, and people go marching up and down it. The back curtains are black but some times there is a pink cyclorama showing and sometimes a yellow drop in the center of the back (this was cut out in performance). The lights are very sensational. The chorus wears blue and the ballet pale green, the mother and father various shades of purple, the lover red and yellow, and the heroine, Iphigenia, yellow. Of course, there are various designs on the costumes.

The singers are quite good especially Agamemnon who is Baclanov.

But now I must tell you of my experience with the group. I am not in permanently as yet, just on trial, as it were. I find it disappointing, and my mind keeps reverting to the fact that I made a great mistake in not following my instincts last fall when I was so very convinced that it was the Wigman school I wanted. Of course, I have progressed at a good pace materially since October first, for I am the only one here with so very little technique. However, I know that my technique has not improved as much as it should or would have under constant training, which I would have received at the Wigman School. Also I have no feelings except greed. I get terrible pangs that I am not striding ahead and then I try to remedy things but it seems hopeless. If I could only find that divine spirit to lead me on. I am sure that I had it at one time, but perhaps that was only a dream.

Mainly I do not like the attitude of the group. They are a bunch of bourgeois dancers, none of them willing to give anything to their fellow men. Those who have been with Miss Humphrey for seven or eight years are better dancers than I am, but not seven years' worth. In that length of time I hope to be something real. My greatest trouble is that I am slow to learn, and I am over-conscious of the fact. I forget to count the steps, etc., and it annoys the other dancers whose brains, it seems to me, must be little adding machines. They must count everything, even lampposts and windowpanes, to be so exact.

I simply cannot keep my mind on what they are doing, and it is only when I feel a movement that I can repeat it the same way twice.

We had our second performance last night and in the audience were—surprising enough—Martha Graham, Louis Horst and John Martin. They all came backstage after the performance, and John Martin gave us to understand that it was marvelous. No one knows quite what Louis and Martha thought, though Louis said he found the Gluck opera very interesting, as he had never seen Gluck given this way before. This morning the whole happy family, including Doris and Charles and Pauline Lawrence [Humprey-Weidman accompanist and manager] and Jose Limon and the three before-mentioned, had breakfast in the St. James coffee shop. The girls seemed to think that it was very unusual and they joked about it. I do not think that they respect Doris enough for she is a great creator, and it is only right that she should be peculiar, which she is in her coldness. They think she is terrible not to go home to see her child over the weekend—that she is heartless. Doris said she was not going home because it broke her mood. That made them all laugh (behind her back), but I think they are the heartless ones not to make exceptions for her.

The other evening we had free (every other we have rehearsed until 12:30, at least) and I went to see *Mary of Scotland* with Helen Hayes. It was marvelous! And I was very glad of the opportunity for I missed it in New York last year. Pauline Frederick played Elizabeth.

Tell me if you are coming down the first of March or around then. And also tell me when the next big production is. Now that I have a few extra dollars, I may also find a few hours in which to get up to see you.

My very best love & do let me hear from you soon.

Sybil

---

3 AM
February 27, 1935
Three Arts Club

Dearest Miss Champlin,

How strange things are; I arrived back in New York about an hour ago and I have just finished reading your letter. We both wrote on the same day.

This evening when I said goodbye to Miss Humphrey and thanked her for her kindness, she told me to come to all the rehearsals, and she would help me to get along as quickly as possible. She really is a dear. But it is impossible to feel close to her.

I want to stop my acting course for I feel I have gotten as much as I can from it, but I am afraid to hurt my father's feelings again. There are so many things I have to do, and I really need to assimilate some of these things rather than just keep going to classes.

The last two days in Philadelphia have changed my outlook again toward the group. I have worked a good deal by myself and I have discovered that the other dancers dislike you for it, but that very dislike breeds excitement and growth, and when you work, they start working too.

I have just started to live the life of a dancer and it is very invigorating. I am sure that any other dancing group has its difficulties and complaints.

I may take a course in composition with Louis. The spring is a very good time to create. I have an almost insane belief in myself, and, in my natural moments, I just hope that it is a good sign. It amazes me how many dancers limit their ambitions to dancing in the group. They all say, "I know my limitations, and I shall be quite satisfied to dance with the group." I could never sincerely say that; I wonder if I am not being too bold? Oh, if I can only create! But Louis can make me if anyone can.

My very best love to you,
Sybil L.S.

March 5, 1935
Three Arts Club

Dear Miss Champlin,

You must share in my joy! I had lunch today with Agnes de Mille. She is charming and real. But I must tell you how it came about.

A month ago Agnes de Mille gave her recital at the Guild. I was so impressed and pleased with her work that I wrote to her. A few days afterwards, much to my surprise, I received a letter from her.

I found her a simply marvelous person full of conviction that she is right in her point of view and her work, but very open-minded and sympathetic as well. I asked her about dance composition and she said that there were only a few real creators and that the word creator was being constantly abused. She said that there are a great many arrangers and then she added, "Now I am a good arranger." It sounded quite funny and I do not altogether believe that she is not a creator, but I do not know her work well enough to judge. Two things a good composer knows are when to discard a movement and when a movement is just right. She said that a thrill of recognition runs through the composer when just the right thing is struck.

I really think that Miss de Mille is one of the few great

dancers today and in a few years she will be even greater, though neither the classics nor the moderns will accept her now because she is neither; she is unique.

She advised me to try to get into the Metropolitan Ballet for next season because things were being changed and they were going to double their corps de ballet with the new head of the opera. Of course, she granted that it would not be great artistic work, but it would be a steady job dancing and better than being in a show because I could always hear good music. She said that she was thinking about getting a group together herself next year, but she did not know exactly what she was going to do with it. However, she is going to California in a week and will be there until the middle of the summer, and will have a group of girls there. She said she would let me know if she heard of anything.

I never would have dreamed that this opportunity could turn into the opportunity to talk with a great person on a very informal basis. Perhaps we will be friends someday. I even hope to work with her as I know she would be a grand person to be under.

Now you know all.

My best love,
Sybil L. S.

March 6, 1935
Three Arts Club

Dear Miss de Mille,

It was so nice of you to ask me to lunch; I enjoyed every minute of it. However, since I left you I have thought of a dozen things about which I had intended to talk to you. But that is over now and I shall look forward to seeing you again next summer when you return to New York. I hope you will have tea with me then.

Thank you for suggesting the Metropolitan Opera Ballet. I shall look into it and brush up on my technique. During the past few weeks I think I have grown in the dance. I feel very energetic and enthusiastic as though I were just beginning to live (probably spring fever).

I wish you the very best luck in your work in California. If anyone can really combine acting and dancing in a ballet, it is you I am sure. I shall be very much interested to see your group concert whenever you present it in New York.

Most sincerely,
Sybil Shearer

[See Addendum II for "A Salute to Agnes de Mille"—describing our relationship through the years—written for *Ballet Review* after her death in 1993.]

5

Dear Miss Champlin,

You must forgive me for writing to you so often and without warning. I have so much to tell you, I would love to talk with you. But I know that when we finally do get together all these things I have wanted to say will be unrecallable and we shall probably waste time becoming acquainted again, for I must say I hardly know you and I find it hard to reconcile the person, who at school one moment frightened me and the next lifted me out of myself, with the person who writes such charming letters to me. If I did not hear from you, I am sure I would believe that you were not a person at all, but a work of art which I had experienced and which had spurred me on toward greater things.

But what I have really written to say is that I have made a discovery this evening. It is certainly not a new thought, but I have just realized it for the first time. After struggling for two or three years to appreciate art (modern, growing art), I have suddenly found out that no one really appreciates art but the artist. The layman is simply not considered. If he has an artistic frame of mind he may gain some aesthetic pleasure from a painting or a dance which he does not understand, but it was not really made for him and if he wants to know what it is all about, he has to spend his life finding out.

I myself have become so involved with the world of art that

I have almost lost contact with any other life. I certainly have lost contact with the layman's point of view. I have lost my sense of fight, for the revolutionary comes so easily that I accept it as a value just because it is revolutionary, and then I pick it apart afterwards. The only thing that makes me fight is conservatism, and I avoid that. The only possible way for the people to find out about art is by education, which is in the hands of, what seems to me, dead men, afraid of everything.

The great artists and their work do not belong to the people. They belong to themselves and their friends. There is Martha Graham, for instance. The same people, all artists, go to see every one of her recitals and rave and claim her great. Practically the same audience moves around to all the recitals, and praises or damns as it sees fit. Where is the rest of the world? Uninterested! because it isn't alive to art.

I am just beginning to appreciate modern painting. I still hesitate to say whether a picture is good or bad, but I have developed a fairly good amount of judgment so that I can sense good composition and, most important, emotional strength. But this is because I am actively experiencing art. I am saturated in good composition in the Humphrey-Weidman concerts, and therefore when I went to the American Ballet I detected immediately the abominable choreography and the complete lack of real art.

The great problem is how to educate the public or whether it is worth it, or whether when one takes on the life of an artist one renounces the world. The communist dancers say it is necessary to have dancing and art in general that means something definite to the people, hence propaganda in art. But I say that the society class as a whole is just as important as the working class and it is just as neglected, perhaps more so, for it has a false idea of art in imagining that it is entertainment. The wealthy want smartness and the poor want their troubles displayed before them. The artist, on the other hand, wants to express an idea comprehensible only to himself and his friends.

How can one link them together? It is really in the hands of the educators. And how many of them have any real intelligence? You have, of course, and you are just the sort of person who can influence others. But then you have your own work and cannot be expected to go out blindly into the world to link the three classes together.

This brings me to another theory which has been occupying me of late: "hero worship" or, in milder terms, worship of greatness. This is not a constructive theory but an analytic one. I think I have found out the "why" and the "how" of a great many things.

Everyone has a certain potentiality for greatness and this potentiality is developed into actual greatness only by contact with greatness in others. Some great people influence their acquaintances and friends by their own personalities and others by their works. But still actual contact with the persons who possess this quality is extremely advantageous, especially to those who are growing.

Everyone who has been touched should decide how he can best impart his gift to others and develop himself in every way into the instrument he has chosen to be. He should not try to do everything at once but rather direct all his faculties toward a greater understanding of what his life means to himself and to others. The teacher should know something about everything and give the student glimpses into the world of knowledge and experience and art, and stimulate the student with a desire for more. This you do beautifully. I want to be a great dancer and therefore I strive toward that end. I have no desire to be friends with people who have not a developed or a developing quality of greatness, which seems very selfish for I am getting and not giving. But at the same time I know that what strength I have does not lie in my personal contact with the undeveloped humans. I must teach them through my art and in order to develop my art, I must receive stimulus through the great—living and dead (i.e., not contemporary). It is a constant source of joy to me to find great people around me. And how often they are most unattractive beings at first sight! Though not always, of course.

I said when I started that this was an analytical theory and I still think it is. I mean that it is the way life stands; at the same time knowing, at last, that things stand thus, it is up to me to see that things stay on the right course. What bothers me is the injustice of it all, for some people seem never to develop. Does this mean that they are just fated not to, or does it mean that they do not happen to come into contact with the right forces? Is it our duty to see that greatness is passed on, or can we just leave everything to our impulses and desires?

If you agree or disagree with me or wish to say anything at all on the subject, I shall be most anxious to hear your thoughts. If you are too busy I shall understand.

My very best love to you,
Sybil L.S.

P.S. The big problem is, of course, should the artist create for future generations of artists, or for humanity in general?

March 15, 1935
Three Arts Club

Dear Miss Humphrey,

It is my duty to tell you, though believe me I hate to, that I have a severe infection in my foot that is not yet cured, and the doctor absolutely refuses to let me dance before next Tuesday. In other words I can attend no rehearsals. I can put no pressure on my foot even to walk before then. Of course, I know I need rehearsals for I have not been out of bed since Monday night. I was not too good in the dances. If you feel that I could not possibly go on without rehearsals before Tuesday, it would be better to ask someone right away to take my place.

What makes me feel so terribly is not the fact that I am prevented from dancing with the group, though heaven knows that is bad enough, but the fact that after you have been so good to me when I was not really needed, I have disappointed you at a time when I could really have been of use.

Though you know who among your dancers could most easily fill in, I want to suggest Maxine Trevor (if you do not think she is too tall) as being a very good worker and a dancer with an interesting style.

Again, I am terribly sorry.

Most sincerely,
Sybil L. Shearer

March 28, 1935
Three Arts Club

Dear Miss Champlin,

Enclosed you will find a letter that I wrote to you while I was in bed with an infected toe two weeks ago, but which I did not send.

Last night Nellie Heggarman called at the studio to watch. She did not know that I was there and she was surprised to see me. I was surprised to see her too, as I do not think I have ever seen her dressed up before. She said there was a big controversy over Hanya's recital that some liked it and some didn't, and that some said the technique was good and some said it was poor. What, please tell me, does Skidmore know about technique?

She also told me that the whole school went home early because of measles. That put into my head immediately that you will have some extra days, and can surely come down to the big city this time before school opens again. Anyway, I want to come up for May Day if possible. If you are not having anyone stay with you, then may I? And may I bring my jeans and help in the theatre? I shall probably only be in the way, but I have the greatest desire to do it. We may have vacation from the middle of May to the middle of June, so perhaps I can stay a few days before going home.

I have at last dropped acting with Ouspie. I could not decide for the longest time what was wrong with her and her school, but it at last dawned on me. She is living in past glories and making no attempt to show us how to live and act now. The only place where there is any real enthusiasm in the theatre is in the communist theatre where they are working for the future.

I saw Bergner in *Escape Me Never*. It was miraculous. The woman does so many little things. I can hardly wait for the movie to come out. Then I am going to sit and watch her for hours.

Very much love,
Sybil

May 6, 1935
Three Arts Club

Dear Miss Champlin,

I enjoyed your splendid letter very much, and I have been trying to find time to write ever since. As I wrote my last letter to you when my toe was infected, I shall write this one with an injured knee. I fell last Thursday, and have not been able to work since. I went to the clinic and was told that I had a severe bruise. It is something internal, I think, but I shall take care of it as best I can. I hope to get dancing again soon. It is an awful nuisance not to be able to work.

To go on with our discussion of the "great" and hero worship in general: first of all, we should really decide what greatness is. I am not such myself, but I shall say that it is that quality in an individual that makes him outstanding as an individual and of value to his fellow man. I agree with you that one must know all kinds of people and all kinds of situations in order to develop that quality of greatness that is in everyone to a larger or a smaller degree. But I am not wholly convinced that it is not the great people who influence us every time in our appreciation of these people and situations, either at the same time or afterwards.

I do not for a minute mean that the "great" are only artists. But mere technicians are certainly not great persons or artists. Their only claim to greatness is in their perseverance. I know several people who seem ordinary enough at first glance, but who turn out on better acquaintance to have a well developed quality of greatness and for that reason I want them for my friends. Later I may become more attached to them and even love them. On the other hand, I have met people who at first sight seem to have greatness in them, and I am very anxious to know them. They remain my acquaintances and never become my friends. Then there is the third case where I see greatness immediately and that greatness soars out ahead of me all through my acquaintance and friendship with that individual. The group which I have neglected, of course, is the uninteresting looking group that ends up in uninterest. I do feel, however, that I have not been fair in my treatment of the human race, because I have not forced myself into acquaintances with enough of the uninteresting looking ones to find out if they have anything.

However, the subject on which we seem to disagree is not so much greatness in individuals as the artist versus the world. I understand from your letter that you believe it is not so necessary to educate the public to the artist's point of view, as it is to educate the artist to the point of view of the "world's people." Miss Humphrey separates the dancer from the "world's people" just as the Shakers separated themselves. This sounds fantastic to the world, but at the same time it is true that artists do live a very different life from ordinary individuals. Then on the other hand, Miss Humphrey includes her dancers with those whom she separated from the world, whereas many of them live exactly the same shallow, accepting sort of life that ordinary work-a-day humans do.

Do you believe, since it would seem simpler for the artist to educate himself than to educate his audience, that there is any way to give the world good art that it can understand and appreciate immediately? Is it necessary to be behind the times in the artist's calendar in order to be appreciated by the world? Could one play for two audiences at once, the artist and the people?

It certainly is true that the dancer cannot wait for her audience to catch up with her. She must go halfway at least and usually that halfway is emotional in the good dancers. None of them will compromise intellectually.

Best of luck and all my love,
Sybil

P.S. May 7—This I must tell you. Miss Humphrey told me not to worry about my knee, that innumerable things had happened to her and she was still dancing. When I told her I hated to waste the time, she said I need not worry about getting behind, for my technique had improved very much in the last few weeks. It is much more sure and even *brilliant*! I just about fainted with joy. Wasn't she wonderful to say that to me? SLS

Looking over my letter sixty years later I feel that we have made a mighty effort to educate the world to art in this century. One cannot renounce the world in becoming an artist, but neither should we compromise. The artist should create for the artist that resides in each individual, now and in the future. There is no other audience for art than the creative imagination. Entertaining and proselytizing are something else.

6

May 28, 1935
Three Arts Club

Dear Mr. Stroup,

[Superintendent of schools in Newark, NY.]

I have a favor to ask you. Will you permit me to give an assembly program some time between June 3 and June 13th? My subject will be The Modern Dance and will consist of a talk and a demonstration of technique. I think it will be very interesting to the students as well as educational.

I shall be very grateful if you will allow me to do this. I feel that everyone should know about the modern dance, and you can use your own judgment as to whether you wish to tell outsiders or not. There will be no charge, of course.

Thank you so much for your trouble.

Most sincerely,
Sybil L. Shearer

June 2, 1935
Newark, NY

Dear Miss Champlin,

I have been trying to find a minute every day this week in which to write.

Suddenly, I have become better acquainted with Miss Humphrey. In the past few weeks we have had several talks, and she says that they want me in the group. Last Thursday we had dinner together after class and had a long and interesting conversation about art and the artist, etc. We have the same ideas on many things, and she agrees with me that the narrative in dancing has been neglected by the moderns and that the middle class audience has also been neglected. She says that the second part of her new dance is going to be dramatic. I am very anxious to work in it. The first part of the dance is marvelous. Really, I am convinced that there is nothing more exciting in the world than being a dancer.

With very much love,
Sybil

June 22, 1935
Three Arts Club

Dear Dorothy,

Let me congratulate you on having become a member of the editorial staff of the *New York Times*. You are wonderful! I read your articles every Sunday since Lydia told me about them. I knew before reading the one on meat, that lamb must be the cheapest meat on the market, because we have it here about every other night. Food is our chief topic of conversation, so do come and visit me again. Then you can write an article on "Food In Women's Clubs."

I gave a demonstration of technique and a talk on the modern dance (in Maplewood) last night. Only 25 people came, and there were chairs for 67. Janet couldn't enjoy the program. She was so miserable about the people she had forgotten to ask, and the ones she did ask who did not come. The people who did come, however, were very interested and they promise me a better audience next fall and a larger place, probably the Woman's Club, in which to perform.

At home I gave an assembly program at the high school on the same subject, and it was a sensation. Everyone wants me to go to all the high schools I can and pass on the knowledge of the art. I must say it is so enjoyable an occupation that I shall certainly do it if I can. It was my first solo appearance before an audience since high school days and it was very exciting.

Most sincerely,
Sybil L Shearer

June 26, 1935
Three Arts Club

Dearest Miss Champlin,

My very best wishes and very best love for the future, and I congratulate your fiancé. He is indeed lucky. Yes, I am anxious to meet him, so please do come to New York.

Miss Humphrey goes to Bennington on the 22nd of July for two weeks, coming down the weekend in between for frantic rehearsals. Up until that time we have two rehearsals a day with performances in Philadelphia at the Robin Hood Dell on the 8th and 9th and in Washington (we hope) on the 10th. Now you know my schedule so please, please come.

Sybil

August 5, 1935
Three Arts Club

Dear Miss Champlin,

I thought of you on the 31st. It was the day we started out for Bennington. I am anxious to meet your husband.

Now please write when you have an opportunity and tell me what you are going to do. Will you go back to Skidmore?

The interlude at Bennington was very exciting and interesting, for many of my friends from last year were there plus the great artist Martha Graham and her friend Louis Horst, and John Martin and his wife. They were all extremely pleased with Miss Humphrey's *New Dance*, which Mr. Martin says is the first symphonic dance in the modern school. It really is a marvelous piece, and I wish you could see it. We are giving a fall concert including *New Dance* in New York.

I know this is a very busy time for you, but when you are settled I hope you will have time to write to me.

My very best love to you,
Sybil

Oct. 5, 1935
Three Arts Club

Dear Mrs. Woolf,
[Virginia Woolf, author.]

Although I have heard your name in connection with modern literature and especially the stream of consciousness style of writing throughout my college course, I had never brought myself to read any of your works until two weeks ago, because I had been so concerned with the works in the history of English literature that my course included.

I had been reading *Tertium Organum* by P. D. Ouspensky when one of my friends suggested *Orlando* because of its interesting use of time. I read it and was quite carried away not only by what you said, but by your beautiful composition as well. After finishing *Orlando* I immediately looked around for more of your books. *Flush* was the only one at hand. I read and enjoyed your style, but the book as a whole did not please me because of the point of view. It was to me quite untrue.

However, I have now started *The Waves* and although I am only on the fourth page, I cannot contain myself any longer. It is necessary to tell you how happy I am that, in 1935, we happen to be both alive and within hailing distance.

Composition interests me enormously, and I feel very uplifted as I read *The Waves*. Because I am a dancer, I compare your words and phrases and images and rhythms to movements. At this particular moment I have nothing to offer you in return for your literature but my admiration. But the dances "I have composed in the future" will perhaps repay you in part for the pleasure I have received and am receiving from your writings.

Most sincerely,
Sybil L. Shearer

P.S. The moment I realized *Orlando*'s enormity in regard to time was a marvelous one. Ever since I can remember, I have been figuring ways to explain why I seemed so much older than my friends, and at the same time so much younger. Now I look at people and think, "Is this person an Orlando or is he still unborn?" SLS

Oct. 11, 1935
Three Arts Club

Dear Cousin Helen,

Last March when I met you at the River Club, you asked me to let you know when we gave our next New York recital. It is to be on Sunday, October 27th, at the Guild Theatre. I am enclosing a leaflet that will tell you something about it. Would it be at all possible to meet you sometime before the 27th? I would like so much to see you again and to talk to you about the modern dance. It is one of the most marvelous of the arts because of its very high ideals, and I am extremely anxious for you to like it.

I have told Cousin Mary and Cousin Ida about it, and I am hoping that they will be able to come. I would like all my relatives to know what I am doing, for it is quite possible that I am leading a more exciting life than any of them.

Please remember me to Cousin Paul.

Hoping to hear from you soon, I am.

Most sincerely yours,
Sybil L. Shearer

Helen Pryibil's father was my father's uncle, William Porter, partner to J. P. Morgan of the Morgan Guaranty Trust. She lived in a complete house in the sixties just off Fifth Avenue, and when I first descended on New York, having read Isadora Duncan's *My Life* it seemed quite appropriate to ask her if I could dance at one of her "salons."

I asked if I might call. She invited me to tea, and I explained my mission. She looked at me in amazement over her cup, and putting it down said, "But all *my* friends are only interested in horses!"

Although we always dutifully exchanged Christmas cards, it was quite a few years later that an announcement of one of my solo concerts included a good-sized picture of me in the *New York Times* wearing a raincoat. I think the coat laid to rest some of her fears about scarves and veils and sequins, because she came in her limousine with friends and sent a note backstage saying she would see me at intermission. I sent a note saying I would see her after the performance in the Green Room, where I received her congratulations.

After that we continued sending cards at Christmas, but never again met in the flesh.

7

December 7, 1935
Three Arts Club

Dearest Miss Munson,

[Martha Munson, English teacher in high school.]

This I must tell you before all others! I am in love! And I am an artist, too—all in one piece. Don't offer any objections, because I won't hear them. I am amazed at everything.

With much love,
Sybil

P.S. I want to see you. Call my Mother to find out when I am coming. This letter must not contain such trivialities.

Miss Martha Munson was one of my favorite teachers. At what I felt were decent intervals—so as not to bother her too much—I would call on her, and have a conversation about Tennyson or Shakespeare, feeling quite grown up.

Miss Munson was tall with gray-white hair piled on top of her head, always the same, kept neat with a hair net, and she had a springy walk.

Several times a year Mama would invite her to dinner. I remember one time in particular when outside in the garden, my half-grown kitten was showing off, I said, "Aren't kittens interesting?" Miss Munson's reply, as she turned to look and smile at me, was, "Yes, but not as interesting as young girls."

I had met Gerald Davidson in August 1935. The Humphrey-Weidman group was en route to Bennington for performances. As I looked out over the landscape from the train window, someone came over and sat next to me. He said his name was Jerry, and he was a new member of Charles's men's group. He had asked Bill Matons about me after watching a rehearsal, and he knew my name.

When my parents came down for the performance, I asked them if I could invite one of the dancers to join us for lunch. I introduced him as Jerry Brooks because that was his name on the program. But it turned out that Charles was in a hurry when the programs were sent in, and had just made up a name for him. So it was not Brooks, it was Davidson. I liked that better. We sat together on the way back to New York.

Then he invited me to the theatre. He knew New York, little restaurants, markets, Coney Island, museums, etc. His conversation was fascinating on all subjects.

I found out that he was almost ten years older than I, a widower with a six-year-old daughter, Joy, living with his parents in Cleveland. It was by that time no great shock. I simply put all that out of my mind and concentrated on the present, which was wonderful. He opened up to me all kinds of adventures, exotic fruits and flowers in ethnic neighborhoods, books to read, walks through the city—a city smell in summer always reminds me of those days—and endless interesting discussions.

The autumn wore on. By this time we were intensely interested in each other, and he began to realize the extent of my dedication to dance, the arts, and its power in my life. I was in love with love of all sorts, and he was my ideal, because he was sensitive and spiritual. He truly loved my talent, my dedication and steadfastness, and my absolute passion for creating through dance. I think this last is what he loved about me most. It was a powerful magnet for him.

I watched him in rehearsal. He moved well, but I could see that he could use some technical help. So I offered my services. I was by that time, of course, an authority having been dancing for a whole year!

November 5, 1935
Three Arts Club

Dear Jerry,

Please let me give you lessons in technique. I watched you last night, and I have a pretty good idea of what you need. I will be much more fundamental than Mr. Weidman. It is really impossible for you to accomplish anything by yourself without someone to correct you at regular intervals. I am really very anxious to begin because I want so much to see you dancing.

Sybil

I hoped he would continue to dance—that was my life, and I wanted him in it. I wrote him another letter.

November 26, 1935
Three Arts Club

Dear Jerry,

No, you must not dance until you are entirely better. Despite everything you might say, I still think that your future as a dancer is much more important than the present. This rest will certainly not hurt you.

Just because you do not consider dancing the most important thing in the world, you should not consider yourself, the dancer, lightly or as a passing thing. I know you said that you would never give up dancing.

So please give yourself a chance in dancing, and don't ever think that you have begun too late. One can only subdue the physical life by getting it under control, early or late.

My love to you,
Sybil

People liked Jerry. His talent was charm. Without going out of his way, he simply attracted everyone. But his concentration was on me, and for the first time in my life, I thought and felt that I had found "the" person. It had been an autumn full of delights.

January 20, 1936
Three Arts Club

Dearest Champie,

Your note arrived and I was terribly glad to hear from you again. It seems like ages, and indeed it is, for so many things have happened to us both since last August. Let us write more often in the future, though I never knew you very well personally, we understood each other through some medium outside ourselves, perhaps, the "fourth dimension."

If you have any hand in the drama where you are, I know that you will lift it out of itself and make something of it despite opposition. I would love to bring the dance to Louisiana, and I certainly hope, some day to bring the dance to everyone, but now my place is in New York where I can learn to dance and create a form in movement for what I have to say. Things are going wonderfully at the studio, and I am very happy. I am enclosing a clipping from the *New York Times* concerning our concert last night, which thrilled everyone tremendously.

The program, which consisted of one long dance in two parts, was Miss Humphrey's idea of life with its continuous struggle in a competitive way and the solution of that struggle which, she felt, could only be found in art where one can make relationships harmonious and even ideal between people who are working toward one end.

The staging would be extremely interesting to you. We used large wooden boxes, all different sizes, and painted three shades of grey, and very tall screens in front of black velvet drops; also three shades of grey. In the first part the blocks were set up to suggest a group of buildings from which projected at various angles and levels, heads, arms and legs. The torsos did not show because Miss Humphrey wanted to indicate how people in general do not use the emotional center of the body, but merely the extremities. The whole gave almost a surrealist effect, and although the movements were extremely funny, they were also so surprising that the audience did not know whether to laugh or to look for the underlying symbolism that the weird disconnected bodies seemed to suggest. The girls' costumes were orchid pink jersey with skirts open across the front, white. Miss Humphrey wore bright yellow. The men wore black shorts and orchid jersey shirts.

The second part was the ideal state and done in a symphonic form. The whole group was placed on boxes in the four corners of the stage, and swayed forward and back together as though they were drawn in to the center by the two dancing figures. Then as the theme recurs, one of the girls breaks away and goes into a side leap across the back of the stage. More come in groups, and finally everyone joins in a fast rhythmic dance. This is followed by a slow sweeping movement with many changes in the level of the body.

Then the men rush on with high leaps and do a dance solely

to percussion. This is followed by a slow processional that works itself into a dance of celebration done by everyone. The curtain falls and the blocks are moved into the center, and the variations begin. These are done by three solo members of the group and myself, assisted by two men and then Miss Humphrey. The dance ends with the whole group on the boxes turning first one side and then the other while the dancers, spurting out from the turning mass to do their own creations. It is so exciting at the end that the audience is completely wound up, and cannot be satisfied with anything less than many bravos and a great deal of shouting and clapping. We have done this second part three times in New York now with always the same result. It is indeed gratifying to me to know that I am spending my time working on real art created by a true genius.

Forgive me if this is too long, but while I write I must tell you the many things that have happened since August. I am supporting myself by teaching. I am Miss Humphrey's assistant at the Academy of Allied Arts where I studied last year. Also, I teach a group of Mr. Weidman's three times a week. Then there is my class in Maplewood. (Janet, by the way, is going in very strong for dramatics in the local club, the Strollers.)

We are giving a concert at Skidmore, April 18th. My one big regret is, of course, that you will not be there. The place will seem extremely dead without you. In fact, just to think of Skidmore makes me feel quite sad.

I have always been so much inspired and encouraged by your advice that at this critical point in my life, I feel I would like to hear from you again. I am in love with the most enchanting person! At one time head of dramatics at Swarthmore College, he is now a member of Charles Weidman's men's group. He has been everywhere and done everything. He has a million amazing inspiring ideas, and I believe him to be one of the chosen great. I am very much surprised to find myself thinking seriously in terms of marriage, for up to now I have thought that a career such as mine could allow for nothing so conventional and restricting, and that a passing love affair was as much experience as I would need. But I don't think I ever really believed in a passing affair. Of course, nothing could change my aims or desires to be a great dancer and an artist, so marriage to me would be a fuller life in a glorious career. If you have any words on the subject, please let me know. There must be all sorts of adjustments to be made about which I know nothing now. At present the path seems smooth and beautiful.

I have surely said enough by this time, and I am so glad that you are happy. I look forward very, very much to seeing you.

With my fondest love,
Sybil

Gerald Davidson and I became engaged. I romantically faced being a mother to a little girl I did not know.

March 7, 1936
Three Arts Club

Dear Papa,

Yesterday, I received a letter from Mama that said you might stop off in New York Friday or Saturday. I was terribly disappointed when you did not come, as I would like to have another talk with you. Letters are so unsatisfactory. As a matter of fact, it is several weeks since I received yours, and I have been planning ever since to write to you.

Yes, I imagine my letter was a surprise. It was a surprise to me, too. It is strange how one's whole point of view can change in such a short time. We don't intend to hurry at all. It is just a matter of time before things turn out the way we desire.

You can depend on it that Jerry is everything I have said he is. We are very much alike in that we are both searching for something, perhaps the ideal, as long as neither of us change in this respect we are wedded forever. However, Jerry's past experiences have taught him the value of money and, although it is not the most important side of life to him, it is important. The only thing that keeps us from marrying right away is, of course, money, because together we could accomplish much more than we could apart. When the time comes, however, I hope we will be able to dive right into our plans and really accomplish something.

You will probably see a change in me, because I have changed. Suddenly overnight, I seemed to grow up, to lose my fear of life and people. The knowledge of love makes me more self-assured than any other knowledge I have yet acquired.

Jerry elected to go back to Cleveland and learn the clothing business in which his brother could supply a start for him. Actually, he was more suited to the theatre, but there were no immediate opportunities. So we continued our relationship by correspondence.

I became ill and went home to recuperate, and the next month was an intense time of letters every day. Without the presence of Jerry, my future in dance and all the problems of creation began to loom enormous again.

March 12, 1936
Newark, NY

Dear Jerry,

I hope you arrived home safely, and that you found Joy [his six-year-old daughter by a former marriage] happy and well. Home seems very strange to me, but I am enjoying it. I am much better. Deep knee bends are still in the future for me, however. I find my mother a delightful person, really quite different since I have grown up. We have been so completely congenial. And would you believe it, I find she has inquired into a correspondence course in writing. Writing has always been the way she has wished to express herself. This was a result of the lecture I gave her on worrying in a letter several weeks ago in which I stressed that creating in some form or other was the only thing worth worrying over. (Papa volunteered the information with a chuckle of the sneering variety from the armchair by the radio).

I can hardly wait to hear from you. My thoughts have been full of you, though I find it difficult with half my head still hollow to collect words to express what I wish to say in detail.

My most delightful experience since I arrived home was an hour that I spent in a dream opera house, not on the stage but in the long and mysterious galleries and halls, thickly carpeted and decorated with dark blue and red portraits. I was a most carefree dancer spinning eight times around and skipping such big skips that each was a little flight of its own with the lightest of rebounds between flights. I think there must have been a waltz in the distance for my heart was beating in three-four time when I awoke.

I brought the Swiss cape home with me, and I wore it out to the doctor's yesterday with the cowl over my head because it was snowing. It was very warm and quite the most romantic costume I have ever dressed in. I am sure the doctor was impressed though he did not say anything. Papa was impressed, and I think a little envious when I told him that you had brought it from Switzerland. (He has never been there.)

Wasn't it strange, in that last hour that we were together, we suddenly became so very happy? It is an excellent omen, I am sure, for you seem quite as close to me now as you did then, and I know it will always be that way. No parting could have been more perfect, because it was a simple revelation of the truth. There is no such thing as separation for us.

I have some things about my acting dancing theories that I wish to discuss with you, but I shall let that go until my head is clearer, and I have had more time to think. You must tell me all the details of fortune hunting.

All my love to you and Joy,
Sybil

8

My Darling Sybil—

The bus ride was a nightmare. It took me over 23 hours to get here. There was fog in the Pennsylvania mountains and, later, rain, as we drove through the soot-covered mining towns.

My father met me at the bus terminal, and we started a conversation which lasted on into the evening with my mother and which concerned, chiefly, the success I surely would have made as a salesman. I was in doubt about their conclusions, but it was not in disagreement. I may have to try my luck, yet.

Joy looks very well. She is an extraordinary child. She went to bed shortly after I arrived, and she was off to school the first thing in the morning, so we haven't had a chance to talk; but, one senses the soul about her that, to me, is like an embodiment of her first prayer—"I pray, oh Life-Spirit, keep me strong and loving and kind."

I love you,
Jerry

March 14, 1936
Newark, NY

Dearest Jerry,

I feel the same violent stimulation that gripped me two weeks ago when I was preparing for the demonstration. I feel that I must be doing something. When I finish this, I shall wrap up my head, put on my cape and galoshes and shuffle through the snow to the post. On the way, I shall have my first breath of fresh air, and I shall take into account all the moving objects along the way, feel them moving in me and make them a part of my collection of moving symbols. If you see any good ones please capture, experience and send them to me for my menagerie. I shall be very grateful.

I didn't walk to the post, because I couldn't bear to rush your letter, and the sun called me out immediately. I walked the other way, and found a boy riding his bicycle and pushing so hard on the pedals that he raised himself off the saddle with the effort. I felt myself doing it, and immediately my own pushing the air came to mind. Marvelous sensation! Then I saw a little dog trot along at a steady little patter. This is much harder to feel with the whole body. I tried to imagine myself dripping off a huge icicle and falling great depths into a snow bank covered with holes from former ones. Then I picked a red cluster from the high bush cranberry, stuck it in my hat and called the birds to feast, but they are not used to me; I have been away so long. All along my path the world acknowledged me, the bare branches stirred silently, the birds chirped, the snow glistened, the wet roofs dripped merrily and even people peered out at me from cars which splashed down the street. Several curtains stirred! I think it was all because of your magic cape with the hood hanging down my back holding in it all the potentialities of making me a medieval princess before their very eyes.

The rest of the afternoon I read *The Ordeal of Richard*

Feveral, and I am in a state of ecstasy over it. Do get it out and read the marvelous chapter called "Treatment of a Dragon."

Let me quote you this marvelous paragraph on love.

> Enchanted Islands have not yet rooted out their old brood of dragons. Wherever there is romance, these monsters come by inimical attraction. Because the heavens are certainly propitious to true lovers, the beasts of the abysses are banded to destroy them, stimulated by innumerable sad victories; and every love-tale is an epic war of the upper and lower powers. I wish good fairies were a little more active. They seem to be cajoled into security by the happiness of their favorites; whereas the wicked are always alert and circumspect. They let the little ones shut their eyes to fancy they are not seen, and then commence.

Do you like this?

Jerry, all sorts of ideas have been coming to me about what is wrong with the modern dance. All that I have been saying about the drama in the form of Stanislavsky and Meyerhold, I am beginning to realize can be said about Wigman and Humphrey—quality of movement and design and movement, improvisation and form—the only thing that can save the dance is the welding of the two. But while I think and experiment for myself, I am terribly anxious to know what Wigman worked out to express her dramatic ideas. I am going to talk to Hanya and find out more, and then if possible take some lessons. I am beginning to understand why and how the Wigmans can have a school and we don't have to. It takes much longer to train a student to develop his dramatic powers than his muscular powers.

I think one reason why no one on the road liked the *New Dance* was because there was no connection between the dancers or the cold and beautiful design of the dance and the audience.

There are two ways to connect with the audience—the cold informal ballet did it by appealing music, Isadora

Duncan by dramatic quality of movement. Miss Humphrey could have done it by her own personal performance in *New Dance*, but she knows nothing of this as Duncan and Pavlova did. Consequently there were two things going on at once in parallel lines—the dance and the audience. In New York it is different. They look for design and forgive everything else. I think, however, that they would welcome a good, convincing combination of the two. Some people think Graham is.

March 16th

The only thing which bothers me about your salesman job (except not knowing exactly where you are) is the difficulty you will have keeping up your dancing. I don't suppose you have yet had a chance to see Frampie [Eleanor Frampton, teacher in Cleveland, formerly in the Denishawn Company; later, critic for the *Cleveland Plain Dealer*]. Will you have a chance to work with her on weekends? And do you think you can do some stretching etc. before bed at night? I do so want you to keep it up because with all that business, the dance will make a nice balance, and it is the dancers who never grow old. Besides, as I told you after seeing *Stock Exchange* [a dance choreographed by Weidman] you do move very well, and all you need is just to stick at gaining control to be a very good dancer. You should practice balancing on one foot, swinging the other leg very slowly back and forth from the hip. Then do it on the toe giving at the ankle slightly as the leg passes from front to back and vice versa. Do all kinds of things for the feet and ankles in the balancing line, remembering the correct posture in the torso, and also using the breath. By that I mean breathe in as the motion with the body is up, and breathe out as the motion is down. Invent your own simple exercises of leg raising and twisting the torso keeping the balance at the same time. So much for the first lesson of our correspondence course.

Well, what do you suppose? The good fairies have brought back my Diana [*Diana of the Crossways*, a novel by George Meredith.]. I shall send it to you as soon as I know your address. Or perhaps, I shall wait until the weekend after next when you will be in Cleveland.

Over the radio there was just an announcement that the snowstorm west of Cleveland is terrific. I hope you are safe, but I am not the sort of a person to worry, so I shall just send all my mental telepathy waves of good luck and love to you, Jerry.

Monday, March 17th

Tonight I leave for New York. I had to toss a coin to decide, for everyone seemed to think it would be good for me to stay until Sunday while I held out for all the sensible reasons, such as teaching, necessity to get back into harness and start working so that I can work gradually into trim, your letters waiting at the Club, the fact that I am much better and able to begin on a schedule. I really would like to stay longer, because New York without you will seem so strange. But I shall certainly take you with me as you suggested though, darling, I would have done it anyway.

Yesterday, we went to Rochester to see the doctor and shop. (I have gained six pounds.) The scenery was one mass of ice in whites and blacks and grays. The willows were pink against the others, and the poplars slightly green. It was very much like our day at Swarthmore. Our country is so beautiful here, so rolling and covered with apple orchards and small woods that the frozen scene (even the grass was quite stiff) was a suitable background for a romantic adventure of a tribe of winter fairies. Fences were almost more astonishing than trees with their fantastic positions of frozen fringe.

March 20, 1936
Three Arts Club

Jerry Dear,

I cannot write long tonight because today has been an extremely long one and I'm worn out. I find that I can still dance, but I have no endurance, and my legs are rather wobbly.

Katie has at last bought a mirror, and it is enormous and very good, no flaws. Kenny said that you had better come back, for the boys class was deadly without you. Bill Matons asked me if I missed you. I said, "Yes, don't you?" and he agreed that he did.

Sunday, March 22,1936

Darling Jerry,

Your plant and your radio and your cape are all very well. I connected the 2nd by myself to the outside aerial, and am waiting for the symphony to start. The flowers have disappeared from the plant, leaving it very green and crisp. I am going to give it some sun on the roof when the wind goes down. Joy's garden of flowers is framed on the desk beside me. So everything around conspires to *remind me of you*.

I just came back from a short look at the Hudson during the intermission of the concert. The wind was so stiff that it was almost impossible to push my way onto the drive, and I had to hold the hood over my head to protect my ears, but once I reached the stone wall and looked over into the purple and brown river whose waves seemed to all be rushing right at me, I did not mind how the wind flapped and swirled around me. The sun was very bright and warm and made everything, buildings and trees and people and green buses, stand out in all their glorious if limited three dimensions.

There was so much motion about me that it was hard to decide which to study in my short stay of fifteen minutes. As much as I liked the bouncing of the gray branches in the park below, I could not keep my eyes off the waves. The white caps, of course, are the most spectacular thing about them, but before I flew back down the street, I noticed that marvelous seesaw motion in quick succession in a way that I had never seen it before. I think I have caught it in my body. When this is over, I shall try it.

I have discovered something about my theory of symbols, or rather about myself in composition which I did not know before. I find it easier to start with a distortion instead of a natural movement. According to my theory, this is wrong. It is, you see, improvisation rather than a development from the natural movement. I am starting first with a technical exercise, and the symbol of crumpling paper because I have captured that.

I intimated in my talk, though I had never thought of it before that moment, that a dancer could start from the natural dance movement and progress in the other direction. It is a little difficult to discover just which direction that is. Whether I should be satisfied with the natural movement I did at the demonstration and start from there into distortion or whether I should create a form in natural movement and distort it by the dramatic quality. I would prefer the latter because it gets me nearer to the real dance and farther from the interpretations of the other dancers of today.

Last night, I went to a solo recital given by the Dance Guild. Eleanor King was the first on the program. The others were Blanch Evan, Jane Dudley, Mary Radin and Miriam Blecher.

Yes, indeed, just as you said, they are children. There are a few thoughts among them, Blanch Evan perhaps. Eleanor did her *Mother of Tears* very beautifully. But her new numbers do not show that she has been experimenting with expression. Just as I said yesterday, these young dancers are taking the surface of the modern dance in their distortions and their dances of frustration. It seems to me that unless they get back to the natural dance, they will never find themselves.

Just arrived home from my first sitting for the sculptor Louis Aiello. But there was no letter from you, which means that I know nothing of you since Thursday evening "when there was a lull in your mental process." I hope it was not due to an illness of any sort. Anyway, I am sending as many good luck waves as I can. Oh, I hope nothing happened to keep you from receiving my letter! If you did not receive it, you must surely think me a beast.

Louis seems to be a very good sculptor. In an hour and a half, he had a good start on my portrait; I still look like Abraham Lincoln, however. He moves very like a dancer, for his strokes are large and sure, and he stoops, balances on one foot, and steps onto his tall stool with ease. The studio was filled with what looked like dozens of musty ghosts, but which were really half-finished clay structures covered with various designs of faded oil cloth to keep them damp. Everywhere was a film of white dust which I felt settle over me in just the short time I sat there. There was another model, an enormous colored woman, who blinked like a sleepy cat and stayed in the same position for so long that I was surprised to see her even move her eyelids.

When you are finally settled, I shall send you some names of dancers in Detroit. When you feel yourself *very* strong, I shall tell you where to find my Aunt May in that city.

Darling, my best love for your success,
Sybil

March 25, 1936

Dearest Jerry,

Write me a letter full of spring. There are so many movements, so beautiful, so exciting that I can't choose. Close your eyes and point to one and I shall take that, for this dance is for you. It is called *In Love, In Love*. It's about spring and wind and life, which are all love. It was born in the middle ages, and I discovered it in Chaucer's "Prelude" and "Aucassin and Nicolette." It was brought up in Ireland and is going to be re-born in America, strange place.

Ever yours with all my love,
Sybil

9

March 26, 1936
Three Arts Club

Dearest Jerry,

I am receding into the past so quickly, that unless I catch myself tonight I may be gone forever. I have gone "back to nature," and the worst of it is that I can see Miss Humphrey and the group from their cynical posts looking on. If only I didn't care, it would not matter but . . .

Jerry, I think Ada will trust me now, for would you believe it of me—I wept with my head on her lap today. She happened to be in the dressing room alone when I escaped from the studio where a man from Ceylon was urging us as artists to unite with other artists by uniting within our group. He did not know whether we were a cooperative group or not, but it was quite evident that we were not by Miss Humphrey's cold and unbelieving receipt of his pleading. She thought he was a fake, but she did not see that what he was saying was true. Whether he was a fake or not was so far from the important point that I could not stay in the room.

Ada stroked my head and told me that she thought she was the only one who was disappointed in the group.

Jerry, I shall have to tell Miss Humphrey or leave the group or perhaps both. This deadening feeling is hitting us all one by one, and I won't take it. I shall fight. Miss Humphrey should know. It is not fair to her to keep it from her, though whether she can do anything is another matter.

Tomorrow I shall speak to her.

My love to you,
Sybil

March 27, 1936
Three Arts Club

Jerry Dear,

Are you surprised? I am going to England this summer. I want to devote my life to the dance for love, not for the critics or the New York audience. I want to go where things are strange and I am filled with wonder, where I see things for the first time. I am going to make as many dances as I can before going. I must dance. I don't want to be an automaton. I know there is a place for me, but not here now. The world needs dancers for love, not dancers for work.

Jerry darling, can you, will you come with me? Or will you meet me there later? That is not important, for we will be together when we have something to offer each other. When I set out for England I shall have my first dances to offer the world. I shall go on a freighter as I hear it is the cheapest way, but anyway I have to find out more about it.

Every day in rehearsal, I shall do a scheduled number of exercises to improve my technique. It is exciting, this starting out. Write to me soon, dearest.

Love, love, love
Sybil

March 27,1936

Darling Sybil—

A note—a note for you, my one. Do not imagine—as one might—that I do not read your letters at every opportunity. There are many words of appreciation I could write, many comments I would make, and in time I shall.

I am enclosing Cartier's [a French mime] program. I happened to be passing, and I dropped in backstage in time to see the last two dances. Well, I'm in no mood to wax eloquent over someone else's vacuity—lest the boomerang . . .

I'm thinking about your problems in dance expression, I promise you.

With my love,
Jerry

March 28, 1936
Three Arts Club

Jerry Dearest,

I have such a long story to tell you. I am finding myself, and where do you suppose I am? I am right in the middle of the Romantic School with Shelley and Wordsworth and Isadora and Wagner. I am amazed, believe me, but I like it. Yes, I am now a child of nature. I don't want to protest against anything, but to preach to glorify nature through the art form of the dance. Have you read Shelley's "Sensitive Plant"? I want my expression to have in it the "significant detail," to light the whole for my audiences. But I must study the elements and feel myself one with them. I am not ready for the modern dance as represented by the sophisticated New York dancers and critics.

Jerry, you must not come with me unless you too become a romantic. It would be wonderful if we could do this together, but if you feel you are not in sympathy with this school of thought completely, by that I mean with complete love and faith, then I must go alone and come out from it to you later. The first symptom I had was one of utter depression, and then when I found myself a romantic, I became stimulated with joy in a way that I have not felt since I first discovered nature about 11 years ago. I feel unashamed of my love for what Martha Graham would call the sentimental. Can you feel so, too?

These dancers are all caught up in critical ideas. I prefer feeling things and then criticizing them afterwards. I have not had a chance to talk to Miss Humphrey, but I shall have to tell her that the attitude of the group is not mine; the modern dance, as she knows it, no longer binds me.

I know that this is not a sudden conviction. As long ago as last June, I was dissatisfied with the group, but decided to take no notice of it. Then as things went from bad to worse, the Bennington engagement arrived bringing you and a whole new world with it. I forgot group problems to a certain degree. But now that you are not here, the whole sensation comes back to me with terrific force. And I realize what Edith and Ada must have been suffering without the distraction of being in love.

I have been reading over all the poems of the Romantic School that impressed me in college, and I find they are even more exquisite than I thought. Here is one of Coleridge's which I think is delightful.

Something Childish, But Very Natural
(Written in Germany)

If I had but two little wings
And were a little feathery bird,
To you I'd fly, my dear!
But thoughts like these are idle things,

And I stay here.
But in my sleep to you I fly:
I'm always with you in my sleep!
The world is all one's own,
But then one wakes, and where am I?
All, all alone.
Sleep stays not, though a monarch bids;
So I love to wake ere break of day,
For though my sleep be gone,
Yet while 'tis dark, one shuts one's lids,
And still dream on.

Here is another marvelous poem.

The Pains of Sleep

Ere on my bed my limbs I lay,
It hath not been my use to pray
With moving lips or bended knees;
But silently, by slow degrees,
My spirit I to love compose,
In humble trust mine eyelids close,
With reverential resignation,
No wish conceived, no thought expressed,
Only a sense of supplication;
A sense o'er all my soul imprest
That I am weak, yet not unblest,
Since in me, round me, everywhere
Eternal strength and wisdom are,
But yester-night I pray'd aloud
In anguish and in agony,
Up-starting from the fiendish crowd
Of shapes and thoughts that tortured me:
A lurid light, a trampling throng,
Sense of intolerable wrong,
And whom I scorned, etc.

This man reminds me of you, and so does Shelley. I have always thought of you as a poet. If only you could throw off this material, cynical world of criticism and become free with the romantic spirit with which you were born. Here is something from "Sensitive Plant." To me it shows marvelous freedom.

> And the sinuous paths of lawn and of moss,
> Which led through the garden along and across,
> Some open at once to the sun and the breeze,
> Some lost among bowers of blossoming trees,
> Were all paved with daisies and delicate bells,
> As fair as fabulous asphodels,
> And flowerets which, drooping as the day drooped too,
> Fell into pavilions, white, purple and blue,
> To roof the glowworm from the evening dew.

March 28, 1936

Darling,

Your letter of March 26th worries me considerably. I wish I could spin out words of advice on your group problems. Unfortunately, I can only surmise the actual conditions you face, but I do feel that there is only one way that a person may freely choose to leave a group such as Doris leads, and that is by going beyond its bounds creatively. To contemplate a change because of the lack of the cooperative opportunity is, in my mind, allowable when the alternative project practically forces attention to its greater possibilities through the kind of creative ferment that can no longer contain itself within the old mold. I see no justification for change, however, simply because of an appeal for the cooperative spirit—as fine and as ennobling as that spirit may be in the ordinary life.

Darling, I know that your scene with Ada was in passing and that whatever you may do will be profoundly right.

With all my love,
Jerry

Dearest Sybil,

I am writing to you soon, I am, even if a bit feebly. I can read your letter and see "London, dance, love, many dances, dancers for love, England, freighter, schedule of exercises, exciting." It makes glorious reading, dear, and I have no doubts or fears about your undertaking a program with such inspiring beginnings. I am confident of the success of your mission as an artist in whom I've seen the world dance.

That I love you is another matter which, I believe, you had best store in some small compartment under lock and key.

You also wrote "we will be together when we have something to offer each other." I agree perfectly. The future may find me with something to offer. Meanwhile, despite absolute physical well-being, I am not able to hold on to the concentration needed for work. For the present, I cannot find words for further explanation.

Did you see Agnes de Mille? Good luck next Sunday night.

Love to you,
Jerry

Wednesday, April 1st

My Dearest Jerry,

Your letter from Cleveland just arrived. You don't know how I have been longing to hear from you. I have saved this letter until I should know your address. I am so glad you approve of my thoughts and desires. But while you are sad, I can never be truly happy. I feel, like you, that I am not ready for the world—that I should go off and prepare myself. I want to thrill my audiences with a desire for a better life and send them home not dissatisfied with themselves but uplifted by more confidence.

But you are my chief audience. Everything I do is for you, because you are the most important person in the world. You are the idealist. My dances are all about you.

That you love me is a matter which I can put under lock and key and keep close to me, but the fact that I love you is a part of my loving which shows in all my thoughts and movements.

Please tell me your thoughts, dear, dear Jerry. Every time you are happy, even the slightest, I am sixty million times as happy.

I felt he needed to create. He was an artist. Just working for a living was traditional thinking. It was not enough. We both knew it.

April 2, 1936

Jerry,

I have been through something that may surprise you. I had a long talk with Miss Humphrey tonight about the group. I told her how I felt about it, and I confessed to her that what I needed was to compose a dance. I showed her my tormented spirit which for some egotistical and unfair reason I have kept from you. She said to me, "Sybil, yours is a bad case of frustration. You should not think. Bring me your ideas and your movement themes, and I will put them together for you. That is fun for me. I like to arrange dances. But you must not think that because you do not do the whole, that it is not yours." Miss Humphrey gave me hope, that in the future I may arrange my own dances, but how do I know that? However, strangely enough, I have hope, I have the romantic spirit.

Jerry, we both have an appreciation of the beautiful. It should be to give the world and those we love some of our appreciation. If we feel first, as Miss Humphrey wisely said, instead of thinking, we may unconsciously create something quite valuable.

Can you believe it; I did not mention to Miss Humphrey any of my thoughts of England, or the glorious art for love. I have been through many stages since this problem first came up, and strangely, very strangely, my problem turns out to be yours. We are both straining too hard for what does not belong to us. Happiness is giving, and we should give the easiest way by living simply and working simply.

Come to Bennington this summer. Charles wants you. Bill Matons asked me to tell you that he is trying to get the men's group together, and he said he thought you wanted to come. It will mean all expenses, including carfare, paid, and we are giving a program of dances to raise money for the group at Bennington to pay for toothpaste, etc. Anyway, Charles is trying to get some extra money for the boys. Bring Joy with you.

Let's be whimsical rather than deep. I am sure it would suit us better. If you hate me for changing then tell me, and I shall know it was not me you loved but an idea. If you still love me, then come to me and we will each live together beyond frustration.

All my love to you,
Sybil

April 3, 1936

Darling,

Only know that I love you and pray for a true light to guide you in your seeking after beauty.

You *are* my belief, my one—and I press a kiss of adoration to your hand.

Your,
Jerry

I had what seemed like a practical idea. What was in my mind was reasonable from a theory point of view. I saw the Humphrey-Weidman group in two sections; one in New York with Doris and Charles creating new works and performing them with the original group, and a second traveling company doing their works on the road. I called Jerry in Cleveland to give him this thought.

April 4, 1936

Jerry Dear,

Please forgive me for my impulsive phone call. It served only one purpose, and that to let you know about things here.

This idea of the second concert group has not materialized yet, of course. I have been going through all sorts of violent changes, and I find that Miss H. is very tolerant and willing to help me with my ideas. This idea we talked over last fall, and she said she wanted to do it as soon as she had enough dancers and someone she could trust to direct it. You and I are just the people for that job. I want to dance and so do you, and you are the born director. Miss H's understudy and scholarship group are full of possibilities for a group. We should get working on this plan this spring, get an agent for the group who books only concerts then we will not have to pay anything to the N. B. C. because it will be an entirely different group. The group on the road will pay a percentage to those in New York who are performing there and creating new dances with Doris & Charles.

It is what I have been really desiring in a vague sort of way for a long time.

If we conduct the matter in a systematic and cooperative way with you as head with the last word of consent, there is no reason why we cannot make a grand success. I know they would trust this matter to you. I think you would have to come to Bennington, however.

I would like to talk to you, because our correspondence is so one-sided. But if you will write me fully what you think it will clear up things.

A telegram arrived.

S. L. SHEARER, 340 WEST 85 ST.
BRINGING LAWYER TOMORROW TO TALK MAN-
AGERIAL PROMOTION PROPOSITION NOTIFY
CHARLES REMAINING SUNDAY. JERRY.

Jerry came to New York with the lawyer. I was not there for the talk with Charles and Doris. But perhaps Doris saw the handwriting on the wall, because she and Charles had left Denishawn taking with them many of their dancers for the new Humphrey-Weidman Company. She knew my strength and my passion for creating, and was aware of Jerry's popularity.

I had no thoughts at all of defecting, but, of course, that could change over time, and a husband and wife team is always a threat to any business. Anyway, Doris was not ready to expand, and I am sure Pauline thought it would be a foolish move—a young company without Doris and Charles would not be salable, and she did all the booking. So it was just another fanciful dream realizable only in an ideal world.

However, everything was left vague. . . .

April 7, 1936
Three Arts Club

My Darling Jerry,

How wonderful it was to see you and talk to you! Now, I know that all is right. I could never have really been straightened out by letter. It seems almost like a dream now; it was so sudden and over so quickly. Yes, our decision is just what it should have been, and I am looking forward to its fulfillment.

This afternoon I had my first lesson with Miss Humphrey in composition. The dear darling just has no power of inspiration. She gave me a few suggestions to work on and has made another appointment for the next lesson. She has suggested a fugue by Lord Berners for the accompaniment. I shall probably use that. If she is my leader, I should take all her suggestions unless I disagree too heartily. The movement was clear to her as far as idea was concerned, so that gave me some hope. I told you the name of it is *In Love, In Love*, but, of course, I didn't tell her that. She said, "It looks as though some new and wonderful idea were being revealed to you." That is the first part. The second is the dawning of understanding—I know for a moment and then it is gone until in the last part is the realization of this and the exciting knowledge of being in love. All my themes are from nature, and so is the dramatic quality which I have yet to work on. I am just dying to get into the country.

[This first dance that Doris was helping with was eventually called *Revelation* and the themes from nature were objects moved by the wind. I had noticed a flag blowing in the wind, and practiced this in all parts of my body. Then I watched all kinds of other things being blown, at the same time connecting them with emotions, and then more subtly with feelings, making my transitions from one feeling to another by changes in the wind as I built up the sequence of what I wished to say through these movements.

It was the body in relation to the surrounding world, the human being humanizing nature, and, at the same time, nature spiritualizing the human being. Later, each succeeding dance was a new discovery. There was no movement formula. In this way I built up my technique and skills. These skills, however, were nothing in themselves. I had to be connected to the universe to make them useful. Louis Horst called me esoteric—I never understood what he meant by this. Everything I did seemed very logical to me, and necessary.

My movements were not the natural movements of the human being—skipping, walking, jumping, sliding, etc. This was so basic that I took it for granted. This kind of locomotion was the human being carried by legs through space, things you did anyway—first as a child, then later mostly walking, and still later limping or shuffling. These for Doris were the natural connecting forms. In ballet the connecting forms were more stylized. (See Addendum III.)]

I am enclosing a card which came with flowers from one of my pupils who not only agrees with my technique of acting but is actually carrying it out in her own development. She is a splendid girl.

This evening I had five pupils again at the Club. So you see I am really reaping the fruits of my demonstration. It looked at first as though no one was going to pay any attention, but suddenly, all these people popped up. I have three classes now.

Really, Jerry, I believe that to inspire people, to stimulate their interest in life and art is the greatest part of greatness.

Best love,
Sybil

After being in the group for a while, but before finishing my dance, I felt the need to perform, but I had to arrange my own appearances. So I asked permission of the Club to use the theatre for an evening, and invited my friends to see what I had worked out—some of which were studies from Doris's and Charles's classes and some pieces of their choreography.

I received enthusiastic applause from Three Arts Club friends. Actually, I thought everyone was applauding. Perhaps they were, but they were not talking. I wondered why I was being ignored at this little reception afterwards. My dance friends and teachers seemed to be more interested in eating and gossiping.

Later it dawned on me. They did think it was good, but they did not want me to graduate too soon. If I had been bad, they all would have been telling me how much they enjoyed it, because they felt sorry for me. So I found that every step I made in any direction was a learning process. I just had to figure out what it was that I was learning. Actually, opposition is a great help.

———————

Even though things were vague, it seemed to make sense for Jerry to come back to New York. He was determined to make his way as a writer. He had two projects—a play about Uncle Tom and a biography of Maurice Silvers, a WPA dancer. He rejoined Weidman's men's group, and in general I felt more positive about the immediate future with a summer in Bennington together.

10

May 10, 1936
Three Arts Club

My Dear Miss Starbuck,

The spring issue of the Skidmore Alumnae Bulletin has just arrived, and I am sorry to have to inform you that you have made a mistake when you say that I am an "interesting example of the success of Skidmore alumnae in a field of work for which I was prepared at college." If, and it seems quite possible, you are identifying me with the physical education department, I must tell you that I was an English major for the last two years and a half, and an art major before that. I never had any connection with that section of the college which claimed to teach dancing, for I found they had no conception of the dance as an art, and I was not interested in dance as physical education except as a necessary alternative for something as unbearable as baseball.

I was very sorry indeed not to meet again and talk to some of the professors with whom I had been very friendly during college. I had hoped that dance club would afford some sort of a reception to make that possible. For the future, however, I shall save myself any hopes from a group that I knew during my own stay at college to be completely spiritless.

I hope you will make the necessary correction in the next issue of the Alumnae Bulletin.

Sincerely yours,
Sybil Shearer

May 17, 1936

Sybil Dear,

A letter from Lilli von Qualen tells me about your visit and triumphal performance at Skidmore. You don't know how glad and gratified I am that you had a chance to show them up there what you can do. I always knew that you would have your innings sooner or later, but I really didn't dare hope that the opportunity would come this soon. Lilli was very enthusiastic in her praise of the whole group, and, since she knows that you are one of my very favorite friends, she took considerable pains to tell me about your work.

Congratulations, dear; I knew, of course, that you were doing fine things, and that you must be getting recognition of a most unusual sort for your steady application and talents. But I guess I have a nasty streak in me that especially enjoys saying "I told you so" to a few of those narrow-minded small-time folks around your Alma Mater.

Thanks for your lovely, long last letter. I appreciated your description of *New Dance*. My one touch with the world that does and feels things is the *New York Times* and I have followed Martin's column all year. He has made a number of comments on that particular piece of work, and I felt very much in the know, since I had your explanation and interpretation with which to fill out his criticisms. I can't imagine anything more gratifying than to be at work with a group of creative people such as you have found, and I know that your own temperament and ingenuity and imagination must be of great value to them. I only regret that I can't see the results of all your study and maturing, and I sincerely hope that the day isn't too far off when I'll be able to watch you in action.

I wasn't at all surprised when you told me that you had

fallen in love; although I never felt like playing Dorothy Dix and assuring you that it would some day happen, I had little doubt that one as wholly alive as you would miss the experience. With my inevitable procrastination I may have waited to write you until the whole affair is either a thing of the past or has taken on an entirely different aspect. You spoke about wanting my advice and thereby made me extremely self-conscious, primarily because I feel that there is really no one who can advise in such matters and secondarily because I feel that I am especially unfitted. I have perfect confidence in your good judgment and in your own clear vision of what you want in life, and as long as one hangs onto those two qualities I can't see much danger of going astray.

I have an old-fashioned theory that there's still enough of the ancient code left in our ideas to make it advisable for any couple to decide which one of the two possibilities for a career is more important and to pool all efforts towards the realization of the superior talents. Sometimes the woman has those talents and sometimes the man; occasionally they are equally divided and both remain great, and that is, of course, the ideal. There certainly is no arbitrary standard, and one has to work out a plan for every situation. Since you and your man have precisely the same interests and would probably therefore find opportunities for the same kind of work wherever you live, you may never find it necessary to concentrate on one line of development. And, I grant, my own sense tells me, in our case, that I would never amount to much professionally anyway, in comparison to the potentialities of my husband. A certain strain of the placid and easy-going in me makes it easier for me to accept what will contribute to the general good of our union than it would be for some career woman. I tried to size up all the possibilities before I decided to marry, and such a situation as this was one of them that I had to admit. Again, I get back to my original contention after much wandering; a good, clear sight into what one most wants in life is about the most necessary bit of equipment with which to go into marriage.

And after all that jumbled mess, all I really mean is that you should more or less let your head and heart both work on the problem.

Since I wrote, so long ago, I've led a pleasant and busy life.

What are you doing this summer? I hope that you'll find a chance to get out of the city and to rest yourself a bit against next year's season. Is it to be Bennington or something of that sort?

Please give my regards to your mother and father, and if you see Janet give her my best. As for yourself, my fondest wishes are always for you and, despite my desultory habits of correspondence, I am thinking of you very often and always with loving thoughts and hopes that I may see you before too many years elapse.

Ruth

May 27, 1936
Three Arts Club

Dearest Jerry,

The prospect of not seeing you until Friday is a little disturbing, especially since this is my last week in New York. I love the Ferde Grofe music which you suggested. But I shan't be able to start that until I go home.

Really, home does not seem as pleasant to me without the thought of your visit. I am enclosing a picture of our garden pool to inveigle you into a serious consideration. I am so glad you are making such strides with *Uncle Tom*. I look forward to the time when I can read it.

Miss Humphrey told us that she would like her next work to be concerning romance and love. (Isn't that wonderful for me? I just think to myself that it may have something to do with my talk to her in April.) She has asked us to all be on the look out for themes either contemporary or in history that would be suitable for a ballet. I suggested *Orlando*, but she had never read it. She said she would prefer a modern theme, but she wanted it to be heroic. Miriam said she thought the reason why love was no longer a good subject for art was because it was no longer the most important factor in life. I jumped on her and some others after me.

Today I tried to pack. My room is cluttered with boxes, paper, clothes, books and millions of letters which I am throwing away (not yours).

Dearest Jerry. I look forward to Friday and you. I expect to have all my packing done, so that all the rest of my time will be yours as you want it.

My love is all yours,
Sybil

Newark, NY

My Dearest Jerry,

The first day of our separation is walking toward suppertime and much to my surprise I find I can eat and relish it. I no longer have a fever and physically feel quite normal.

But it is delightful here, and you must come if possible. The house has been partly redecorated, and I think you will like it. Mama is quite antique conscious. The garden is so lovely, and the breezes wonderfully warm. I lay out in the sun for a while this morning, and played some records this afternoon, and stretched a little. Tomorrow I shall start work.

Please send me the names of the plays we decided would be good for ballets. I shall read them while here.

Tonight, as the air becomes cooler, I feel inspired for us both.

All my love,
Sybil

June 3, 1936
Newark, NY

Dearest Jerry,

Today has had its place, but it was not important for I have not really settled yet. The climate seems to make me sleepy. This morning I practiced on the lawn, because the parish house has not been cleaned, but tomorrow I start there clean or not. I have thought out the *Prelude* to the end, and shall try to put it into real movement when I have the space.

I have read over *A Dollar* and find it to be even a better play than I thought. It suits my sentiments of today to a tee, for it shows how completely money can distort values. I think it will make an excellent ballet if only enough thought can be put on it to make the movements as significant as the words.

All my love,
Sybil

Wednesday, June 3rd

You darling one—

Yesterday was the crisis for me. I guess I was really sick.

Actually, I wasn't alone for a moment all day long. Maurice and I made excellent progress on the biography both morning and evening (we didn't go to rehearsal—Maurice notified Charles by phone), and Don Saks came in when Maurice left at midday and stayed on for dinner with us when Maurice returned. Don is such a pathetic soul. I gathered my strength to help him clarify his thoughts about his projected play, but I am at such a ragged end by the time he leaves and he is so unaware of the damaging effect he has on me that, in the future, I'll have to be a little more hard-boiled and refuse to allow him to exploit my energy. Still, he's such a miserable one and lonely; and in the midst of our discussion, he suddenly got a notion about a certain medicinal jelly that he insisted on running all the way to 4th Avenue to get for me. Ach! the contradictions in people. To live with them and to find them acceptable without the support of an organized religion requires the strength and vision of Jove.

I love you, darling! I had visions of you yesterday, and always I saw you smiling and off on your toes in a green setting that I helped create—nest-like—

I just received your letter, another of your "revelations" of you to accompany me wherever I go.

The plays and scenes we decided would be good for ballets are:

Pan, by Charles van Lerberghe, in French
The Magnificent Cuckold by Fernand Crommelynck, in MS
The Little Clay Cart, in Sanskrit
Pelleas and Melisande, by Maeterlinck
Uncle Tom's Cabin, by us or "Sybillus"
A Dollar, by David Pinsky
The wind scene from *Orlando,* by V. Woolf
The Lady From the Sea, by Ibsen (or scenes from it)
The Last Night of Don Juan—Edmund Rostand
Chanticleer, by E. Rostand (or parts of the last three acts)
Lilulu, by Romain Rolland
Joan of Arc, by "Sybillus"
Scenes from Moliere, *Le Bourgeois Gentilhomme*
Tartuffe
Scapin, etc.
Pippa Dances, by Hauptmann
Certain Biblical characters and stories like that of Ruth
Poems of Shelley's—What about "Cenci"?

And all the musical symphonic poems, and the operas. And modern themes and interpretations.

Darling, the world teems with its offerings if only we can create the needed ballet forms to give them "altar"! But you are doing just that, my darling, and you will, and I shall be with you loving you always.

Jerry

My kindest regards to your mother and father, J.

June 4, 1936
Newark, NY

Dearest Jerry,

I was so happy to receive your letter this morning. Thank you for the long list.

This morning I worked for a good two-and-a-half hours at the parish house, which had been excellently cleaned for me, and I practically finished my *Prelude* and started on my next dance. I also did *Revelation* for the first time since the performance. It was quite a satisfaction to feel that it was a real dance and had already stood the test of two performances. Nothing has been done about my appearance here. Mama seems reluctant to start, and she is always trying to get me to rest, etc., which is all very absurd. I am quite well. All I needed was a change of air and scene.

I think my father is rather surprised that I get up before he does, and my work, I know, has gone up in his estimation because of it.

All my love,
Sybil

Sybil Darling—

I received your second letter, and I was glad to know that you were entirely well.

The Dollar is certainly good material. From your account of it, I can recognize a certain Rabelaisian gusto characteristic of the "commedia-del-arte," which was theatre at its most pantomimic. I agree that it could be turned into a riotously funny dance—the broader its humor, the better—and that, at the same time, it would bite below the surface with its "dollar" implications. It's worth thinking about, pending the time when you will have the people.

I'm hurrying Maurice as much as possible. Yesterday was our best day. We worked morning and night and covered about 8500 words. He is rehearsing with Charles and Doris for the WPA on the stage of the Daly Theatre from 12 to 4 each day. It seems that the music isn't ready, and the opening performance in Brooklyn is to be postponed to some later date than June 8th. I wonder when Doris and Charles intend to go on their vacations.

I can feel the pull of Newark. It must be because of your hoping, you sweet one. Of course, miracles can happen. I may be there yet.

With my love,
Jerry

June 5, 1936
Newark, NY

Jerry Darling,

I am sitting in the sun on the terrace as I write and I am experiencing the feeling of great heat which I can use in my dance, but not depression which the heat is supposed to express.

The plants in the rock garden are marvelous. I feel like a giant when I stop and look at them in the crevices and drooping over edges of rocks that I could imagine to be almost mountain-like. Some of the plants are rubbery to the touch and covered with many round leaves, and some are like spun green silk dotted with tiny white stars. There are thousands of varieties. I would love to be little and lost in the woods and the caves of the rock garden.

My very best love,
Sybil

June 5, 1936

Dearest Sybil—

It's a quarter to three, and I haven't received your letter yet today. I hope you didn't suffer a kind of relapse in your illness as I did. I won't be able to go to Charles' rehearsal this afternoon, but I expect to be doing handsprings by tomorrow.

According to Maurice, Doris notified the WPA group that she accepted an engagement with Smallens at the Stadium for July 2nd and 3rd. She said she would do *New Dance* with her own group and *Prelude*, *Gigue* and *March* with the WPA people. This would seem to mean that you'd have to stop in NY before going to Bennington, and possibly somewhat in advance of July 2nd for a few rehearsals. I'm afraid that this necessitates a change in your June plans, but you should hear from Doris or Pauline about the matter.

Last night I dreamt about you, doing your *Prelude*. It was all so sparkling and gay, and it was on a grassy plot in the outdoors. I remember I was sitting on my haunches with my head and face upturned following your turning and bending from side to side. There seemed to be an ecstasy in the air, because I knew you wanted to create warmth, and here I was basking in a veritable flood of sunshine shooting off in starry sparks from your face and hair and dress and feet and hands!

My darling, separation is endurable knowing that you are daily weaving just such visions for dreams. I am in love with the "revelations" moving around me.

Your,

Jerry

Jerry Dearest,

What do you suppose has been rushing into my head again? England!

I went to the doctor yesterday, and he said that he could see nothing wrong with my tonsils, but that my blood pressure was way below normal and that I was very tired. I really don't feel tired. I simply feel the pressure of life on me, demanding immediate results. But I refuse to conform and I am sure that will help just as long as I don't feel that I am being rebellious, for rebellion is wasteful too.

I have more or less come back to my senses today after a lone drive through the country. We really live in the country. I never realized it before. The trees and houses of Newark were cutting off my vision, but as I rolled back into the village after my drive through the cozy country roads over the hills and in warm green valleys, I knew that Newark was just a gathering of houses and people that puckered up the country-side in one spot like a smocking stitch on a summer dress.

My dearest one, I love you so very much. Because we are not normal people who want to settle for the sake of our children's children, we will always find it hard, but we shall know great ecstasy and our greatest ecstasy will be when other people know it through us.

All my love to you,

Sybil

Dearest Jerry,

Now I am playing Tchaikowsky's Swan Lake Ballet Suite. It is so beautiful. I think the classic ballet must have been at its best when it inspired such lovely music. I bought it my senior year in college, and played it constantly and never tired of it.

This day is one which brings up memories—nothing definite, nothing pleasant or unpleasant, but still not restful with all the peace. I cannot help thinking of Mrs. Woolf's lines from *To the Lighthouse* which I am reading:

> . . . but Minta still sobbed, all the way up to the top of the cliff. It was her grandmother's brooch: she would rather have lost anything but that, and yet Nancy felt, it might be true that she minded losing her brooch, but she wasn't crying only for that. She was crying for something else. We might all sit down and cry, she felt. But she did not know what for.

In this frame of mind I ought to do a good movement for my dance of depression. I shall try tonight after supper and if anything comes of it I shall for some strange reason be happy again. I am always optimistic even when most depressed. But I have also decided that in a solo composition, instinct alone and not theories carry one through, just as in literature, plays and novels must have theory, but in lyric poems the writer uses inspiration and intuition.

Dearest this is the extent of me for today.

Sybil

Monday, June 8th

Darling,

I saw Mathilda Naaman's recital last night. It was childish, uneven, shallow, badly managed, without excuse. I was more than disappointed; I was shocked. You know, little Dotty has shown such an all-embracing faith in Mathilda—and then you had such high regard for Mathilda's technique studies— that I was prepared, at least, to see an adult performance. Well, what I saw could have only pleased their mammas and papas, who were there in abundance. What gave me further cause for sober reflection as I left the place was that Dotty ran over to me after the last dance full of buoyancy and confidence, exclaiming, "Wasn't it good work? Aren't we good? We've got a future, haven't we?" It simply means that there is a point where optimism becomes synonymous with ignorance or insanity. The poor kids. They weren't dancing, that's all. Not one minute of the time.

How, in a creative art such as dancing, can so many modern dancers have turned their backs on beauty in expression? Because ugliness is strength and beauty is weakness? Never was such the case.

My darling, you have the pure love and the strength, never compromise that which you have.

I love you, sweetheart,
Jerry

June 10, 1936
Newark, NY

My Dearest Jerry,

The news about the group is a little disturbing, especially since you will not be able to come here at all, but you must go to Bennington. I couldn't bear it there without you.

Evidently they do not need me and probably will not call me. I am really quite glad.

I am at last come out of this depression or whatever it is that has been weighing me down. I have started on my dance in a methodical way. I find myself making long lists of symbols and ideas that will help create designs as well as qualities of movement, and I find myself very much exhilarated. Please don't worry over my moods, for I know they are passing things even though when they are here they seem endless.

The *Prelude* is at last beginning to feel like something. I wish I could see some of the movements in a mirror, but there are none around.

Well, I have my first engagement for the fall. On October 8th I am to give a concert demonstration (half & half) for the Maplewood Junior Woman's Club (with pay!)

Yes, I am feeling extremely blithe and gay and worthwhile again.

We were very close Monday night. I felt your presence and for the first time since coming here wished myself back in New York with you with all my might, and could think of nothing else for ever so long.

I look forward to Bennington because of you, and I swear to have my dance done before then to show you.

Sybil

You Sybil one—

What is Virginia Woolf doing to you? Your Monday letter makes you seem so forlorn—or at least Sybil-lorn. I can't endure the thought of your being in low spirits.—I knew the depression wouldn't last. Your Tuesday letter which just arrived (it's 3:15 P.M.) reassures me, as you were already in the process of thinning down the line between the air without and the air within; but while your dark periods continue the impulse that carries me toward you is almost more than I can restrain.

We rehearsed again this morning with Doris. It was mostly technique with some attention given to *New Dance*. It is hardly likely that Kenny and George will be absent for the two concerts, so you need have no concern about your variation. If you haven't heard from Pauline yet, it must mean that Doris decided not to bother you with anything in addition to *New Dance*. She goes on her two weeks vacation this next Monday, and I suppose she'll want you here on her return to rehearse the last week before the concerts.—I hear that the program will include *New Dance*, *Prelude*, *Gigue*, *March*, *Piccoli* (by Charles, Jose, Beatrice and Edith), the Handel composition for Doris and Charles, the Stravinsky Suite!! (Jose and Letitia). I understand the above selections were influenced primarily by Smallens' musical requirements.

You darling—I have to run off now. I intend to find more time later.

Jerry

June 10, 1936
Newark, NY

Dear Mrs. Woolf,

Enclosed you will find a letter which I wrote to you last autumn but never mailed, because I never had time to look up your address. Now that I am on my vacation, and I have found it at last in an old Who's Who, I hope it is still the same. Our library is so far behind.

Since the last letter, I have read *A Room Of One's Own* and *To the Lighthouse* both of which I admire immensely, and I have composed a dance of my own called *Revelation*. When I was composing it, I read again the marvelous passage from *Orlando* in which the wind comes up and blows Orlando and Shel indoors to be married.

This spring I had a great urge to fly to England where I awoke when I was 13 and where I hoped I might be able to meet and talk to you. Believe me, of all the authors I have ever read, you are the one I most wish to know. But instead I made my dance. Heaven knows when I shall ever get to England, but when I do I hope I may offer my admiration in person.

Thursday, June 11

Sybil Darling—

The rehearsals continue unabated. There is nothing new to report except that I noticed that K. Litz is rehearsing Letitia's variation, to be ready in case the latter doesn't show up. I received your June 10th letter today, and I was very glad to hear about your engagement for Oct. 8th. I hope you will be successful in finding other similar engagements. I consider it especially important that you attempt to build up your own list of bookings as long as the group atmosphere is such as Doris and Charles create. Did I remember to tell you that there will probably be a change in the policy of the WPA project for dancers by next September? Charles said they expect all dancers to be unionized and to be admitted on the project—if they meet with the higher standards—even though they were not primarily on relief. I managed to get to see *Macbeth* last night [a WPA production directed by Orson Wells]. I was thrilled with the jungle scenes. I felt that they had made a production out of the witches' scenes and that all else was pretty much of the kitchen variety. No one can come near the blacks for their voodoo effectiveness, but to call it *Macbeth* seemed to me a bit specious.

Always—your—Jerry

June 12, 1936
Newark, NY

My Dearest One,

I am getting quite tanned and I sing in the sun when I am not reading in order not to waste time. I am giving exercise to my voice every day now as well as my body, and I am teaching myself to read aloud. The ideal drama, it seems to me, would not leave out the words altogether. They should come as the crowning point of the meaning—movement is the root of all. And when there is no speaking or when there is only one person on stage, then there should be music. But everyone in the cast should be essentially a dancer with the movement interpretation for all meaning. I think it is possible soon, and should be worked for beginning now. I am working more of my symbols into scenes. It is devilishly hard, but very good practice and a basis on which to create.

I liked most of *Macbeth* very much especially the sleep walking scene. Tell me why you don't think it should be called "Macbeth"? I also liked the banquet scene where light was used for the ghost, and in fact was quite moved by the whole production. I thought L.M. and her husband, though he could have been better, very sympathetically portrayed.

Yours forever and ever,
Sybil

June 14, 1936
Newark, NY

Dearest Jerry,

It seems ages since I last wrote to you (day before yesterday) and eons since receiving a letter (same), and today is Sunday full of church-going and dressing up in one's best and dining out. I have a new hat, very large, which I pray that you will like, for I shall have to wear it anyway and that would be too bad.

Yesterday I received a letter from Doris telling me all the news at the studio. She said she hoped I would be back on the 29th, because they needed me and that I could be in the Roussel Suite if I came the week previous. However, I don't expect to do the latter for various reasons.

My mind is extending itself out in directions that I may not be able to get to for some time, but anyway, things are starting to move. I imagine three dances to come before *Revelation* and one afterwards to complete the whole idea. My trouble so far, I have discovered, is that I have been trying to put too much in the dance I am on now.

Yesterday was the big event in our household—the flower show. Mama tore around madly to get things ready and arrange flowers and boss people and entertain judges at lunch, etc. etc. She was going so madly that she couldn't stop even this morning but must get breakfast early, go down to see how the flowers kept overnight and then dress and to church. Even after that, when one might expect an ordinary person to relax before dinner, she had to take the mop, mind you, and go over the hall floor and pick up odd bits and books and straighten and arrange and dust, until I thought I'd go mad and called out, "Sit down! Relax! Sit down! Relax!" to no avail. It was the reflex action like Charlie Chaplin on the machine or a chicken with its head cut off. But now things will settle, I hope. No more cameramen in the garden, so that I can bask in the sun content. One would think we lived on a showy estate the way we have been treated, but I must say, Papa's garden is nice and larger than most, though not enormous by any means.

Now dozens of visiting Garden Presidents and their families are milling around the pool and finding mutual acquaintances in their conversation.

Monday

Last night I had supper with Miss Munson. I made her my audience for all my creative difficulties and, walking home in the dark evening, I felt lighter.

This morning Mama asked me why I was so aloof. She seemed to sense something about me that you have noticed, and she asked me what was the matter, but I could not tell her for I did not know. But I discovered when I began to practice my dance! It all came out, and I did it in an hour and a half. What I have been struggling with for so long? Of course it is not finished, but I know the form and the outline and some of the qualities. It is such a relief.

Now I have one more to do which I am going to make short and sophisticatedly cynical if possible and that finishes the dances (first draft) coming before *Revelation*. After it can be the rest of my life.

My dearest one, I hope you are well and in good spirits and

able to work. I hope to hear from you soon. There was no letter this morning.

Sybil

11

June 17, 1936
Newark, NY

Dear Mr. Martin,

On packing to go home for a vacation I came across your Italian notation system again, and my conscience smote me when I thought how long I have had it. I want to thank you again for the use of it. I am sorry to say, however, that the Italian newspaper never responded to my request for the third copy. As you said, they were probably far too occupied with Ethiopian news.

But I am glad to have this opportunity to tell you how much in sympathy I felt with your article concerning the dance congress. I am sending a copy of it to Helen Priest who is in Germany studying von Laban's system of notation. Miss Humphrey writes me that the dancer's association issued a special bulletin attacking you. Of course, you expected it, but the truth and sincerity of your opinions make anything the bulletin might say seem quite pale to those who have some conception of the meaning of dance as an art. Your statement that it "stemmed from honest ignorance" was to my mind the core of the whole situation. I was amazed and embarrassed to find that with the exception of those few who are obviously artists, no one else seems to have any idea what the dance really is. Some think it is technique, some content, some form, some projection, but very few put them all together. It makes the fight very hard.

I remember from my first week in New York your idea that the dance is the basis of acting. I am very much interested in that point of view and have worked out some ideas along that line which I would like to discuss with you some time at Bennington this summer.

Most sincerely,
Sybil L. Shearer

Sunday, June 14th

Darling one—

I am resting this on my knee, thinking and trying to put into words what you will have to know eventually in a fuller account.

Oh, darling, so much has happened that I preferred not to relate to you because there was no sense in bothering you with stupid details.

Without elaboration, these are the facts. For reasons unbeknown to me, Doris has been going out of her way to make me more than a little uncomfortable, until on Friday after the rehearsal when she told me I wouldn't be needed for the stadium concert. Of course, I saw the justice of her saving the $20 by putting George in my place in all the dances (since he was to be in *New Dance*), but when I asked her why she picked on me rather than Harry Cole (who is a WPA worker—you know the group decided to eliminate the WPA people whenever possible), and she stuttered and finally reminded me that Harry was more of size with Jose, and George and Bill Bales—I began to realize that the incident was actually the culmination of a series of digs she had been giving me all week long. Of course, the next day she told Maurice to tell me that she had talked to Charles and that they were going to include me in some arrangement satisfactory to the group; but I had already made up my mind that I could no longer work with people who didn't trust me. . . . So I'm through dear. And that means Bennington, too. It's probably all for the best anyway. Do please be glad about it, because it's about time I broke with the dance adventure, and because I'll manage to get to Bennington to see you off and on, no matter what happens. Please, please, please don't mind this hectic note. It's not so awful.

Darling, I love you!
Jerry

June 18, 1936
Newark, NY

My Dear Jerry,

I have read over your Sunday letter a dozen times. Of course, I think it is for the best. I am just disappointed that you are not going to Bennington, for it will be awful being separated from you so long. Also, I had hoped that we might collaborate on writing a ballet. However, there is plenty of time for that, and if you can get *Uncle Tom* finished this summer, it is much more important; you should work at it every day.

As for Miss Humphrey, we both know her weakness of not being able to see through people. I can't believe she is actually malicious, but also I can't easily forget after this her complete unreality in relation to people. Heaven knows what hands she might fall into.

However, I am really glad that you are out of this school-room atmosphere and into the world, for I feel that only when you are the master of yourself in a worldly sense, can we be really united forever without constant interruptions from people like Miss Humphrey or worse, people who might actually intend to separate us. Don't ever forget that I am always with you in spirit. And am working with all my might as you are to make it possible for us to be together. To that end I am thinking along lines of a theatre of dance drama, for in that we can be together and our interest will be centered together. I hope because you have always been interested in this idea, even before meeting me, that you will also think about it as an ultimate aim of a practical nature. No more dreaming, please, but let's get to work with all our faculties. I shall do everything I can at Bennington to further the idea.

I have no wish to destroy the Humphrey–Weidman group for I certainly believe that they are true genius and the best choreographers in existence. But I feel there is another system (though there may be quirks in that too), which we and all those who are interested and have the artist's point of view can eventually bring about—a system quite different from the present group in outlook as well as output. The two groups would not really be comparable, because of their different aims; and I would be loath to ever hear anyone say that one was better than the other no matter what we might think privately. I believe there should be no time limit for its completion.

I shall be in New York on Mon. the 29th, unless for some particular reason you wish to see me before then.

My dear one, keep what you want most always in mind and let nothing, not even your own moods, stop your progress toward that goal, and I shall do the same.

I am always yours,
Sybil

Once Jerry had cut ties with the Humphrey-Weidmans, there was nothing I felt I could do except rethink the situation and stick with him. The decision had to be his. From a theory standpoint, one wonders what was actually going on in Doris's mind and why, and what were the causes that brought about the thinking and the actions that followed?

Were these reactions thought out, or were they instinctive? Did custom or habit of thinking influence decisions, or was it the old fear of, or distaste for, the outsider?

Seeing what has always gone on in dance, especially "modern dance" where all sizes and shapes are pitted against one another, either for design reasons, or because of availability of bodies, Doris's choice of "closer in size" is something to ponder. Actually most of the men were quite large, and size might have been important to her choreographically. Also since choreography was more important than human relations (except in theory), she did not know how to handle the situation. Instead of taking Jerry aside earlier, and explaining her size preference for artistic reasons, she prepared for this decision by making him "more than a little uncomfortable."

However, when she saw his reaction, and heard his reasonable question, she realized that she was not just replacing one body in *her* choreography, but *losing* one body for Charles as well, and Charles did not care about size. So she tried to patch it up.

Then there was Pauline's point of view, which was usually the deciding factor in human relations. She was a great one to have noses fixed, and smiles placed on faces, and decisions as to who should be in the front and who in the back. Jerry was definitely of a different caliber than the other dancers, better informed, popular, and perhaps a threat. But he was an outsider—dance was not his first passion, so perhaps she had the feeling that Jerry and I wanted to take over the group. However that was, I always felt that Doris Humphrey needed a good director to stand between her and the world—the audience *and* the dancers. Pauline Lawrence was not good enough. Pauline was more an antidote to Doris's personality. In that way she helped. But her level of thinking was way below

Doris's, and her level of taste was inadequate for the subject matter. She was a good booking agent, but she was of necessity given too much peripheral power.

Standing in one's mind beside Louis Horst, who was in a similar position in the life of Martha Graham, Pauline seems frivolous and worldly in a personal way. Louis was protective of Martha, but he acted from a more universal point of view, not trying to do everything, rather firmly pointing out directions through artistic principles.

These two women, with similar artistic backgrounds, were equally talented in very different ways. Martha's accomplishment was more concrete, largely because of Louis, Doris's more nebulous, largely because of Pauline.

Jerry turned entirely to his play and his biography with renewed force after this decision. On the other hand, looking back, perhaps he expected me to encourage him to reconsider this decision and come to Bennington. But although I was highly emotional on a daily basis, I lived by principle and would never have interfered with a decision he made on that basis.

Also, since I lived in the future, I was not aware of how much he needed me at that very moment. I see now by his letters that he tried to tell me this, whereas I only felt the necessity to work even harder at the dance-drama project during the summer at Bennington—something that Jerry and I should have been doing together if it were to be our future life. Since it was my initiative and my action, this made the situation unbalanced.

I was in love with an idea, my idea. I wanted him in my life, and he wanted me in his. So I had to go to Bennington without him, and without my knowing it then, we moved farther and farther apart.

June 17, 1936

Dearest Sybil—

I have your letter about the garden party and flower show. I can just see you so beautiful looking in the midst of it all. My sweetheart, I hope you are keeping patient about the lack of news of my doings and whereabouts. I am working very hard to attain a certain end. Fortunately, our relationship at the H.W. Studio was more than friendly only in rumor, so that your independence of me will continue so, and obviate any necessity for your making any explanations. I'll write again soon.

I love you anyway—any way,
Jerry

12

Dear Polly White,

Your letter arrived just before I left New York to go home for a short vacation. Thank you for writing me Miss Humphrey's opinions on dance notation. No, she has never told me them, and I am rather surprised, and a little shocked at her point of view, for it is so different from mine, and I could never, despite the fact that I believe in her as an artist and a choreographer, agree with her idea of notation for I think she leaves half, the most important half, out. Nor do I agree with her as to what a dancer is or should be. It is truly amazing that I have been with her for two years and have just found out what she really thinks. Perhaps it is because we have both been believing in our own points of view so strenuously that we have taken for granted that the other believes the same.

In the first place Miss Humphrey does not believe, you say, in the dancer as a "paragon of versatility," that is, I would say, because she is thinking in terms of all dance rather than in terms of dance as an art. When she speaks of Oriental dancing she is speaking not of art but of folk dancing. She is not taking into consideration that there may be many American choreographers in the future each of whom would have a different style, but each of whose works would be moving and well worth recording for future performances. Miss Humphrey does not seem to think of the dance as a theatre art, perhaps because she is so much in the studio herself. The future of the dance, to my mind, is in the theatre with the works of many choreographers to choose from. Without that there will only be those choreographers who are living at the time who will put on their dances. And how many great people in any art live at the same time?

In painting, which Miss Humphrey compares to the dance, the actual canvas is handed from one generation to another, but in the dance, as in music, the composition must be brought to life again by performers who have nothing to do with the composers, in order for it to mean anything to the world at large. Paintings of the past are not merely educational documents, but moving works of art.

Of course, notation has an enormous place in education, but in the long run it is impossible to make great choreographers just by teaching a few rules. And when great works of art appear, they should be preserved for everyone as great works of art.

Then there is the exquisite and moving dancer who is a born performer, because with her brilliant technique she also has dramatic genius. I refer to Pavlova. She made almost none of her dances, and yet to have lost her because she could not create would have been to me, for one, one of the greatest losses possible. There may be other Pavlovas, and Miss Humphrey has not considered them. They should have at their command all the solos created by artist-choreographers in the world.

To my mind, again, dancers who move like their masters do so more from habit than from conviction, so they might have chosen their own master. A dancer, to be a good performer, should never allow the peculiarities of style of any one master to change her own style, or prevent her from using that of another master.

I think Miss Humphrey means here that each member of a group should be creating dances in the style of the master of the group. But this is virtually impossible, because very few of a group are choreographers at all. Most are performers only. However, it is a very interesting and idealistic point of view which I like. The argument is really—are choreographers and performers two different sorts of people. I say yes; Miss Humphrey says no.

However, I am convinced enough to ask you to consider my ideas as one side of the question in your article. I will see what I can do about gathering other ideas at Bennington, and will send them to you.

We are giving two concerts at the Lewisohn Stadium on July 2nd and 3rd, so that I have to go down to New York to rehearse and perform before going up to Bennington. I don't know any news just now because I have been away for so long. Let me know what you think of this letter.

Most sincerely,
Sybil Shearer

June 18, 1936
Newark, NY

Dear Miss Humphrey,

It is positively amazing to me that I have just this minute, or at least not more than 15 minutes ago, discovered what you meant when you told us that morning in the studio that it was your idea for all dancers in the group to create, and that you had changed your mind about the fact that some dancers do not have to create because they are performers.

I have received a letter from Polly White, the girl who interviewed you about notation, and she tells me that you think a dancer is more like a painter than a musician, and her followers should attempt to create like her, because of an inner conviction of its being the right way.

I think it is an excellent conviction on your part, and I think that you should try to bring it about as much as possible, though I have discovered that most dancers in modern groups chose that group because they like the technique and the dances of the choreographer from the point of performing them, and not with the idea of ever creating like the choreographer.

It would make for much greater group spirit if we all had your conviction. We are much too individual in our outlook, but it is a dream outlook, not a real one for we each dream of being ourselves by ourselves, and we don't seem to realize that individuality will out no matter what.

One person asked me once if it was necessary to create several dances before being admitted to the group.

I hope we can give more studio recitals next year, considering them, of course, an artistic necessity, and not a duty. I think that with the proper incentives even people like Miriam (who seems hopeless now because of her suffocating inferiority complex) will blossom out and actually find themselves in creating new combinations of movement. I know that Miriam is interested because, last year in Charles' class she was one of the few who came right up to the last for help on her dance. With sympathetic encouragement, she can develop because she is devoted to you, but I know she has a positive horror of being made to feel like a child in school who has failed to do her lesson, and she is constantly finding herself in that position because of her fear.

Yours is a very idealistic point of view, and I like it for that, but I do not wholly agree because I believe that there are definitely two kinds of dancers, choreographers and performers, though some people have the luck to be both. However, if you are more interested in the choreographers, then it should be those whom you gather around you with the expectation that they will respond as you wish. If they happen to be performers as well, then all the better, but the first requirement should be choreography with, of course, a proper background of technique with which to work on their dances and yours. With a group of this sort a real art center would be formed, and you would truly live on in your followers, and their followers down through the ages.

Am I right in putting these two together (what you said to Polly and what you said to us)? Sometimes my thinking carries me way beyond the point. But I feel I must know what you are thinking, and you, my thoughts.

I hope you're having a restful vacation. You certainly needed it. And I hope that the WPA program went off as you wished. I am gaining energy and enthusiasm again, and have at last picked myself out of a depressing gulf.

With much love,
Sybil

June 20, 1936
Newark, NY

My Dearest Jerry,

So many things have happened since I wrote last. In the first place this delightful picture appeared in the paper. I am afraid you will at last be disillusioned about my beauty. It doesn't speak well for the dancing profession for one of its "stars" to look so suspiciously like a librarian. And poor Mama, but I much prefer her to me! Then to make this edition the illustrated special, I am enclosing a better picture of Mama and the pool.

The next news is that in the same mail with your last letter came one from Mrs. Markloff telling me to come to the Club and they would try to put me up, but that in the fall I would have to get a studio of my own because I could not go on using the theatre as I have. Also that my clothes are too extreme (my practice suit), and that several board members have commented on it. She sent me an adv. of a very high-sounding apartment with studio. I don't know where she thinks I am going to get the money. She probably thinks my teaching brings in plenty of profit. So I have written to International House to see if they can take me for a week in order to get acquainted with it and see if I like it. But Papa threw up his hands in holy horror and said I was socialistic enough as it was, and that that place was a den of socialists and communists. When I said I had never heard that, he accused me very unjustly of being purposely ignorant (at which point I was too dignified to stamp upstairs). Will you please inquire and find out for me the truth? I expect to get an apartment with Helen Priest if she comes back from Germany in the fall, but in the meantime I have no desire to enter the Club unless I have to. However, since this has come up, I expect to leave here Sat. night and arrive in New York Sun., the 28th. Will you be in New York at that time?

Oh, Dearest, I have been wishing you all kinds of luck and love, and though I am not impatient to know what you are doing, I am very interested, and look forward to the time when you can tell me.

But strangely enough I have discovered something about Miss Humphrey that I was unaware of and I like her better for it, though it shows her idealism and lack of contact with the group. This is it. She thinks a dancer is more comparable to a painter than a musician, and that the members of a group should all create and be influenced by the master because they have a conviction that it is the right way, and they agree with the master's point of view. In other words, it is her desire to gather around her choreographers. I think this is an excellent idea, but it is quite obvious that we don't measure up to standard, nor have we been aware of what was expected of us, though she did remark that she thought we should all create. Perhaps it will come about some day.

Then the latest and best news is that Mama stopped in at my place of work this morning to bring me something, and I showed her my "cycle." She thought my *Prelude* (which I may call "Faith" or the "Joy of Faith") thrilling, though I did not do it at all well. She also thought the movements of *Cynicism*, which I was able to show her, quite effective. But after *Depression* she said that she was carried away and that it was certainly an inspired piece. I hope it is not just because I am her daughter, but she was really moved, I could see. *Revelation* she also thought very stirring and inspired. Because I have done *Depression* all myself, I find it quite pleasant to have it praised. But the thing which pleased me most was the fact that she could feel without any effort the changes of mood and said that each dance was distinctly different from the other.

So by fall I may have some kind of a repertoire, for after this (and I have another dance to do in this "cycle" called *Hope* to something with the idea of future in it) I plan to do a group of fantastic dances for children which I may be able to show in schools. My plans are unbounded, but I'm so anxious to see you and hear from you.

My greatest love,
Sybil.

Monday

Darling—

This will have to be one of those hasty notes that you probably detest. Thank you, a million, for your marvelous letters. I'm in N.Y. again. I hope to be here when you arrive. Nothing in particular has panned out, so that I'll have to let you know definitely as to my plans later in the week. I love you for the dances you've created—and for you alone—my one.

—Jerry

P.S. About ten years ago, Anna [Jerry's first wife] stayed at the Int'l House. It seemed to be satisfactory then. Why don't you stay there the one week in June? That's the only way you can really find out about it without knowing one of the residents.

June 23, 1936
Newark, NY

My Dearest Jerry,

I received your note this morning. Of course, I don't detest such notes. I hope mainly that our week in New York together will be a marvelous one, which will give us strength to keep going through the summer.

Let me know as soon as you can what your plans are, and if you don't have any, make some up. I have been watching the pool with its fish and frogs and dragonflies, and that is all I can think of, for I was studying movement. I have done nothing since I last wrote, but sit or work or read or eat, so there is nothing to tell except that Mama fidgets continually about where I am to live, though it doesn't bother me. She hopes you will be in New York to take care of me. Otherwise she would come down herself, but I assured her that I would be in competent hands.

My darling, I love you so much. Please do your work and forget this stupid world.

Sybil

Wednesday, June 24th

My Darling—

Why is it that I can't bear writing to you whenever I'm caught in a low spell? It puts me into a positive rage to face the ordeal. But I do know why. Bob Cooligan is to marry Rosemary in Dayton, Ohio, today. Then, there is your picture that I love—I worship; and the thought of Bob and Rosemary comes to me. Even Mac and Mae—let alone Bob and Rosemary—drive me to distraction. Yesterday, I was working on "Tom" again, and in the evening I was told that Charles wanted to see me this morning. He saw me this morning, and this afternoon I'm back with "Tom." And so on without progress. Darling—your letter—your picture—do you think—do you really—give heed to your father's opinion, dear—take example from Champie's adult choosing. Certainly when you return to the H.W. group, be prepared to dismiss remarks about me with unconcern. If to take care of you were merely to love you, the incomparable and sustaining beauty of a Persian pattern would carpet your life forevermore. I'll meet you at the depot Sunday if you come then. I hope I shall be ready to meet you truly, then.

There's only you, Sybil dearest—Jerry

June 25, 1936
Newark, NY

My Dearest, Dearest Jerry,

Your letter has just arrived. I know you have been having a bad time. I did not write yesterday because I was entertaining Miss Munson and her sister at tea. Afterwards, I showed her my dances and asked for criticism. She said she was unable to criticize, because she was fond of me and all the dances were Sybil to her. But her sister said that she thought she would have enjoyed them whether she knew me or not.

And last night, I completely forgot that it was midsummer's night, although just before dinner I was out in the garden and felt a peculiar spell over everything. It wasn't until I read the postmark on your letter that I realized it had passed.

I am so looking forward to seeing you that I think of it very often. Will you meet me at the 125th St. station, because I am going to be at the International House until July 1st? We can spend Sunday together before my return to the group. I hope you are in good health. Dearest one, I will show you my new dances if you will read me what you have done on *Uncle Tom*.

The train leaves Newark at 9:41 and arrives at 2:30. To be with you will be a great joy.

All my love again and again,
Sybil

June 25, 1936
Newark, NY

My Dear Mrs. Markloff,

I received your letter telling me to come to the Club next week, but my plans have been slightly changed.

Thank you for the adv. about the studio. It looks like a very nice one, but I am afraid that I could not afford to move into a studio right away. I am sorry not to be able to go on teaching at the Club because all of my pupils come to me, not I to them; and I know they got a great deal out of it, for my rates were very reasonable and I like to teach. As for me, it did help to pay for my room and board, but I received no profit, for although I may appear on the surface to be financially successful because I have been artistically successful, it is not altogether true. I have just managed to make ends meet all year. And I am not receiving support from my family. Most of the dancers in the group live with their families, a thing which I obviously cannot do.

Of course, some day I hope to have a studio, but that cannot be until my fame has spread far enough to bring me enough pupils to pay for it. Until then I know my mother would never be satisfied to have me in surroundings unlike those in which I was brought up.

You speak of my clothes being too extreme. I am very

sorry, but I was not aware of it, unless you refer to my practice skirt which I wore to breakfast only for convenience. However, if you think the board members would prefer me to wear regular skirt length, I can have my suit shortened to wear at the Club.

Trusting this will be satisfactory to you.

<hr>

June 25, 1936

Darling,

I'm high this morning. I sit with your photograph alongside me, and I can hear harmonies and feel a new coordination surge through me. How completely I respond to the image of you! I always believed in miracles and saints, but I never hoped to be suffered such nearness in my lifetime. By all the Saints, how I love you! This will be my final note to you before your departure. I shall expect some communication from you as to the time and place of your arrival. I want to be there, of course. Yesterday, I finished the first act (of the 1st draft) of "Tom." I started on the 1st scene of the 2nd act this morning. I think it may go along quite speedily from now on. (You dear—ain't I the crazy one with my fits and starts?) Maurice's WPA section is opening tonight at the Neighborhood Playhouse. Archie's in town, and we're going to see the performance together. I was to call Charles this morning with my final answer on the Bennington matter. I called to tell him I definitely would not go under the circumstances.

Have you engaged your living quarters yet? Is there anything specific that I can do before you get here? I hope you'll have a restful ride on the train.

My only love to you,
Jerry

My Dearest Jerry,

Just a note to tell you I received your wonderful letter this morning, and that I am happy at your progress, and that I can hardly wait to see you. Also, Mama is giving us a picnic lunch to eat on Sunday somewhere together. I can hardly believe the four weeks is over, but I am certainly glad to think of Sunday.

All my love to you until the day after tomorrow when I may say it in person.

Yours always,
Sybil

13

So began my third summer at Bennington—the first as a student, the second as a professional dancer, the third as an assistant teacher. The best part of it all was being included in the faculty dining room where I could listen to conversations by dancers, choreographers, teachers, and visiting artists. I took advantage of being able to sit, listen, learn, and once in a while chime in, ask questions, and air my own opinion. It was fascinating to find out how these various members of the dance world thought. I was at the same time full of reverence and full of judgment—on principle, of course— and I loved every minute of it.

At first I thought to keep up my creating, but the strain of business at hand and lack of time put an end to this after about a week and a half, and I decided to just enjoy being there. My daily letters to Jerry recorded all this. However, I have none of Jerry's letters from that summer in Bennington and I suspect it was very hard for him to write. Nothing was going well for him, whereas I was loaded with energy and verve. I was into another world. I wanted to know more of what he was doing. He really could not tell me. So I leave out most of my questionings, protestations of love, and hope for the future. They make redundant reading.

July 8, 1936
Bennington

Jerry Dear,

How much I think of you. But I have not been able to think clearly until today, because of the change of climate, I suppose. Everyone is sleepy. Now, however, I am going to dig into my future tooth and nail. We have heard nothing more from Jose about the "little group," and I don't know when we can possibly find time to work. Last evening I wore my Austrian dress which you haven't seen (bright red pink with bright green trimming) and caused quite an uproar. Everyone was mad about it. While in it I had a short talk, to be continued later, with Mrs. Martin about her technique of acting for dance choreography. She seems suddenly quite open and friendly, as does her husband, though up to the advent of my becoming "faculty," they seemed quite unapproachable. Now, John Martin actually makes jokes with me, and talks when he really has nothing important to say, which is quite nice, because he is the only one around whose small talk is not dull. Both Katie and I landed on him for suggesting that people might go to sleep in his classes. But I think it will take him longer than that to be convinced of his bad psychological approach.

I am unable to rent a bicycle, but Miss Humphrey has one at their house which she says she will lend me.

This morning, coming from breakfast, I saw a very large caterpillar, and stooped down and leaned over to see it better. Just then Louis Horst hurried by, as best he can hurry, with the fleeting remark, "Morning prayer." I almost fell on my head—it was so funny.

Dearest one, are you well? Take care of that chest cold and get over it soon. Only in the summer can you build up resistance against such things in the winter, and it is really bad if you let it go and expect it to peter out in the fall. I think of "Tom" and know it is good, and wish you concentration, and I send you all my love and any excess energy that the country air gives me. Let me know when and all about your trip to New Haven.

Yours always,
Sybil

My Dearest Jerry,

Oh it is so hot. Can you bear it in New York? It is 120 degrees in the Middle West and it might as well be here. The sun is brighter than any place in the world, and I have to squint until sundown. But in the evenings, the cool grass is a reward. We are working terrifically hard. I don't see how the girls with no vacation can stand it. My knees ache. The whole workshop is covered with bruises, especially those on the knees—enormous.

If I could only write poetry—tonight is the time for it. I am too tired to dance, and after supper this evening, Humphrey (the baby) had a birthday party of ice cream and cake and many presents, like Christmas only in yellow instead of red. We all wore party paper hats and watched the baby perform. He is quite a dancer, and not a bit afraid of an audience, though very shy when spoken to directly. All the girls sighed and laughed, but I guess I am a little hard, for I can't bear to see him so surrounded by stalking grown ups full of admiration.

Here comes bad news. We found out today that for working our heads off, we receive $33.33 apiece, for there is a blanket sum of $100 for the three of us for the summer. The only advantage we get is sitting with the faculty.

I guess I had not read your letter correctly this morning before sending mine, and I find that you say Joy's visit to New Haven is off. I am so terribly sorry—it is a disappointment to you both. Perhaps she can come on when the measles are over. What are they, the German measles or the regular two-week kind? I hope the former.

All the wives up here are sighing for their husbands. Katie acts very blasé and I sigh to myself.

My dearest one, all my love to you and all my thoughts toward the continually approaching reunion,

Sybil

July 9, 1936

Jerry Dear,

Such a day for changes—it has been hot, then rain, then sun, then violent cyclone (several trees knocked down), then hail and now sun again, and all the while voluminous changing clouds, and thin layers of mist speeding across thick slow moving billows.

I feel something tugging me to you. I must start on my ballet tonight. I always think of that when you are strongest in me, because through that and where it leads, we are inseparable. I love my free time, and am actually beginning to get over my sleepiness so that I can use it.

Today I received a "fan letter" from Janet. She seems to be very much moved by the dance, especially my dancing. I think her ecstatic love state has something to do with it, but I am very glad anyway, for that is what I wish to do—move people. She has secured $25 for me from the Jr. Woman's Club, seemingly without effort, which is also encouraging. Oh, if only all this time were mine to use as I wish.

Last night we rehearsed for a demonstration tonight. I always feel like a trained bear at those things, and tonight will be worse because of the critical audience.

Mr. Martin answered my questions at dinner last night, so I don't have to ask them in class. I find he is very sympathetic and an idealist at heart, but like George he has another face for the world.

———————

I just received your letter and was very excited to know that you are forging ahead with your play. I am interested very much in knowing what you are doing. I wish you could tell me by letter, the way you told me by word that memorable week.

The discussion this morning was quite interesting, and I aired my views about critics being creative writers. Mr. Martin wanted to know if I had been listening in on the seminar course in criticism for they had decided just that.

My dearest Jerry, I send you all my love.
Sybil

———————

July 12, 1936
Bennington

My Dearest, Dearest Jerry,

Did you go to the beach? Did it rain? Are you well? I love you and wish we were on a desert island away from the world. I am in a rage, all because Louis and John Martin raised their eyebrows when I publicly admired Pavlova. But it will blow over, I know. I must steel myself against these all-knowing critics. I have been quite happy until now when all my desire to flee to England comes back. I curb my desire, however, and so must you. It is not even fair of me to rouse you. It is not time to push off. I now only know that I must retreat into myself, and let Bennington go hang.

By the way, raising the voice is good, for we are now to get $50 apiece for the season instead of $33.33.

The demonstration was very successful and everyone was actually thrilled. Jose said I did brilliant work, and many people who were here the first year I was have come and told me how much they liked my dancing. I had no idea that it would be at all impressive and was quite surprised at the general reaction.

John Martin says he is going to publish a paper to print the criticisms from the seminar course called, "Big Bennington, no cause for alarm." Very quaint, eh what? Yesterday, I took a walk into the fields and came to the magic garden where only blue flowers grow, and rock and short grass. It looks almost cultivated in an airy offhand way. Beside it is a wood full of birds with red spots on their heads and white spots on their backs. Following the path I came to a brook, quite wide, with a plank for a bridge and purple dragonflies hovering over it. I learned the value of a waving wand; animals and insects respect it whereas they flee from a human hand.

I am calm again, and love you with all my heart in a sane and sensible way.

Yours always,
Sybil

July 13, 1936
Bennington

Dearest Jerry,

The tables have turned again, and John Martin and I are friends once more. I find it a little hard to get along with Louis, as I don't know what to say that won't be sat on in some way or other, but Mr. Martin very kindly lets me have my innings, and I find that we are really on the same side of the fence though expressing ourselves in such different terms. To him everyone is guilty until he proves himself innocent; to me, just the opposite. In other words, he takes nothing on faith, and I take everything.

I am slowly getting acquainted with the different people here who, on the surface, seem to be just people, but upon second and third looks have extremely interesting backgrounds. (Isn't this in accordance with your idea of biography?) One girl is Mrs. Jerome Boyer, from California, where she says she has a group of 25 for which she does choreography all year. She was married last summer, and she and her husband spent one month in New Mexico. Then he came to New York, and she stayed in California for ten months, and she just saw him again for a week in New York. So, of course, she wants her husband with her up here. He is coming up to finish his book which he has been writing all year on the dance. In it, she says, he has laid out several themes for ballets. I hear that he gave the best talk of anyone at the dance congress, and everyone was wondering who he was. She says he really does not want to talk dance nor see dancers, because he is getting a bit tired of it all, being originally a lawyer, then a musician and now a writer. She is a very interesting and nice person. She found it hard to talk to Miss Humphrey, so she came to me, and we went over the dance and its problems, and her problems with a very sympathetic feeling.

I am now taking time off in the morning to compose by myself, so I shall have to end, darling. I love you more than ever. Be good and careful and write soon.

Sybil

July 14, 1936
Bennington

My Dear Darling Jerry,

It seems centuries since I heard from you, so I suppose you went to the beach. I hope it agreed with you. The warm weather has disappeared here today, for it is very cold this morning, though it is too early to judge what it will be at mid-day. It seems that I have been taking it easy for these two weeks, so now I have to begin teaching group three on Monday which adds one hour to the day's work.

The Ballet Caravan, or little group from the American Ballet, will be here Friday and Saturday nights. Lincoln Kirstein will give a lecture one afternoon with the ballet demonstrating. That ought to be interesting.

Last evening they had movies here on plant life. The movements were quickened so that we could see the growth of a plant in fertilization, and the opening of flowers, etc. But I did not see them, much to my disappointment, because Charles had a rehearsal in which I was supposed to partici-pate, but I really did nothing but sit and wait.

The husband of the girl of whom I spoke in my last letter arrived yesterday, and he is one of the homeliest men I have ever seen. I think he is quite temperamental for he did not like the rooms she picked for him in North Bennington, and insists on staying at the hotel in Bennington which is very far away. He is so uncomfortable that he doesn't wish to stay after being here six or seven hours.

Then I met another girl called Eloise Moore from Chicago. She is very attractive and is a concert dancer with a large solo repertoire and a manager who gets her about 35 concerts a year in and around Chicago. She is also married (and has been for six years, though she looks like an infant) to a feature writer on the *Chicago Herald Examiner*. He seems to be an ideal husband who lets her do anything she wants, to the point where she says that all of their friends are lined up on his side ready to testify at the least disagreement that she neglects her duty and her husband for the dance. She said she would give anything to be in the Humphrey group for a year, so I said I would exchange with her, both of us knowing that any such change would be impossible.

Yours always & always,
Sybil

July 15, 1936
Bennington

My Darling Jerry,

I showed your clipping about the birds to John M, because he has been telling us about just that in his lectures, and he thought it very interesting.

The bad news now comes. I can't do my dance because Miss Humphrey won't let me do it to the Victrola, and it is impossible to get the music, as it does not come written for piano, and I would have to get the orchestra score from N.Y. and have it transcribed, etc., etc. and it might not sound good anyway. I am terribly disappointed. However, I wonder if you would try to get me the score for piano of Ferde Grofe's "Painted Desert" from the *Grand Canyon Suite* and also Debussy's Chimes Through the Leaves or Cloches à Travers Les Feuilles, then I can do those dances. Try the cut-rate music shop on 50th St.

The Ballet for which I get a ticket on Saturday is arriving today in all its finery and is staying at the Mayflower Inn.

Last Saturday evening Bill Bales took Lilly, K. Litz and myself out with two other boys, and we had quite a gay time. One of these fell for Lilly and now calls for her at the armory everyday in his swanky car, and every evening he is seated, waiting, outside the commons building. He is a summer resident of Bennington and quite nice, I guess. Bill and I had a riot of a time dancing together, improvising ballet fashion, modern, old Ginger Rogers, etc. We had everyone in the hall doing variations. Bill is so boisterous. It was the first time in my life I was ever worn out enough to let go and be just as crazy myself.

I send you all my love.
Sybil

14

July 16, 1936
Bennington

Dearest Jerry,

Martha Graham is here, but would you believe it, she won't come out and show herself. It gives the whole place a tense expectancy. One sees stray pupils of the Graham technique doing stretches on the lawn. Frances Hawkins [Martha Graham's business manager] struts madly about with her business-like face. Breakfast came, luncheon and still no Martha. Perhaps it will be tonight she comes. This Graham cult is a marvelous thing. I can't help admiring it, as one does the Catholic Church for its persistence.

The Ballet also arrived today and Mr. Riegger, so we shall have a full dining room. (Only the heads of the ballet will come here.) We rehearse tonight while the ballet does the same, one floor above us.

———————

Saw the ballet rehearse by sneaking out while Doris was concentrating on Bill, and decided that there is nothing worse. They lack all sense of movement and imagination in design and are generally awful, poor things. No wonder they are scared to death of us. This is their debut.

Martha came finally, and all of her admirers were in a formation outside of the commons building after dinner with concealed cameras ready for the attack. I could not stay to see her received. It seemed a little embarrassing.

After the rehearsal last night, I went in with Katie Litz and Louise Allen and Ada, and we began pouring forth our complaints with the view of finding a remedy. I presented our idea of dance drama with a written ballet and a director etc., and it was just exactly what they wanted. We got very heated in our plans and decided to ask Mrs. Martin to give us a course in acting, and we would also take voice. We decided that in our theatre (and we are going to work like mad). Louise will have the group in dance technique, you will be director, I will be a performer and also Katie Litz. George will be the designer and Katie J. has a friend who is interested in writing ballets. Though, of course, we will all have a chance to do what we want to. We feel ourselves very inadequate as performers, and will work toward improvement in a choreographic manner.

I spoke to Mrs. Martin this morning, and she was telling me that she is going to be connected with a new school of the theatre which is going to be located in the Roerich Museum, and that they are interested in dance drama; she would like to take us on and develop our ideas and guide us to new fields using the technique of acting. It looks as though this ought to be a very good beginning, because Mrs. Marquis, who seems to be the head of it, wants to combine dance and acting and even wanted Doris to transfer her teaching completely over to their school.

Anyway none of us could sleep thinking of it.

Do write soon.

Sybil

152

July 17, 1936
Bennington

My Dearest Jerry,

What an amazing organization this Humphrey-Weidman group is! Not only the feelings of various members of the concert group are continually being trampled upon, but also those of the workshop group. The latest tragedy is that of Anne who has studied for a long time with the above masters; she is quite proficient in the technique except for various peculiarities, such as being not good looking and unable to control the small of her back too well. However, she has expended most of her energy, money and devotion on the dance. Charles asked her to be in one his dances, and then after she had been to several rehearsals vibrating with joy throughout, he changed his mind in the true Weidman manner, causing long hours of weeping behind closed doors. I found out about it through Eloise, and am in my usual rage at injustice.

Also, though perhaps I am imagining it, I feel as though Miss Humphrey does not wish me to do *Revelation*, for when I spoke to her about having it transcribed by one of the musicians here, she agreed, but in the same manner as she used when I so subtly divined that she did not wish me to do the Stravinsky in the studio recital in May.

From my experience so far in life, I am beginning to feel that there will always be situations like this, which is not a pleasant prospect. But it is consoling to know that it is the struggle toward the whole that is important.

Well, darling, the tragedy of Anne is a thing of the past. I went to Mr. Weidman and explained the situation of which he seemed to be uncannily unaware, and he was very contrite and said by all means he would use Anne. So she is back in the dance, thank heaven, and both he and she feel much better, I am sure. We went on talking after we passed the point, and we talked about Mrs. Martin's course, which we agreed it would be good to take, and about my dances, etc. It is the first time Charles and I have had a sympathetic conversation, and we are much better friends than ever before. The man is really a child, completely unaware of other people's feelings unless told point blank.

I received your letter about the music. I am sorry I was so thoughtless about the money, and am sending a check for $5. I don't suppose it will be that much, but you can give me the change when you see me. There is no great rush. I should have told you that also. I cannot try out for the New Dance League concert because the auditions are tonight. But there will probably be another opportunity to dance.

It seems centuries since I heard from you, though it was yesterday. You really said nothing of yourself, however.

Tomorrow begins a hard two weeks. I lose one of my practice hours in the morning, and I teach one more hour in the afternoon.

I went to the ballet Saturday night, and have felt ill ever since—just plain disgust that grew from indifference on first seeing it. It cannot be called art, and therefore cannot be compared with our dance, but it is really not entertaining either because of its depressing influence. It tried to be so light and gay that it became strained, just as a gushing society butterfly becomes strained as she grows old. A feeling of reminiscence comes over me for some reason, and I feel strangely in the air and distant from people.

But tomorrow we must come down to earth with a bang, because Louise and Katie L. and I are starting our experiments with my technique of acting. I have given them homework in the form of my four types of movement for which they must think up as many symbols as they can.

I love you,
Sybil

July 20, 1936

Dearest Jerry,

I was so happy and relieved to know that your trouble is only a summer cold. You must remember, however, that even that is wearing to the system and should be cast out as soon as possible. I am also glad that you have gotten into the middle of the last act, and I am interested to know how you described the pantomime or dance drama in the first scene.

Thank you for your efforts about the music. I sent the $5 in the last letter, and that will cover the expenses.

Well, all sorts of things have happened here, including the fact that half the workshop group is brewing revolution which may or may not come out. It happened last year too, however. But Martha Graham stormed all over the place, and Doris will do nothing. Selma from Philadelphia (perhaps you have seen her around the studio—very ugly with dark, red hair) has openly expressed the desire to transfer to the general program. It remains to be seen what they will do about her.

Last night, we had tea in Joan's room. The guests included Mimi (Joan's sister), Edith, Miriam, Bea and myself. Later Katie M. came in. There the conversation was mostly joking about why Doris had not chosen Edith for the young girl in the ballet, which is a romantic tragedy. She (Doris) has chosen Katie Litz because (so K.M. says) she (K.L.) is the type of young innocent with her spiritual expression and blond hair. Edith and I are the only ones who have no parts at all yet, not even eight counts like Joan. And the poor workshop group thinks it is merely making a background for us. So the undercurrent grumbling is constant, and I think more strongly than ever that the dance drama is the ideal. We, K.L., Louise, Ada and I, started on our experimentation yesterday. We are trying to discover a basis of natural movement upon which to base our technique and it is really fun discussing it. For only by that can we arrive at any conclusions by constant interplay of ideas.

Ada has marvelous ideas for symbols, and she is evidently

very observant of movement. We meet every night just after dinner.

Love to you as always,
Sybil

July 23, 1936
Bennington

Dearest Jerry,

Absolutely nothing has happened since yesterday of importance. I had the fullest day I've had yet, however, for I taught three and a half hours in succession in the afternoon, and then right after dinner Ada, Katie, Louise and I had a meeting again. We have decided that the Humphrey-Weidman technique is not explicit enough and we are going to get down to rock bottom.

We discussed some of our symbols, and it is amazing to find the different movements that they have experienced, and it opened up to us all great horizons. Ada described the movement of the octopus which was marvelous, and also of the flying fish and the bumblebee; Katie, the movement of a giraffe and a mad rooster.

Tonight we hope to work out some combination of natural movements to begin with. Their only distortion will be the fact that they can be repeated over and over again, and therefore have form. It is a wonderful feeling to know that these people are enthusiastic and cooperative in this matter, because each of them is an individual with her own responsibility and interest in the plan.

Yesterday I received a letter from George enclosing his homework (lists of symbols). He is a dear, and a good person, and he works out his ideas for our group (he knows nothing about Louise, Katie and Ada yet) and asked me to write out my thoughts on the subject. He is a very sincere person, and devoted to the dance and the theatre as an art, and will do everything in his power to forward it. We have quite a little nucleus in the six of us, I think, and will eventually be able to accomplish great things.

I have not been able to work by myself for about a week as time is unbelievably scarce. It is really good you didn't come up here if it was only to be with me, because we would never get together until late at night which would be bad for us both.

Last night, Charles started a new dance about the D.A.R.s. I am one of them, and it is lots of fun. The dance is so crazy. We come in bringing a garland. So far I think his works are better than Doris' because they are more dancy.

I shall say good-bye now, darling.
Sybil

July 23, 1936
Bennington

My Dearest,

I have not yet had the time to look up the article by Stark Young, but I shall. I was so glad to get your letter yesterday. The idea about the dramatic image is excellent. Do you have one in your play? Things are getting more complicated every day, that is the work is, and I am truly sick of teaching, especially someone else's technique. Every time I tell my pupils one thing, Doris turns right around and says something different, merely because she has completely forgotten what she said in the first place. It is constantly embarrassing. I would like to work out a method by which movements can be consciously changed for consciously different reasons. Doris seems suddenly to have forgotten all about breath, and has people breathing every second time or third time instead of *with* the movement. Everything is very slipshod. She knows her choreography, however, and I certainly wish I knew mine. I must do some, though I have to forget about it while here.

So much for complaints. Last night Bill Matons was very sweet to me, wanted me to sit by him in the bus and escorted me right to the door of the house. While on the way, I asked him if he was going to see me all the way home. When he said yes, I told him it was sweet of him and he replied "Oh no, not at all. I am a materialist." I roared laughing and asked him what he wanted. He never did come out and say what he wanted, but he began telling me what a good dancer I was and that I had dramatic understanding, etc. Of course, he wants me to do a dance with him. He has been asking me for a year, and now he is bound to get his way, if not by my interest then by his own "polite" aggressiveness. The day before yesterday I told him for the nth time that I had too much to do. He and Beatrice did a dance which ended in a grand argument, and an embarrassing performance for her before Louis Horst and John Martin at the auditions.

I didn't tell you to go ahead and buy the whole *Grand Canyon Suite* but I meant to because I do want the "Painted Desert." I don't have as much time now as usual because I overslept this morning, so I shall have to say goodbye as the bus to take us to the armory is due soon.

Sybil

Bill Matons was a most interesting example of what was going on in the dance community. He came out of the nowhere and went into the nowhere after a few years. In the meantime, he was very much in evidence on the dance scene.

It seems Charles had put an ad in the paper calling for men dancers—no experience necessary. Bill was a truck driver, but destiny put this paper in his hand, and he appeared at the studio holding it. He was big, brawny, and very curious. A few turns around the room and he was into a whole new world. He not only started to dance, he started to read everything on esthetics, to observe movement everywhere, and with book in hand he was pointing to passages, enthusiastically sharing every bit of knowledge with the other dancers and anyone else who would listen, including waitresses in restaurants.

Of course, he was considered rather ridiculous by the sophisticated who figured he would settle down and obey orders sooner or later. But for Bill dance was also creativity.

He was in the process of making a dance about a spotted fish he saw in the aquarium when he ran into *The Communist Manifesto* and the *Daily Worker*, both of which were being constantly discussed by many dancers. With the same gusto he gave to esthetics he now turned to Communism, which became the subject matter for all his creations. So with literature in hand again, underlined in red, he was explaining dialectical materialism to one and all.

Bill firmly believed that the "revolution" was imminent, and he had to get all his satires on capitalism on the boards before that happened. So he got himself a loft where he created a theatre, and swarms of young dancers came to perform and to look. It was a fascinating experience to be in their midst. None of the big three—Humphrey-Weidman, Graham, or Holm—were into Karl Marx, and I was considered a "humanitarian," which was a tolerant way of saying, you are harmless, you can watch. So again I was the observer, critical only artistically.

During all this activity, Bill was also a member of Charles's group, and he was especially good in *Traditions*, a dance in which he was the rebel breaking away. This dance was one of Charles's best, but never as good without Bill's interpretation.

July 24, 1936
Bennington

Well, Jerry, here it is almost three weeks. The time is just about half over.

Yesterday was a big day, for the representatives of the von Laban Notation System in this country were here and gave us a lecture. It was fascinating and really looks excellent. I think they should give a course in it here next year. They ought to at least set 15 or 20 people of different dance techniques to work on this system and in that way judge how workable it is for all dancing, how quickly it can be learned both from the writing and the reading (which is much easier) point of view, and altogether find out its value before puttering around with experimentation in something entirely different. However, I still think that movies of dance are extremely important.

I was talking to John Martin and he seems to think that it is marvelous and eventually will do the trick on notation. The Martins and I and the two von Laban women and a couple of others sat at the same table both at noon and at night, and we had some interesting conversation. When Mr. Martin introduced me, he did not call me Miss as he did all the others, but Sybil Shearer and then added, Dear Sybil. I was rather embarrassed, because I thought he was making fun of me, so I told him I thought he had the wrong impression of me when he insisted on calling me La Sylph, etc. He protested, and said he liked my ideas and ways of doing things (going for walks alone, etc.). I felt quite warm, nevertheless.

Yesterday morning in rehearsal, Miss Humphrey stamped out the revolution that had been brewing by a cleverly constructed talk and the addition of more difficult movements on the dance for the workshop people. So now all is well, though for a while things really looked serious because a bunch of girls, (mere hoodlums who tell each other wild stories at night and drink themselves silly, though in the day they appear, at least to me, to be sweet, naive little girls full of life in a school-girl manner) decided that they wanted more to do in the production, and that they were just making a background for the concert group, which was quite true. Things have changed, however. I told Katie Manning what I thought would be the solution, and Miss Humphrey did it, though she had very likely thought of it herself first.

Au revoir again, dear Jerry, until tomorrow,
Sybil

P.S. You never tell me how Joy is and whether she is over the measles. Let me know. Pussy [Humphrey, Doris' son] has mumps.

July 26, 1936
Bennington

My Dearest Jerry,

We have the afternoon off! so I am writing to you, but I would have written anyway. Don't think of my being "over faithful," silly, I love to write to you. The reason you don't hear from me Mondays is because there is no outgoing mail Sunday, and the Sat. schedule is always distracting to letter writing. Of course, I like to hear from you, too, but you are creating, and it is difficult, I know, to write when you think you have not accomplished as much as you wish.

I laughed at your itemized account and especially the half-cent stamp. It had the Barrie touch. I hope you don't mind that I laughed. I love you so much.

I have just spent an enjoyable and profitable hour working and creating movements for my next dance, while a Mr. Leonard [Clair Leonard, professor at Vassar] composed some music in the same room. We both accomplished a lot because of the double concentration, I suppose. He is not composing

161

for me, though I hope he will some day because I like his style. He is going to transpose my Lord Berners' music, however. Last night before Mr. Martin's lecture, we were all gathered in the lounge during the rainstorm, and Mr. L. was doing musical portraits of the different people in the school. Joan asked for me, and he did a very nice one with a Debussy feeling to it. I remember after the concert at Madison Square (what a marvelous night) you told me I should dance to Debussy.

Monday

Last night was the New Dance League recital, which was quite interesting. Anna Sokolow did half the program and was excellent as usual. Bill did his solo *The Well Fed*, and a duet with Edith, *American Rhapsody*. I saw him do it with Grusha and thought she was more of a partner for him. Edith looks as though she belongs to an entirely different class of society, and in that way spoils some of the dramatic meaning. If she knew about theatre she would have gotten herself down to his level. As it was, I can't feel that it was truly important because of its decorative quality. They were just doing the dance together socially.

I must say goodbye now until tomorrow, dearest one, write to me.

Bennington

My Dearest Jerry,

I was invited to go on a picnic last evening with Joan and some people she collected, but I couldn't because I did not want to go out and through my enchanted garden with a whole bunch of people. I want to be with you or alone. I have promised to take individuals there, but it must be at long intervals apart or I feel as though I have been dissipating.

Joan was telling me that she never ceases to wonder at nature, and she can't help exclaiming aloud when she is moved, but she is content to just wonder and finds it perfectly satisfying to relax in the beauty she sees. I could not help comparing her point of view to mine for (and especially since I have grown up) beauty is not contentment but rather pain to me. It is pain that I either can't say what I wish in some creative form or pain of actually putting my feelings into a form.

I have finally settled myself down to a good three weeks. There is no sense in wasting my time here wishing myself away. I really have wasted no time so far, but I feel as though I have by accomplishing nothing. But suddenly I have a great love for humanity and I have a desire to know and love a great many people. But that cannot come quickly. I have discovered the few friends I have here by very slow processes with intervals long in between.

I have discovered suddenly that I am no longer a schoolgirl, that my reactions are quite different in a school atmosphere than they ever were before. A schoolgirl applies herself as she wishes and when she wishes but I apply myself at someone else's bidding to a task that is not my own choice. But it seems to me that I am getting extremely heavy, so much so that my head is bobbing up and down leaden with the pulse from my heart. Who knows what I might do today if I had time. I cannot bear that this wild feeling in me should go untamed and escape off into space unused.

Mimi has come in and brought me back to life by demanding to know why I am always writing. I told her it was my philosophy of life and I sent it out in a correspondence course.

My darling, I hope I hear good news of you today. What is this coma that surrounds us? It is ridiculous. Tomorrow you will see my awakening.

All my love to you always—S.

July 26, 1936
Bennington

My Dearest Jerry,

Yesterday morning at rehearsal at the armory, Pauline called me over and asked what the matter was. I said nothing and then added I didn't mean to look pained. She said it wasn't that, I was simply aloof. She is the third person who has seen me that way and commented on it. I was quite unaware of it until she mentioned it, and then of course I knew that I really was miles from the spot.

But the whole day was so full that it was impossible to keep aloof for long. After the armory, we had to rehearse for movies by Bouchard [Thomas Bouchard, a well-known dance photographer], then lunch, then costume measurements, then Eloise showed me several of her concert dances, so that I could get an idea of what Chicago considers good. I found it very interesting but too limited in body movement. She has a fairly good sense of design and a good sense of space. Her dramatic powers are a little lacking, however, and she has a delicacy about her movements that does not seem to be her own but an added feature from Berta Ochsner, her teacher. But I am to see more later as the hour was up too soon.

Then I taught for two hours the workshop and one hour general course. Then I tore back to the house to review in my mind and body my *Revelation*, because I had to do it for Mr. Leonard so that he could tell if the music could be done for two hands instead of four as he thought at first. He seemed to like it, but I really didn't do the poor dance justice in my exhausted state. We got talking terms, however, and discovered that it was too late to get dinner. I was too tired to care, except that I had another rehearsal in the evening, as Mr. L. had a car at his disposal we went out to eat and continue our talk of terms—money.

I discovered that he really doesn't want to do it because he has never tried it before and doesn't know how long it will take, and also he is doing some composing for himself which he wishes to get done. But if he did do it, he wouldn't take any money but would do it as an experiment. It is against his principles to take from those who can't afford it. He said he learned music and composition from a master who made a special rate for him because he was poor. Now I ask you, have you ever seen or heard anything so complicated? And to make matters worse I told him that it was all right if he didn't want to do it, it was just that Doris had suggested him, because she said he didn't have as much to do as the other composers, but if he had work of his own I was very much in sympathy with his point of view. Then his conscience smote him and he thought he was not working for as much as he was paid if he didn't do it. Well, the situation is practically insoluble as far as I can see, because I want the music, and any other composer would demand money, so I am willing to pay etc. etc. etc.

Do you like him from this description? He is really a very sincere person, and I am sure will be a lasting friend if we ever get past this difficulty, and even if we drop the whole thing, I shall keep him in mind as a composer for our theatre of dance drama because of his character and his interest in the dance as the basis of the theatre. (I managed to bring that into the conversation before the meal was over.) He is doing something for Hallie Flanigan [head of the theatre section of the WPA as well as drama head of Vassar College, and a powerfully lively personality], composing music to a poem she has written and which was printed by the *Theatre Arts Monthly* in Jan. 1935. That seems to be his big work.

Yours with all my heart forever and ever,
Sybil

July 29, 1936
Bennington

Dear George,

I was very, very glad to receive your letter, and I have been wanting to write to you, but have had absolutely no time off from duties. You don't know how happy I am to find that you are coming up for the concert. I certainly hope it works out, for I would be very disappointed if it didn't.

As to new horizons in the dance, I feel that your premise is absolutely correct. I believe also that only a collection of individuals, each with his own initiative and sense of responsibility and interest in the basic premise, can accomplish a worthwhile life for all. Also, I do not believe that rebellion is conducive to art, but peace, not in the sense of world peace, but rather peace among ourselves. Each of us must value the talents and abilities and the good character of each other member of the group. I do think we can draw on people outside ourselves to aid a professional theatre which we must have, rather than just a studio, but we must have the same requirements for those individuals as we do for ourselves.

Mrs. Louise Martin is giving a course here in choreography from the standpoint of technique of acting, which involves design in relationship to objects around one. We have spoken to her about taking us on in the fall to direct us in her ideas. At the same time there is the problem of being treated as students, unless we would take her completely into our confidence. Both Mr. and Mrs. Martin have our ideals about art, but Mr. antagonizes people by his smarty remarks. However, I like him very much, and agree with him almost entirely. He is just a little cynical toward talent and never takes anyone on faith, which it is my habit of doing.

But I have met a musician here who seems to be the kind of person we want around us. He is a composer, Clair Leonard, and is thoroughly good and honest, I believe. It is well worth our time to discover people of this sort.

I want to talk to you about these things and am looking forward to seeing you.

Most sincerely,
Sybil

July 31, 1936
Bennington

My Dearest Jerry,

How happy I was to receive your letter full of good news. I have been writing all week, so I hope you receive what I sent to New York.

We have been working madly here. I am glad you are not under Charles now. He has hurt his foot, and is therefore in a triply bad mood with nervousness about finishing and polishing the dances. It is like the machine age in dance choreography. Every day something new is turned out to take the place of the old, until the whole structure of things is so changed that it is impossible to keep up. Doris' dance is progressing rapidly. I wish you could come up for the concert. We are not having a vacation afterwards, or I would beg you to, and then you could go home with us (Mama, Papa and me).

Mr. Leonard had consented to do the music, or that is try it. We agreed to go to Miss Humphrey about the price. However, after trying it for an hour and a half, and having done eight measures, he thought it was going to take too long, and that it didn't sound right anyway. He played it for me, and I thought it was very good, so I told him to just go on doing it for the rest of his life, and let me know when he was finished, and I would do the dance then. He said he would do it at Vassar this fall where he teaches. Charles has asked him to compose for one of his dancers, and he is very anxious to do that now.

Martha Graham dances tonight. George is coming next weekend and will stay the rest of the time.

Best of luck to you darling,
Sybil

<hr />

August 3, 1936
Bennington

My Dearest Darling,

I hope you have received all my letters. Just think, only two more weeks! I am just beginning to reconstruct myself, however. Today I had a long talk after dinner with Mr. and Mrs. Martin, and she is anxious to take us on as an experimental group of actress dancers and actor dancers. She understands that we have no money, and while that is an important omission, still she is interested in us as serious artists who wish to form a group of responsible experimentalists in the field of dance drama. I told her of Louise, Katie L., Ada and myself and several men whose names I didn't mention, but I was thinking of you and George. She wants to work with us, and she and Mr. Martin have been planning this for 20 years, so he says. Anyway, the Roerich Institute is starting up again with a dramatic school, and they are interested in experimentation, so something may be able to be done. J. Martin also told me as a deep secret (so you mustn't breathe it to a soul), that he has a ballet on the lines of a musical comedy with popular appeal, but based on the soundest principles of the acting-dancing combination that we as a professional experimental group could work out. We will have a theatre, not terribly good, but something with which to work, and our publicity and production will be paid for so it really sounds marvelous. I really had all this in mind before I came up, but it has taken Mr. Martin a long time to put enough faith in me to talk as seriously as he did today. I am glad that it has at last happened, and that we have come to an understanding.

Friday evening Charles and Jose and Kinney (a girl from Boston) and I went to the Hotel Pullman after rehearsal and had two beers. Well, I had been in a very bad mood during rehearsal. Suddenly I became full of gaiety and self-confidence. All of us began to spout Shakespeare, much to my advantage with my English accent and my latent dramatic ability. You would never have recognized me. I was so funny. Better than Bea Lilly, Charles thought, though of course not at all vulgar. I couldn't be that, but I did *As You Like It*, Lady Macbeth and various other things on the first glass, and then we all started in on French on the second. Jose has been quoting me ever since at dinner and roaring with laughter. He thinks I am a brilliant *charrracter* actress.

Last night was Martha Graham's recital and it was superb. She is a dancer of moods, and this was one of those unforgettable occasions when all of her dramatic power came into its own, and pointed up what ordinarily seems to be pure design, so far abstracted from nature that it is unrecognizable. She is a solo dancer, and should dispense with her group of supple but laborious dancers.

I am looking forward to your next letter.

My very best love to you, again and again,
Sybil

August 4, 1936
Bennington

My Dearest One,

Your long letter arrived yesterday. It set a mood of confession. I certainly hope you can love me without being possessive, because my love for the dance, which is so great, will be a constant annoyance to you if you cannot. However, I am sure that as soon as you find yourself doing as you wish with your writing, things will even up and we shall be extremely happy. What do you think of the Martin idea? I am extremely pleased with your work and I want to know more of it.

Doris asked me to understudy her part in the dance and of course I am very pleased. Charles has taken new interest in me, since I established myself as a "charrracter" actress and last night he took me downstairs during Doris' rehearsal and outlined his solo dance for my approval, and showed me a lot of his movements and explained his duet with Doris and quite wore himself out in his excitement. I think he is doing a marvelous job, but he is getting so keyed up that it is almost impossible for him to relax.

Yesterday, we started reviving *Theatre Piece*, and found we remembered most of it without effort up through the hunting dance. It was fun working on it again, only I missed you because it brought back memories. I am beginning to enjoy it here immensely. I like the people better and I am acclimated and the work is heavier but more dance, and I have relaxed as far as my own work is concerned and don't try to do a million things at once, or worry when I don't accomplish a new movement.

Louise and I have worked out a basis for our technique of movement. We call it our textbook, and now all four of us are going to work out combinations upon which to start working with quality tonight.

As usual, I belong to about six different sets of people and enjoy being with each separately. I always feel sorry for those people who have to stick to their own crowd, either because they don't like any other, or because they are afraid they are horning in. This noon a whole bunch of us, mostly miscellaneous in interest—librarians, dancers, musicians and one Latin teacher—all piled into Mr. Leonard's car and tore over to North Bennington and back. One of the girls drove over, and I drove back. It was packs of fun. I am getting a little all around rowdy what with my bicycle riding, tree climbing, auto driving, etc., but it is the most honest to goodness fun I've had since I was a child.

Today I slipped into Hanya's class and had a marvelous half hour under her excellent tutelage discovering my body. Their technique is wonderfully inspiring. I wish I could take a great deal of her work.

I am looking forward to another letter soon.

P.S. I spent an hour last night drawing a set for Doris' dance which she liked very much. She is not using it, of course, because as usual she has a much better idea, but it was loads of fun. Yes, I am full of energy and enthusiasm. Catch some of my sparks!

Love to you, dearest,
Sybil

August 5, 1936
Bennington

My Dearest Jerry,

I got your letter off last night by a friend who took it to North Bennington at 11 o'clock, so you should get it today. I am so happy about your play, and I wish I could read it. To have a whole play on your hands to take care of is a job I know, especially when you are aware that your child is a genius, and that it just needs the proper bringing up and pruning and adjusting to make it perfect.

I certainly am disturbed to hear that Maurice has not forwarded any of my letters, for I wrote every day last week.

Do you remember Malcolm who used to clean the studio on 18th St.? Well, he is up here as one of Hanya's accompanists and has become thin almost to emaciation. I can't remember how he used to look—he is so changed.

Last night I went for a ride with the Martins, just over the state line to get some gas, because I had to be back for rehearsal. But John is the biggest fussbudget I ever saw. He was bound to get me back on the dot, and he kept counting the minutes we had been away, and the number it would take to get back. He puts me in mind of my Uncle Harold who, when I took him into the garden at night, drew a circle around himself and said he couldn't go beyond that line (else he would get his feet wet in the night grass).

Both Doris' dance and Charles' are going to be wonderful. At least, they are that in the making. The individual movements are grand, and the dance done for the workshop group is really excellent. It is the dance of search when all the townspeople are out warning the mother and hunting down the girl. Katie Litz is the girl. I wish I were she, but I am not, so that's that.

Yesterday, I was angry with my class for making fun of the movements, and I called them down. I was sorry afterwards, because I certainly think that is no way to teach. I knew there must be some reason on the part of the different members for being so disturbed at each other, and thereby making me disturbed. I hunted it down in the case of Eloise, who I like very much and whom I was sorry to speak crossly to. I find she has no end of troubles at home and is beginning to feel herself at the end of the rope now that the movements are becoming so difficult. I was very glad that I went to see her, for contacts of that kind make me more tolerant. Miss Humphrey laughed when I told her they had made me angry, and said, "Sybil's learning about life from the workshop." She meant the seamy side of life with all its disagreeableness, but I could not let it go like that. Both Miss Humphrey and Miss Graham think people are essentially uncooperative, but I prefer to be like Hanya Holm who sees not perverseness in people, but outside disturbances which prevent them from cooperating. If you delve far enough, it is sure to be that way.

Mary Track is the most impossible of human beings. But I think if she were given the chance to be thought good for a short time and received some encouragement, her terrible inferiority complex, which upsets herself and everyone around her, would disappear and she would be a normal human being.

Well, my dearest one, I shall say au revoir until tomorrow. Let me know immediately of any change of address.

All my love,
Sybil

August 6, 1936
Bennington

My Dearest Jerry,

Being in the country has at last gone to my head. I controlled myself just so far and then, but I knew it would happen, though I did not know just what "it" was. Now I know that hereafter, for a time at least, all my dances will be dithyrambic, and my masterpiece will be the time I fell in love with a satyr. You have never known me in this kind of a frenzy, dear, and by the time I get back to New York the only trace of it will be in my dance, which is as it should be.

Have you ever seen me do the camel's humph? It is a voice exercise for relaxation which I learned at college. I did it for Charles and Jose the night of our revelry at the Putman, and the knowledge of it has managed to travel all over the campus, so that I am asked to do it six times a day, at least. I don't always conform, but those who have seen it go into gales of laughter, and think it is the funniest thing they have ever seen. Those who have heard others talking of the camel's humph in connection with me, but who have not seen it, expect that it will be a dance. They never seem to be disappointed, however, when they finally experience it. I have become quite famous, thanks to my voice teacher, Mrs. Howk.

Well, today is the day for all those who have caught the

mumps from Pussy boy or Pumba the mump carrier (Pauline) to show signs of the disease. I certainly hope no one does, especially Doris who has never had them, and who at this point it would be almost impossible to give up on account of the production.

Yesterday I tore madly around without a moment's relaxation, except that I am not in very many of the dances and could sit and watch quite often. Today it is pouring rain so I shall have to keep under cover as much as possible. My mother sent me one of those transparent rain capes which you don't like, so I shall wear it out here.

I am not in a good letter-writing mood today, and besides I have to write to Mama, so I shall stop now.

All my love to you, my dearest,
Sybil

August 7, 1936
Bennington

Jerry Dear,

I think I am beginning to learn what I have struggled for so long, and that is love of humanity, love for its own sake, for it is the greatest force in the world. I never knew it before in so many words, but I am a collector of people. I pick out the honest and sincere ones and love them with all my heart, and so call up love in them for me. I think this surge of feeling is due somewhat to Hanya's presence, for I take technique for a half hour a day from her and feel her marvelous benevolence.

Yesterday my class was wonderful to me, and I felt each personality separately as though I were endowed with the power of inspiring mutual love. Why is Joan so unfortunately constructed that she antagonizes people? If it is so, that some people have power and others not, then it should be up to the ones who have it to be generous. Doris is inhibited, however, and I think I am slowly but surely losing my inhibition! I never can see why I should be so blessed with love, but because I am, I must work harder to distribute it. Do you think it takes away from a performer to be good and full of faith instead of cynical? For Martha Graham is the latter, and she certainly was divine the other night.

Most people say such unpleasant things about their students behind their backs. They are so bitter. I think that attitude must be what destroys teachers. I hope that I can benefit by teaching rather than being embittered.

Dearest one, my letter to this point reminds me of something strange, perhaps medieval confessions of a young nun. I have become a fantastic creature since I left you. All the energy which I ordinarily put into my work on dances and dancing has been used on people the last few weeks, and I find that I like them as well as I do trees and dragon flies, etc.

George will be coming tomorrow, and I shall be so glad to see him. Maybe if he is in the right mood, I shall find a moment to whisk him off to the enchanted garden.

I do hope I hear from you today, and that you have heard from me, and also received my other letters sent to New York.

All my love, dearest Jerry,
Sybil

August 10, 1936

My Dearest Jerry,

How are things with you? This last minute feeling is getting me down. I don't feel as though I have accomplished anything this summer, except quite personal experiences of joy and love and anguish which I have not put into form.

I expect to be back in New York on Sunday evening, Aug. 16, on a train that leaves here around four o'clock in the afternoon. I can hardly wait to see you, but for some reason, I dread going back to New York. Probably, it is because I am in such a dazed state that I can't decide what to work on first and how. But perhaps I can collect myself before then. In fact I feel strength surging up in me right now. How strange to suddenly feel one's self going right out of pain into pleasure. I am a little breathless at my easy and quick assent, though I am not near the top really compared to my ecstasy of last week. Autumn's approach always makes me feel extremely sad, as though I must have a thousand resolutions for the new year of accomplishment.

This morning we are supposed to have free, but it so happens that the workshop group demands attention again, so I have to teach for an hour. Then I think I shall walk in the country, then take Hanya's class. She is a wonderful person (as I have said before). George and Kenny came yesterday, but Kenny went back immediately. George is staying for the week. They both look wonderfully well and very tanned. I hope you are both. My tan has faded almost completely. George has been working out some experiments in his theatre work which sound very good. I shall tell you about them when I find out more.

All my love to you, my dearest Jerry. It is less than a week now.

Sybil

August 12, 1936
Bennington

My Dear Jerry,

I received your note this morning and thank you with all my heart for the flower. I wish I knew more of what you are doing. But I shall soon. I am really getting anxious to do some real work in New York, as beautiful as the country is. This last week may be hectic, but my spirits are high and I hope yours are too.

This morning I at last had my pictures taken. The sky was not clear, however, so when I see how these come out, I shall decide whether I want more. They are action pictures. You shall be the first one to have one. It was a beautiful morning, but the grass on the field was very wet, and the clouds were heavy and brilliant with the effort of keeping the sun hidden.

Last evening I actually discovered some new movements. I was bubbling with creation. I listened twice yesterday to Stravinsky's Symphony of Psalms. It is glorious and the whole world danced as I listened. Then I did a little improvising in the evening by the lamplight, and we had a marshmallow roast, most of which I missed coming in at 11 after rehearsal.

I think I am going to get to know Hanya this time, so that I can see her in the winter and talk to her. It is marvelous to look forward to. I took her class today, and have sat by her several times at dinner. Now I must relieve Joan from her teaching job for an hour. She is practically a wreck with all her various ailments and should take a real vacation after this.

Until tomorrow, Darling. Please let me know what you are doing and how you are.

My dearest love to you,
Sybil

15

The relief I felt at Bennington from the two problems of worrying over Jerry and producing solos of my own, which caused this giddy fling I was having the last two weeks in Bennington, ended abruptly when I returned to New York.

On our first meeting Jerry and I were walking across 57th Street when the realization of the predicament I was in came, and it came like a thunderbolt. As we sauntered, we stopped to look in a window full of new cars, and Jerry said, "I wonder when we will be able to afford one of these."

Suddenly I felt as though I were drowning, and my mind flew, not backward, but forward—a car, a house, dishes, furniture, sheets and pillowcases, children! This was not what I intended. In a flash I looked at him, then turned and ran as fast as I could to the Seventh Avenue subway and home.

Jerry called and said, "I don't want you to live the legend." But the peak had been reached, and after we met the next time, he told me that he was jealous.

I feel now that he was jealous, and that I was guilty. But he was also down to earth about himself in relation to Joy, and I was not ready. This was the separation that I had dreaded, and it had to come. This was the love affair I so desired and the marriage that I always really knew I could not handle. Before we met I was already in love with and married to the dance and any attempt to circumvent that defied destiny.

I wanted Jerry to join our group. But he wisely went his own way and returned to Cleveland and Joy. I really missed him terribly—I remember well the feeling of dryness. I tried to grow up and take other people into my life and face the fact that not being in love was really my choice.

August 18, 1936
Three Arts Club

Dear Clair,

I write to tell you what a marvelous evening was last Sunday and to thank you for the introduction to the great Hallie Flanigan. I have never before been in such an emotional state nor felt so many vibrations at once. I was so glad Eddie was along or I never would have been able to stand the trip back to New York. He seemed to be a weight at my side to keep me from flying off into space.

It was a memorable summer, Clair, and I hope, if you have time, you will let me know what you are doing, and what is decided about Vassar.

Most sincerely,
Sybil

August 20, 1936
Three Arts Club

Dearest Champie,

For months I have been wanting to write to you to thank you for your marvelous letter and help. What I am writing for now is to tell you that if you are north now, or will be soon, you must make a point to see me. I expect to be in New York for the rest of the summer, and I have a great deal to talk to you about. I was on the staff at Bennington School of the Dance this summer. I had a marvelous time and met many great and exciting people. My career is at an important point now, for I am just about to carry out the thrilling idea of combining the dance and drama in the theatre. We have an experimental group headed by John Martin and his wife.

Sunday, I met Hallie Flanigan through a mutual friend, and had supper with her. She, too, is interested in dance drama. She reminds me of you in personal magnetism.

My private life has come to a standstill at this particular moment, and I feel nothing but my work. It will pass, probably.

September

Dear Clair,

For two weeks, I have been in a state of complete schedule, which is a marvelous sensation of accomplishment. But today I had a distraction in the form of a girl who has been here for several weeks and to whom I have only spoken once before. How strangely one stumbles on these people glistening through their human forms. As I look back, I have been conscious of her presence all along and, almost without knowing it, saw at which table she sat at meals and with whom she talked in the library, but I was too busy with my own affairs to put myself in contact with her energy. And how different I am myself. I remember once when people like her caused me such agonies of jealousy, because I could never be them! I was so devoted to Joan of Arc and Florence Nightingale that my own position in life was unbearable by its very insignificance. Now, I feel that the selfish artist in me is excused by the fact that, once I make myself a proper instrument, I can give to the world instead of just a few individuals. Now I can talk with this girl and feel that at least I have something to give, too, if not now, then later.

But what about these people who do not glisten? Can it be that they are not born yet? I can no longer believe that they are dead souls.

Have you heard of Lauro de Bosis? He was the Italian poet who flew over Rome distributing pamphlets against fascism to the liberty-starved people of Italy and who never returned from his deed of heroism. He has written a poem called "Icarus," and Eleanor King has created a dance drama out of it, and we are dancing it. She knew this poet when he was in America about eight years ago and said she found him truly great, a hero and an idealist. It is thrilling to do his poem, especially since Eleanor has captured his spirit within herself and within the movement of the dance.

How marvelously vibrant people can become about other people and their creations. Creation breeds creation. I feel tonight that I could dance myself to distraction. But tomorrow I shall objectify this madness.

Best of luck with your orchestration. You will do it before October first, and then I hope to see you.

With love,
Sybil

And so Miriam Wallace and Mary Baker Eddy came into my life for a brief spell. This terrible emptiness at losing Jerry had somehow to be replaced by hope, and when I met Miriam Wallace at the Three Arts Club on my return to New York, she handed me the spiritual bridge I needed in Mary Baker Eddy.

I can remember thinking that physical healing was simply a matter of timing, and that although it seemed to be a miracle of replacement—or change from sick to well—it was rather like the magic in the movies where the action can go forward or backward quickly at any speed without omitting any of the actual process. "Time heals" was an old saw that one took for granted, but I suddenly realized that the difference between time and eternity was a matter of rhythm and speed. Christian Science brought me back to the wonder of the presence of the Christ, which my upbringing had suggested but not clarified.

October 10, 1936
Three Arts Club

Miriam Wallace
Westport, Conn.

Dear Miriam,

Thank you for your note and the quotation. I shall certainly think of it often, in fact, I have used it already. You know, of course, that I am in a transition period and because of you and your great love and strength, I have been able to hang onto and strengthen the connections of which I first became aware in Bennington last summer.

I really feel that the last two weeks have definitely started me down the right path. Even such little things as the goodwill I felt for the green grocer who sold me five Jonathan apples yesterday, and the merry nod I exchanged with the garage man on 10th St. whom I have passed every day before as though he were a telephone pole. These things tell me that I am a different person, and that the illness of unrighteousness is leaving me. Of course, I still forget that these two-legged or pronged individuals, as Carlyle calls them, are human beings, but I am confident that this blindness is a temporary thing.

I am very anxious to read Mrs. Eddy's book, because right now I definitely feel a sympathy for all her teachings, but not a true understanding. Although much of my life and experience has been mental and spiritual (up to now) still I find it hard to genuinely comprehend the supremacy of mind over matter for more than a fleeting second at a time.

Our friendship, I am sure, will be lifelong, for nothing can stop it as long as we continue to live creatively. But no matter what may be in store for us, those two weeks are already eternal. Don't you think so? I have only seen my college dramatic coach once since I left school, and yet I have merely to think of her, and I find myself renewed by my admiration of her spirit.

But there is no need to talk in terms of eternity, really, for I certainly hope I shall see you soon, especially that you will come back to live at the Club. I expect to be here for a good, long time.

Nancy left today, and I find it necessary to look around for congenial friends who are alive, so this evening I sat with some girls I had never seen before. I was pleasantly surprised. Of course, during the conversation we traveled around to the coming election. I, for the sake of a reaction, said that I was a communist, and the girl on my left looked at me in amazement and said, "Are you an American?" I howled, of course, but I managed to redeem myself somehow, for she even agreed to read *The Communist Manifesto,* and asked me to stay longer when I got up to leave the table.

I wish you very good luck living at home, and I hope to hear from you soon.

With love,
Sybil

<hr />

October 10, 1936
Three Arts Club

Dear Clair,

Last Thursday evening I gave my first demonstration and concert of the season. It was quite successful, and strangely enough the audience liked my second dance the best, the one I was so worried about because it was so hard for me to get into the mood (cynicism) and because I had no accompaniment for it at the last minute. I wore shoes and beat out the rhythm with my feet. It seemed to cause quite a controversy, because I used my face. Most of the audience had been under the impression that modern dancers were always completely blank.

George went over with me and worked the lights, pulled the curtain, turned the pages for Edith, and helped me with my makeup, and carried the bags. I don't know what I would have done without him. He is a very dear person and, as I told you, an idealist. We are working together on the dance drama idea. He thinks I should go through the West giving demonstrations this winter at all the places we will touch on our tour next year as advance advertising, and he said he would go with me. We would create some dances together, and I would talk about the dance, etc. etc. We are very excited about it. But to convince the Humphrey-Weidmans of the value to them, as well as to us, will be another matter.

I hope something can be worked out about my going to Vassar. I have a tentative engagement over in Brooklyn which I have to arrange about on Tuesday.

Miriam, the girl I told you about in my last letter, has gone back to the country, but before she left I found out, just as I expected, that she is a truly great and creative person, and we will be lifelong friends.

I hope to hear from you soon, Clair.

My love to you,
Sybil

When I found we would touch Cleveland on tour, I wrote to Jerry.

Dear Jerry,

On Friday evening, October 23rd, I am going to be in Cleveland performing with a small demonstration group that Doris & Charles are taking out for several performances—the others—Bea, Katie Litz, George and Jose. We are performing in the Little Theatre, but perhaps you have seen the folder that Eleanor Frampton has sent out. I expect to do the knocking dance from *Candide* with Charles, though we haven't rehearsed it yet.

All this leads up to I hope you will be there and that I will see you after the performance or, if not, perhaps I can see you some time Friday, for we arrive at midnight and will be in Cleveland until Saturday.

Our dance drama group is very interesting and successful so far. There are something like 18 or 20 members, and we just began working on acting this week with Mrs. Martin. We have been working steadily on diction and Eleanor's *Icaro* which, by the way, has turned into a truly beautiful dance. Eleanor is slowly, thanks to Perry-Mansfield this summer, freeing herself from that restricted feeling of the Humphrey-Weidman group. And this whole new dance drama idea has broadened everyone's viewpoint to the extent that Doris and Charles are much more cooperative with and appreciative of us. Our new group consists of quite a few members of the old group as well as Jack Cole and Alice Dudley whom we are very glad to find interested.

Louise Allen has blossomed into a really interesting person, plus showing great imagination in acting which Doris never gave her credit for.

But more when I see you, Jerry. Believe me when I say I do want to see you very much, and I hope you feel the same. We have been very good friends, and I feel that that should always be.

Sincerely,
Sybil

P.S. Charles, in his disappointing way, has decided not to do the knocking dance!

———————————————————————————

October 18, 1936
Three Arts Club

Dear Miriam,

I was very glad to receive your card. Have you been in the midst of moving as it seemed to indicate? I would like very much to spend a weekend with you some time. This next weekend I shall be on the road with Doris & Charles giving a short demonstration tour in Cleveland and Detroit, etc. I think it will be a great deal of fun because, as usual, I have the wanderlust, not having moved out of New York since the beginning of September. Are there still bright, colored leaves on the trees? I hope so, for I am looking forward to some beautiful scenery. We shall be traveling all day Thursday.

On Nov. 6 I am giving another demonstration in a high school assembly program in Brooklyn.

The other day, I stopped in an old bookstore on Sixth Ave. between 12th and 13th Sts., and asked if they had any of Mrs. Eddy's books. The woman, whose husband died nine months ago and left her with a 100 foot deep bookstore, the walls and low ceilings of which are lined with everything imaginable in print and gave one the feeling that if you walked too heavily the whole would cave in, causing a cloud of dust to rise miles into the air; this woman was fascinating, alive and attractive with excitable eyes, hair sticking out at every angle. She had a bowl of brilliant red flowers which she asked me to admire as she ducked behind a mysteriously narrow door and hunted out two faded looking books, one *Science and Health With Key to the Scriptures* and the other, *Retrospection and Introspection*, the latter was a thin lavender book, out of print, so she said, and it was marked $5. However, I may have it for $2. Of course, I can't pay that, especially since it is advertised for $1 in the *Herald*. But I want so much to go back and make this woman's acquaintance. I am tempted to just take her some flowers, and then look around at her other books.

Dottie wants to be remembered to you. She is the grandest neighbor. I like her better every day.

I hope to hear from you soon.

With love,
Sybil

P.S. This evening, I went for a short walk on the Drive just before supper. It was growing dusky, and the new moon was between two stars in a pale blue sky. There were few people out, because the wind was blowing. The river reacted with quick undulations alternating blue and black. I was ecstatic and put landscape above man until, on reaching the soldier's and sailor's monument, I met a man, young, I am sure, with a grey beard and grey hair ruffled up by his overcoat collar. He smoked a pipe and was springing up and down on his toes in the wind when I saw him. Then he walked and I was amazed at his light step. Then, believe me, he put one foot on top of the stone railing and stood stretched, the other foot on the ground. I bounced up and down with excitement, and was just about to go up and say to him, "Zarathustra, you are a dancer," when I saw a dark man looking at me, and I was afraid. Some day I shall be calm enough to speak to whom I please.

October 20, 1936
Three Arts Club

Dear Miss de Mille,

By John Martin's column, I see that you are returning to England right after your appearance at the New School. Of course, I shall be there, but I would like to see you before then if possible, because I have some things to tell you about the new Dance Drama group that has been formed by George Bockman of Charles' group and myself and 17 other interested dancers. The group is just two months old, but is functioning daily and has great hopes for the future.

I am busy every day until 3:30 and Thursday I am going on a week's tour with Doris and Charles. After that, however, I hope you will have time to have tea with me some afternoon. It would be better if you would set your own date as your schedule is probably more irregular than mine.

I see that Howard's *Hamlet* received a good write up in Boston. I am very anxious to see it.

I certainly hope to see you soon.

Most sincerely,
Sybil L. Shearer

My suggestion to have tea resulted in an invitation to a showing of Agnes's new dances at Martha Graham's studio. Martha was not there—on tour some place—but everyone else was. I had never been in a room with so many celebrities. I was the unknown critic and beginning dancer, there among Agnes's many acquaintances and friends from the stage and the literary world.

It surprised me to find that these dances were in the making, "works in progress," and I think everyone else was surprised, too. Her pieces were not ready choreographically, nor were they finished from a performance standpoint. I think her idea had been to get friendly criticism that would help her. But the light only dawned during and after the event that this was the wrong move.

The moment it was over everyone left with as few polite words as possible, nothing like, "Call me Agnes, I want to talk to you," etc. I was the only one remaining, and I went back into the dressing room where Agnes lay "stricken" on the chaise longue, her mother preparing a cup of tea which she handed to me to pass to Agnes. I was stopped in my tracks, however, by a cry from Mrs. de Mille followed by, "You are disturbing the money!" I had stirred the sugar and the bubbles were evaporating! My mother, too, was always careful to drink the bubbles before they burst. Bubbles seemed to be money in the old days. But the bubble had already burst for Agnes. She was mortified by the unforeseen outcome of the evening's display.

All three of us were miserable because I was the only one in that audience who cared, and who was I? But I went home and wrote my opinions and advice anyway. Later, from England, Agnes wrote back to thank me.

Oct. 28, 1936
Three Arts Club

Dear Miss de Mille,

Because I know that you must value my opinion to some extent, or you would never have asked me to see your dances, I want to tell you what I thought. When I said it would be easier to write to you than talk, I meant easier than talk right then and there, for if there were time and calm, I would certainly prefer to talk. I regret that you will not receive this before sailing.

Everything I shall say to you comes to you both from my head and my heart, for I am fond of you as a person and I admire you as an artist, perhaps more than I do any living soul.

Certainly, I have been more moved by you and your dances than by any other.

I still feel that *The Witch Spell* is the best dance. That may be, of course, because I have seen it in performance before, and the others will take better shape in my mind later. With you, more than any other dancer, it is the actual performance rather than the form of the dance that connects you intellectually as well as emotionally with your audience. *Witch Spell* however, can stand alone, and it suits your movement completely.

The second Stravinsky was not clear to your audience before you began. I didn't understand your point of view during the dance and therefore was forced to concentrate on the form. What I found was a dramatic dance, which I am confident would reach your audience in performance but could not reach us at such close range because there was too little actual dance design in the movement, as most of the dance was within you rather than objectified in the movement. For that reason it was not able to exist apart from you as much as the first Stravinsky did. It therefore does not seem to be a step ahead in choreography from the first Stravinsky, although the actual theme is deeper and more moving.

You saw that practically everyone was more impressed by the *Song of the Sea*. I feel that it was because of this very choreographic fact. Your meaning was much more tangible in movement, which is the form all of us deal in and understand, rather than the more difficult to achieve dramatic form. Your little conversation with your mother about cutting out spots that were technically difficult was interesting. Strangely enough, my mother said exactly the same to me in a letter not long ago. And it is true, especially in your case, that it is your dramatic power and quality of movement which will put your dance over to your audience, rather than any technically difficult movement. I know that for your own satisfaction, however, you desire to deal in dance form regardless of its technical difficulties in order that you may have more range for your dramatic ideas. Actually, in the case of this dance, which is so full of imagination, anything you might cut to make it easier would not be missed, because the movement themes are good, and the feeling projected by them is full of freshness.

You have said to me several times that you are unable to cope with an abstract form, and therefore always deal in terms of drama. I understood this to mean that some people have one approach and some another. Not until last night when I realized why you have the approach you have did I understand why you are different from the other modern dancers. It is purely from the technical point of view.

The others—Martha Graham, Doris, Charles—had not only ballet as a background, but also a great deal of oriental which made them conscious of all kinds of distortions—the movement in every direction of every part of the body—and they continued along these lines in their own experimenting. Mary Wigman approached the dance from the point of view of rebellion against the ballet and developed a technique which I have always thought was more universal than any of the others in the light of pure movement, not taking choreography into consideration. The followers of all these dancers are consequently very much concerned with movement for its own sake and composition in terms of movement, instead of in terms of a dramatic idea which is your approach.

Your background in the dance, as far as I know, has been ballet, and although you certainly do not use the technique in your compositions, I feel it has limited your scope in movement and kept you from the full play of your imagination.

You have the marvelous faculty of picking out the significant movements for the dramatic idea, and that is the gift of genius—the arrangement and development is to my mind merely a technical difficulty, overcome by constant experimentation. I must confess, however, that I never noticed any technical lack in your actual performances, because I am always carried away by your feeling for the idea. It was only seeing your dances in an unfinished state which made me realize that your next step in developing yourself as a modern dancer, which you are already in point of view, is a technical one and you should develop a technique of your own for training every part of your body to move in any desired direction with any desired quality; by quality I mean those abstract technicalities such as the succession of movement and the rebound or bounce and the breath rhythms, suspension and relaxation, etc. The other modern dancers have begun with movement and are working toward drama, whereas your approach has been exactly the opposite: thus, in your development toward complete expression, you are unique and alone.

Your pantomimic dance was a revelation to me to find that you were actually uncertain as to its being understood by the audience. This gave me great encouragement in my own things, knowing how clear your compositions always turn out in performance.

But I wish you did not have to tear off so quickly. I would like to be with you more, and I shall certainly make every effort to go to England to work with you next summer, but before then I hope I shall see you. The group is very enthusiastic about working with you, and if you have a composition which you would like us to work on in the spring, I think it will be possible to give you the third section of our year as we have nothing definite planned yet for then. Until Christmas we shall work with Eleanor King, during the winter with John Martin, and I hope in the spring with you. George Bockman, who is really the chairman of our group, heard your talk last Tuesday, and was very much impressed and feels that to work with you would be quite inspiring.

I wish you the marvelous success you deserve in England with your concerts, and I look forward to seeing you in February. Thank you for inviting me to see your dances, and I hope my point of view, which has been steeped in the modern dance for two years, is of assistance to you, though I am aware that you probably know all these things already.

Most sincerely and affectionately,
Sybil L. Shearer

16

November 13, 1936
Cleveland Heights, Ohio

Dear Sybil,

I was in the audience during your performance at the Little Theatre, Cleveland, and I was pleased and impressed by the sureness and finish of your movements. It was quite evident that you had completely mastered a medium of expression that will stand you in good stead as an art form for any discovery or convictions that may arise within you.

I trust that you are having jolly times and that you are full of plans for the future.

With the best of luck,
Jerry

Nov. 16, 1936
Three Arts Club

Dear Archie,

Today, much to my surprise and pleasure, I received a note from Jerry. Do I have you to thank for that? Whether I do or not, however, I was extremely glad to hear from him.

I have been thinking of you, because you said it was after the 13th that you would get in touch with me. [Archie had borrowed money from me.] If you are not yet ready to see me, however, don't let it disturb you for I want to see Leslie Howard's *Hamlet* anyway, so perhaps we can arrange to go out, at $1.10 apiece, or whatever the lowest seats are. I saw Gielgud's *Hamlet* last Saturday, and I felt that the acting was good, but that the production, especially the direction, could have been better. So, of course, I want to see what Howard will do along that line.

I also have some things to tell you about our experimentation with acting and dancing. I think, am quite sure in fact, that our acting methods will open up a whole new field in play writing.

In the meantime why don't you become a radio announcer? Hasn't anyone ever told you that your voice over the telephone is most pleasing? Of course, you'll say well it takes this and that, "besides I'm an old man," at which I shall laugh out loud, as I always do when people say they are "so old." And for some reason, I have to do it often, for in the presence of my impossible energy, people reproach themselves with old age even though they don't mean it. I wish, of course, that they would have the opposite reaction. But these quotations which I ran across the other day, if thought about and applied, seem to me to solve the whole problem of time and old age and sad unpleasantnesses, which I have denied since childhood, though I am by no means a perfect example of timelessness. I believe "that time represents the accumulation of still unfulfilled prophecy, the aggregation of unsatisfied moments" and that if discernment of any kind—intellectual, emotional or spiritual—"were always accompanied by objectified achievement, time elements would be eliminated." And so there would be no more old age. How delightful! That is what I hope for in myself. It is an exciting thought, and I am telling it to you not as a sermon (please heaven forbid!), but just from one friend to another. And I hope you will find it logical and sensible, and for that reason, useful. But don't be afraid of me on account of it, because I promise never to speak of it of my own accord. Everyone sees these things differently.

I hope to see you soon,
SLS

Dear Jerry,

I was very glad to hear from you, and to know that you were in the audience in Cleveland. That performance was the best of the three, I felt, for the audience was the most responsive. Also, I had prepared myself mentally before the performance and was better able to dance for that reason. *New Dance* had more meaning and renewed interest for me, both because I was in the mood, and because Miss Humphrey danced it as she never did before, marvelously, and I gave her everything I had in response to her dramatic intensity.

I have discovered the value of mood, not merely as an idea, but as something powerful, which includes every part of me, and I have been able to use it once or twice. It is that, more than anything else, that I am working on now. And this concentration on the reality of thought that I am learning from various sources, especially from the acting with Mrs. Martin, is an important part of the new life that I have suddenly stepped into this fall.

I am so terrifically busy working for everyone else—Miss Humphrey, Charles, Eleanor—that I have only a short time in the morning, 6:30 to 8:30, and a few evenings to work on my own compositions. At present, I am still creating the fifth of my suite of five dances. It is the hardest one of all, and takes much thought as well as physical labor.

If you could spare the time, Jerry, I would like very much to know what you are doing. I have heard from Maurice and

195

Archie that you are working with both dance and theatre, which seems very good to me. I hope you are still working on your play, too. George Abbot's was quite a flop. I am enclosing a postcard of Van Gogh's boats, which I bought for Joy in Detroit. Maurice showed me a charming picture of her taken, I suppose, at the Great Lakes Exposition, for I recognized the background from my walk around Cleveland the morning of our demonstration.

Very best of luck to you, and thank you for your note.

Most sincerely,
Sybil

December 1, 1936
Three Arts Club

My Dear Mimi,

This is to let you know that I think of you during the week, even though I do not have time to see you. Tonight, I am going to see *Hedda Gabler* and hope to be thrilled by Nazimova's performance. I have never seen her before. Now as I write, I am at the same time fighting to hear Tchaikowsky's Fifth Symphony through two other stations. It's amazing how the persistent voice of a fat little German and the strains of a popular jazz melody sink into nothing the minute I allow my mind and body to relax in the strains of the music I really want to hear.

I did not tell you of the girl I met on the subway whom I had seen before last week. We got off at the same station, and both proceeded to the music library. I arrived at the door first and opened it and said, "I saw you last week on the Westside subway," and she looked at me and said, "Oh, yeah." she was a very nice looking girl too, pretty, Italian, perhaps.

Good luck to you—till Friday,
Sybil

Sybil—

Your letter again reveals to me the remarkable parallelism in our thinking. In recent months, I have adjusted my life to what I call the necessity for the supremacy of mind, and in your last letter I find you laying stress on "concentration on the reality of thought." Are you acquainted with the life and works of Paul Valery? I think, at this time, that you will find his ideas much to your liking. In thinking about you and me and our experiences together, it occurs to me that parallelism was the verse form used by the old Hebraic psalmists. Without numbering the syllabic feet or rhyming the final sounds, they gave each phrase its balanced counterpart in thought content and imagery, and the whole effect was one of ecstatic freedom of being soaring on the full organ tones of religious fervor. As I say, somehow, in a symbolic sense, this reflection seems to apply to something that was born between us.

Judging by your working schedule, your days must be far too short. Your new life that you speak of is evidently so crammed full of activities! I hope, some day, to be able to see the results of your new discoveries in compositions of your own making. Very likely, the fifth of your suite of five dances is many leagues removed from your first *Revelation*. When the time comes, you must grant me the privilege of being part of your audience. I look forward to the event with keen anticipation.

I am working on various ideas. The fact that I am again dancing should interest you. I have a group of 15 or more Negroes and whites who are working on technique with a view to eventually creating an Uncle Tom ballet based on my play. We are all very enthusiastic and forward looking. And—do you remember Alice Marting at Bennington? She and I work together three or four times each week on ideas for new dances. We have one gay little dance that is practically finished to Pick-Mangiagalli's Les Petits Soldats (Charles' *Piccoli Soldati*). We wanted to have that ready for a certain occasion. Next Friday evening (that is, tomorrow evening) we're all going to Eleanor Frampton's recital in the same Little Theatre where you performed.

Other things are happening that I'll tell you about when I write to you again.

Joy and I were very grateful for your gift of Van Gogh. She made a copy of it.

I love you sincerely,
Jerry

December 20, 1936
Three Arts Club

Dear Jerry,

It was so good to hear from you again, and to know that you are doing such interesting things. And I am very glad you are dancing again. Of course, I remember Alice Marting. I liked her very much. I recall now that she came backstage in Cleveland, and I was surprised to see her. A very short boy with a bright face also came backstage, and we had a short conversation. Is he in your group?

I have been so busy that up to now it has been impossible to get hold of the life and works of Paul Valery, but I am looking forward to reading it. The 15th of January is the big moment in our lives about which we are now concerned, for that is the Hippodrome performance [*With My Red Fires* by Humphrey]. When that is over, heaven knows what may happen. Charles may go to Hollywood. We all hope he does. He is the bane of my existence at this point, for his rehearsals take all of my free time, which I would like to be spending on my own dances.

You were in my thoughts constantly just before your letter arrived, and I had secretly attributed the reason to the royal romance across the sea, but evidently you had been thinking of me, too.

To me the important thing, as always, is love in the form of creation, and more important, recreation, or performance. I really am confident that by concentration, both can be accomplished by me.

But what I have found, and think you have found, should eliminate these ordinary difficulties.

Tonight we give a demonstration at the New School, and I have a new variation nicknamed by the group, the variation of the squashed bug. Its real zoological name, however, is a variation on a theme from the hunting dance (*Theatre Piece*).

I have sent a scrapbook to Joy, and some pictures I thought she might like. She can add her own collection to this and probably some of her own pictures. I always think of her as a very grown up little girl, because of the very beautiful picture of the garden she drew last Christmas, but I hope I have not over estimated this grown-upness, for I am constantly surprised when I remember that she is only seven.

Merry Christmas to you, Jerry, and please let me know of the "other things" that are happening when you write. I look forward to news of you.

Sybil

December 26, 1936
Three Arts Club

Dear Jerry,

For some reason which is now unaccountable to me, I neglected to say all that I wished to tell you in my last letter—my struggles and problems, which you so ably told me by your letter that you could understand.

During Christmas I came down with the flu, and all activities ceased for me—both mental and physical. The cause of my illness was a terrific dilemma which had been piling up on me during December. I have myself so involved in both the Humphrey-Weidman group and the Dance Drama group, that I began to experience that terrific frustration that comes when nothing creative comes out of me for any length of time. I had no time to work, and I saw no possibility of ever having any without completely severing my connections. My problem now is so complex that I would almost rather not begin, except that I feel you will understand and perhaps help me. The "necessity for the supremacy of mind" concerns me deeply, but as in all concepts or situations that have come into my life, the adjustment involved takes long and is terrifically painful. The one thing that bothers me so much, and which is the basis of all the troubles of the world, I am convinced, is selfishness. If I could only find some way to overcome this trouble in myself, then I feel there would be a marvelous and creative life to look forward to. But, as you once said, the mind says one thing and the emotions another. But in order to overcome selfishness, I must know what the self is. Understanding this and comprehending it with my emotions would mean living.

I know that unselfishness is not just giving to others, it is wanting to give, and then just over the line is wanting because it pleases yourself, but it is no good to give and not want to. There must be a higher understanding than just the physical act of giving or not giving.

The compassion I feel for Miss Humphrey, working with people who are not interested really, but who stick to her like leeches because their worldly reasoning tells them that she is the best, and they would be helpless by themselves. This emotion is genuine in me, but true compassion would also include these people whom my emotions scorn, and I am really one of these people whom I scorn.

I go into the country and look at the hills and the trees and feel refreshed because of the calm, but the minute my eye strikes a town with people residing there, I receive a sharp pain, because I feel the tumult of lack of understanding and the intenseness of selfishness. And I know that a great share of it is mine.

One thing does convince me, however, and that is that if I can capture these essences of unselfishness, then whether my form is absolutely intellectual and above the head of my audience or not, still they will receive my message through any dance form and will respond to it. For that reason, I collect my courage to leave New York and the dance world and go out to create for people and to teach them, though I am afraid it will be they who will teach me.

One thing that I need is absolute discipline, and not one of my associates in New York can give that. I must get that for myself, and it comes only through the mind. I am sure that it is impossible to die if one's mind is strong and active. So it is up to me to create one, and the mind I have cries out that the most good for everyone concerned will come from an attack on myself and not an escape into a group of people that will cover me up when I don't wish to be seen and praise me when I do.

You know that one of my greatest desires is to be a member of a company of creative actor-dancers, but so few of the people here have my vision and George's, and he has no command over people, and I have a secret, and perhaps unfair, desire to also be a solo dancer. We are crying out with all our strength that we want theatre! theatre! theatre! And we are tied hand and foot by every imaginable obstacle, the worst of which is selfishness. Only by living together for an idea can people live cooperatively, and consequently, happily. The sadness that seems to permeate the world is the lack of cooperation among humans who are marvelous in themselves, but cannot connect with others for some material reason.

I love you, Jerry! How long will it be before I can say that with no reservation on account of this selfishness which eats into me? But at this moment, as I write, I see a clear spot of calm compassion and love, and everything becomes warm for a second during understanding and light. Oh, that I should never have to sink back! I am definitely in a transitional period now, so that although I know little, I feel much. Your letter pleased me, because of its calm clarity, for as I said, it seemed as though you had such a balance between the two worlds. I look forward myself to a time of calm and a creative acceptance, in which I am not a stranger to reality, when my questionings may be put into dance form. (And with that I hope that we may meet again.)

January 16, 1937

Now the Hippodrome performance is over, and I find you were almost here. Eve [a student of Jerry's] came in the morning and asked for me, and we had quite a talk while I put on my makeup. She told me all about your successes, your play and your new job. You must tell me when the former is going to be presented. I would give anything to be there. And the fact that you are going to direct in the WPA Theatre is really exciting. She was also very enthusiastic about her acting with you and the dance drama idea.

Mrs. Martin has not given us any emotional problems at all yet. Of course, my idea is one that leads to character, and so far we have just been ourselves, but Eve tells me you have been giving them problems in emotion, and that you keep them working like mad. I envy her having a director like you who can work up the enthusiasm of the group. The one time you directed me, although you seemed to think it was a failure because of my temperamental fit, was the only time I have been led on to greater ideas by suggestion since college when Champie used to help me.

I have asked Eve to work with me Monday morning. She seemed very pleased when I suggested it, and I am looking forward to it, too, for I am always thrilled to meet new people with ideas similar to my own.

I am so sorry you couldn't come to New York, but that job

will be worth more to you than all the Humphrey-Weidman performances on the face of the globe. We are giving a performance in Columbus on our tour. I was telling Eve, and she said she would drive you there, so I hope I shall see you soon. I feel as though I must see you again and know you and be with you before I can know any real calm.

Eve mentioned the fact that Alice said she thought she would give up the dance. Do you suppose she meant this? And if so would it be possible for me to have the job? It may seem foolish of me to want to leave all of these great people who know so much more than I, but deep down I know that things here are not right.

Let me know what you think of the idea of my going to Cleveland, Jerry. I look forward to news soon. I want to work with you enthusiastically, for the love of it. I want to be a help, Jerry. Let me know your thoughts.

This is one of those rare moments when I feel the limits of space and time have lifted for a minute. Ouspensky says the seeking after knowledge for its own sake is the ideal state and I believe him.

Good luck always and always, Jerry, and give my love to Joy. I am so glad she liked the scrapbook, and thank her for the picture. I like it very much, indeed.

My love to you, sincerely,
Sybil

Jan. 28, 1937

Dearest Sybil—

Your letter reveals again the exquisite balance of a finely attuned mind. It gives me such joy to follow the clear line of your thinking! If it were merely lessons in understanding that you required, it would be a simple matter for me to offer certain thought-suggestions to help you through what you call your transitional period. However, I've always known and loved and respected the keen awareness of your mind that positively rises to heights of clairvoyance. You look out at the world unflinchingly. That is your way. That is your genius. I am convinced that you do know what the self is and that you will not benefit by trying to break it down into emotions. I think, rather, that it is your *mind* that is demanding recognition of you. It is not that you are caught on a seesaw of selfishness between mind and emotion, it seems that you persist in denying the *will* to *believe* what you already *know*. Be guided by what you know, and instead of being a battleground for a mass of turbulent emotions struggling to unseat a calm-spirited Goddess of Reason, you will become that disciplined being you are now seeking—full of self-pride and sure knowledge, whose servants are the humble little emotions deflated to normal size.

My darling Sybil, I love you, I always have loved you, it can never be otherwise. I couldn't possibly give up the hope of some day creating beautiful dances with you. If, perforce, I have had to dream alone of music and your dancing and my writing and our schedule in the peace and union of love, I have at least become strengthened in my faith in the future.

In your letter, you say you want to be a help and you ask what I think of your coming to Cleveland. Dearest, you *are* help in that you actually write that you want to be. It is difficult for me to face the wisdom of my better judgment, but I don't think that Cleveland is quite prepared for your advent at this time. But I want to be with you, Sybil, planning and creating things in heavenly motion and I shall do all *I* can to make a reality of the wish. I know New York. I know what it can do to one. Frank Lloyd Wright is a true prophet in calling it "the Disappearing City." Sometimes I used to feel that it had the perspective of a mote in a madman's eye. Wright said that it has grown "Argus-eyed and enamored of 'whirl' as a dervish." You write that you go into the country and look at the hills, and I know that you and I know that true creation is not a machine-made product but of a spiritual conception.

I saw Eve last night. She adores you. She was so happy that you told her she had possibilities as a dancer. She said she saw you and your mother one night when you were wearing a cape and hood. It thrilled me to the core.

I'll tell you more about our dance group later on. I'm going to do Chanticleer by Edmond Rostand with my WPA group. The Gilpin Players are to produce *Fresh Out O Heaven* for six nights February 17–22. Tomorrow night Alice Marting and I are going to Marjorie Schneider's for an evening with John Martin—after his lecture.

I send you all my blessings and love—Jerry

Feb. 1, 1937

Dear Jerry,

Last week was one of the most emotionally eventful of my whole career. I was preparing for an audition of my dances at the New School. All my fears and worries were over, however, when I received your marvelous letter.

Last week seemed a month long and I have come out a new person with a new prospect of the future, a new understanding of life, a new appreciation of people and even a new room at the Club with a view of the Hudson and millions of lighted windows to the south and a wide streak of sun all day. Also I dreamed of warm waves washing me up on the shore, and that means new life. And when I dreamed that, I knew your letter would be as marvelous as it was.

But tonight I am so tired because of this long week of thinking and working on my dances which I auditioned last night that I can no longer comprehend all that we said and thought last week. I can only ask when will Cleveland be ready for me.

Sybil

But on our next short tour we danced in Columbus, Ohio, on a stage that was wide and shallow with no curtain and American flags at each end—some kind of town hall, somehow a bad omen. From there Eve and Jerry took me to Cleveland.

Then during and after my visit in Cleveland, when I showed Jerry my dances for the New School performance and met his group, I had the foreboding that I did not and would never belong there; that the idea of a future life with Jerry was fantasy; that no matter what the reality of my past incarnation might have been or my next one might be, this time around I was a soloist and that eventually I would realize this truth in a positive way.

I was not a Pisces for nothing—two beings swimming in opposite directions, the social being and the recluse.

I had, however, a huge urge to set myself and everyone else straight, to encourage them to create, to make them understand that creating was the most important thing in the world. I inspired Jerry because he too was aware of the importance of creativity.

But I felt that there was something else waiting for me. There still is. I had to move on. Sometimes I was floating above the scene, sometimes I was on the beach, but I was always saved by each new wave. Over the top it comes, and I can hear now the water rushing on to the pebbles.

High tide and low tide and high tide again. Someone said—but you are always happy—not always, but in the movement of the swinging back and forth, I have never been lonely.

Years later all this was in my dance *In the Shell Is the Sound of the Sea*, my most profound piece, and I only needed to do it once as a symbol of the all.

I was afraid of being lost in surface form. I needed, and still need, to find deeper form. I was told to keep fluid, so what I have always been searching for is form in movement. In a sense this is what all artists have been trying to achieve—the balance of creativity between the flight of improvisation and the ground of habit, both of which, in the extreme, are impediments to growth because they camouflage the reality.

Surface forms can be the "image" of the answer, but the real answer is not on the surface. Somehow I felt that I might be caught in the net of the ballet or of marriage, two forms I was not ready to face until I could make forms out of the movement that seemed to come to me as a gift from some being, or beings, I could not see. In the end, this was for me the real marriage.

I felt that the ballet was good only as a training ground for the physical body. And one must be careful not to let the door of this cage snap shut, because the world loves surface forms. They are recognizable signposts and I would be caught.

In between these signposts is the fluid search, the eternal receiving and giving back. It is feeling, seeing, and finding oneself within the totality of forces, the evolving eternity—something I have always found to be fulfillment.

17

Dearest Champie,

We are now on a tour with the Humphrey-Weidman Company which takes us out to California and back by way of Texas. We have been gone since February 1st and have been performing practically every night. But this is a real rest cure for me because for the last few months I have been doing double duty with the Humphrey-Weidman group, and the Theatre Dance Company. The latter gave its premier, including a ballet composed by me, on January 23rd, and on the same day in the evening the Humphrey-Weidmans also gave a premier of two new numbers; in fact all of January was a series of preparing for and giving first nights.

The Theatre Dance Company, as you gathered, is a group of younger artists who believe in bringing the dance and drama together in a theatrical form that is not only art, but appealing to a normally intelligent audience as well. Of course, each member of the company has his or her own idea as to how this is to be brought about. But I have just recently discovered this, for I was under the general impression that they all were working and believing along lines I felt to be important; that is, I thought I could win them over, but after much thought and discussion with people who were my good friends and artists at the same time, I feel finally that it is impossible to get a bunch of people who already consider themselves soloists of importance to accept the ideas of anyone else for practical purposes, although they may agree heartily with the idea. But all this probably means nothing to you, whereas really it is the beginning of a new and vital and terrific revelation to me.

It was through George Bockman and myself that the Theatre Dance Company came into existence and flourished with the help of a few staunch believers. And then we find that these people whom we have gathered do not and will never believe with us. So I am asking for a leave of absence from the H-W group from the end of the tour until Bennington, and then I shall work by myself without all this wrangling, and really find something. Up to now it has been a case of a minute here and a minute there for any accomplishment.

Two years ago I had the bright inspiration that real movement should be traced back to nature, that is natural human movement essentially, but natural movement from all sources such as animal, plant life, etc. In fact I worked out a whole theory and started to put it into practice in a suite of five dances which I performed at the New School for Social Research last April. It was a good start, and then this duty to the idea of the group took all my time, and my own ideas sat until I started screaming inside.

But I met a Russian, an artist, a cellist, who had been inspired by Isadora Duncan and who worked out during the process of his career a scientific system of natural movement, which I have been studying this fall two mornings a week from 9 to 10.

Also, during the fall and last winter too I worked with Louise Martin (wife of John) on dance choreography from the point of view of the technique of acting. We gave a very revealing demonstration at the New School this January and convinced many dancers who had pooh-poohed the idea all the time we were working on it. I am really quite proficient at sense memory now, and can drink imaginary tea from imaginary anything, as well as fall down a steep rocky cliff on a flat surface, etc. It is packs of fun, and I have learned a great deal. We try to work up genuine emotion from dramatic situations and then use those emotions to call up dance movement that will be convincing. That plus complete control of the body should be the solution to everything, but it takes time, not just over a long period, but concentrated time, and it is a thrilling procedure to look ahead, though I imagine all kinds of trouble will beset me in the form of frustrations and anxieties. I do have some idea of choreography though, and shall soon be able to use it.

I have met so many marvelous people in Bennington and New York that it would take a much longer book to tell about them than I have here. Though I wish you knew them all— Thomas Bouchard, the famous artist-photographer who specializes in dance photography has been an excellent friend to me, very encouraging and full of wisdom. Also, Dane Rudhyar, the superb composer and author of some marvelous essays on art as a release of power, as well as many articles and a book on astrology. He, I think, may compose with me if my ideas turn out to be bright ones. Also, Louise and John Martin who have helped me a great deal. John often comes to class to direct us. And Agnes de Mille of whom I am a great admirer has been very friendly, and has asked me to work with her, although there has not been any good opportunity for it as yet.

Also, one summer at Bennington I met a composer, Clair Leonard, from Vassar College, and he inspired me to great heights. The man I intended to marry, and about whom I wrote to you for advice two years ago (can it be that long?) has gone out of my life temporarily. We took your advice. He believed me to be the important one in the match, but because he was an artist too it was not practical, for he always had hope for his own talent and so did I, although it was a trying time for him, and he had no opportunity to prove anything to himself or to me. I didn't need proof, but he seemed to feel it imperative, so after the usual anguish I now consider the affair as belonging to the future, no matter how distant, perhaps several hundred years, who knows. In the meantime, love, admiration, devotion to an idea are so kaleidoscopic that a normal life (like the one I was brought up to be a part of) seems out of place, and certainly out of desire.

I have decided, however, out of all this and more too, that possessiveness is the "fruit of all evil," and I try to keep myself from being that, though it were probably better, and I hope it will be possible, to make my aim a positive rather than a negative one. That too is part of the new revolution. But it seems that no matter how marvelous the idea, the details—the people in other words—get in the way and upset things temporarily and too often.

As to the picture and my having grown up, I am not anything as glamorous as I look in the picture. In fact I am wearing all the same clothes that I had in college, including the hats and a few pairs of lisle hose. My mother has replenished my wardrobe from time to time by copious knitting, but I don't think you would find me much changed. I went through an intellectual critical period, but always with the feeling that I was being poisoned, and have finally arrived back, or perhaps ahead, at the idea that the fourth dimension can only be properly expressed by complete control and application of the first three for, to be more modest, an understanding experience of real life. (Now all I have to do is go out and experience it.)

As to Hanya, her concert was beautiful and as grand and promising as John Martin said in his article, though many people in the dance world think he stretched it a point. Strangely enough, it is Hanya whom I need now, and her understanding and knowledge of choreography. Of course, Doris and Charles have given me a great deal, but I have always missed Hanya, and shall make it part of my leave of absence to visit her and to get to know her. I have kept up with her from time to time and always go backstage but have been too busy to really visit.

I must say good-bye now, and if you have time to drop me

a letter on the trip I shall be delighted to hear, more than delighted to hear from you.

Feb. 15, 1938
Madison, Wisc.

Dear Bouchard,

The trip so far has rendered me more or less unconscious. I am not used to being with so many people so constantly, and find it difficult to think in a crowd. The chief topic of conversation is dance, of course, and the subject though always interesting begins to pall now for I desire not so much to tear down as to build up.

I am one globule in this nebulae called the H-W group, and float across the country. One day one of us shines more brightly than another. We don't even penetrate any further into each other, though at times one of us will disintegrate from lack of sleep and show broken edges, and another time one globule will close up and be silent for private reasons.

This tour, which is like a dream, keeps leading me over miles of territory. My main regret is that I do not really penetrate into the soil or the people, I just write at their desks and sleep in their beds and eat at their counters without knowing any of their thoughts or desires.

Until Chicago it was difficult to do anything really constructive because of the necessity of finding the easiest way to live and get a proper amount of food and sleep. But in Chicago Katie and I went to the Art Institute and saw some sculpture, and above all the drawings of three artists, all brothers, the Tiepolos. Have you heard of them? The drawings were marvelous, full of movement and had the flowing quality of Blake to a certain extent. Up to the time when I entered the room containing these drawings, I had been sitting on each bench as it presented itself along the way, for my body ached in every part and my head throbbed from the stuffiness of the place. But these pictures, so full of space and light and solidity and movement, were a transforming power, and I did the rounds again and again in a state of concealed excitement.

Also we went to see the Bahai Temple in Wilmette. Rudhyar mentioned it as a new form of architecture in his book *Art as Release of Power* (which by the way is out of print). It was very interesting indeed. We were led around by a believer in the faith of Bahai, an enthusiastic man. He told us many wise things. The temple is not yet finished but promises to be very beautiful and a little mysterious.

Then we also went to see the Chicago WPA Dance Theatre which is filled with excited young dancers who were refreshing after the New York wranglers. Grace Graff, wife of Curt Graff, showed herself to be a passionate, imaginative and beautiful dancer. I was very happy about it. Katie, knowing the Graffs from *As Thousands Cheer* days, we went out with them afterward along with Charles and Jose, the latter of whom showing always in his big-chested, strange manner that he was after all superior to these Chicagoans with their German influence, etc. Although he said nothing to convict himself, his manner was so patronizing that we were divided constantly between our affectionate admiration of the Graffs and our murderous sentiment toward the Indian. The electric sparks flew unseen but not unfelt in and out of the glasses on the table and around the low candles fading out in low conversation at one corner of the table and flashing back into action at the moment the Indian opened his mouth or wiggled his head.

And now we are on our way again and I would like to hear from you and know what you are doing somewhere along the way. Perhaps, Seattle 3–5 March, or San Francisco, Curran Theatre 8–13.

February 18, 1938
Sioux City, Iowa

Dear Mr. Martin,

The Humphrey-Weidman Group sends greetings from the Middle West. We are here for a couple of days rehearsing *New Dance* before showing it on the coast. The tour so far has been delightful, good houses and very good audiences, and even good reviews, and once we were treated to filet mignon all around after the performance!

But you will be tremendously interested in our contact with the famous Margaret D'Houbler, mother of the modern dance, and perhaps the only one who has retained in full her original concepts of what it should be. We met her at the reception after our concert in Madison, Wisconsin. Miss D'Houbler came over and entered into conversation with us. Her manner was so engaging and her enthusiasm so genuine that we recovered almost immediately from the surprise. Miss Humphrey and Mr. Weidman were surrounded by students, and Miss D'Houbler chose us. We asked questions and she answered rapidly, and we asked more about her views and her teaching, and in no time at all she was telling us about her system of rhythm and movement from life, etc., and we were writing things on paper. Before we knew it the reception was at an end, and we begged her to let us visit one of her classes, but that was impossible because there were none the next morning and our train left at 12:30. So we asked her if she would talk to us again and perhaps give us a class (that a little timidly), but she received the suggestion so gaily that we all jumped for joy and arranged to have a class from 9 to 10 the next morning, and a continuation of the talk from 10 to 11.

And we did. We were ushered into Miss D'Houbler's large studio at the university. It was lighted by a theatrical dimmer system so that it could be used for studio performances, and curtains hung all around the walls behind which at one point there were shelves upon shelves of percussion instruments and Victrola records and at another point many mirrors with adjustable barres in front for use whenever needed. It was like entering some unknown castle miles away from civilization and finding there all the things of which you had ever dreamed.

The lesson proved as interesting as we imagined it would. Miss D'Houbler started right at the beginning and explained everything simply, and then we improvised rhythmically the different kinds of movement. Before we knew it we were working out rhythms on paper and agreeing upon fundamentals. Her belief is (as I have always felt, too) that the modern dance should be so basically creative that there would be no room for clichés or classicism of movement. She was marvelous, young, gay, and enthusiastic to the point that she started a dozen things at once and tried to follow them all at the same time so as to leave nothing out. To find the real modern dance so far from its New York center seemed unbelievable. How *we* all need her!

February 28, 1938
Train between Salt
Lake City & Spokane

Dear Mr. Rudhyar,

I have been trying to read your article in February's *Astrology Magazine* amid cries of communism, modern dance and miscellaneous matters, but being completely unable to concentrate on astrological principles my mind turned to you, and I thought you might like to hear about some of my adventures. There is no time now to put all this violence into a form of power through the dance, but if I can recall it in the spring, great things may happen! I shall tell you only something about Salt Lake City.

It dawned gradually for we arrived at night, and the next morning we arose late and went immediately to rehearsal and into a matinee. The audience was warm but quiet, and we came out of the theatre feeling normally gay. Someone glanced to the right as we went into the late afternoon sun, and we all cried out in delight for the mountains were white with pink and blue ridges and shadows—a truly unbelievable sight.

Then after the evening performance we met the people—wonderful people—mostly Mormons. Virginia Tanner was responsible in the most unheard of manner for bringing the group to Salt Lake—she left college and worked day and night for a month trying to get people to sponsor us and finally got the high schools to put up $100 apiece and a donation. She wrote articles and did publicity and sold tickets and arranged receptions and sent us each a corsage after the performance.

She was a wonderful human being, enthusiastic, loving, and unselfish. When we arrived, she looked pale and tired and as she is naturally sallow and looks at people through the top of her eyes with her head bent forward, it was difficult to imagine at first that she had really done all that work by herself. As soon as we met her companions, however, her mother and sister and friends and pupils, I could see how this enthusiasm for life and the dance was aided constantly by their sympathy.

At the reception I met a young girl, Elsa Jordan, with a German accent and straight long, blond hair. She seemed out of place in all this homely Mormonism and yet completely at one with her surroundings. I was at once fascinated by her manner and appearance, perhaps because she reminded me of Hanya. I found out from her, for she talked quickly and with great spontaneity, that she had come from Hollywood in the fall. A girl came into her class there who was alive and robust and full of enthusiasm for the dance, and that girl was from Salt Lake. Elsa said, "If they're all like you, I too shall go to Salt Lake." And she did. She was inspired with the modern dance by Mary Wigman in 1933 and had been working ever since on preparing herself to be a concert dancer. I went to her studio where she has set herself up as a teacher and where she creates.

If you have ever been to Salt Lake you will know how the Mormons must have felt after traveling over the plains to enter into that valley surrounded by green hills and snow-covered mountains, and how Elsa felt when she arrived looking for a place to settle and create, and how I felt when the mist lifted out of the city and I saw the hills, the mountains, the canyons, the lake, the city, and felt the excitement of an artist like Elsa and a student like Virginia all vibrating together in sympathetic understanding. The Humphrey-Weidman group passed into the valley and would pass out having left an indelible impression on their minds.

Virginia's sister, Lydia, told me that the night Virginia met Elsa they stood at the corner of the street and talked of the dance for three hours, and the next day they met again, and the next evening they talked all night, and that they still had things to talk about. So I know our concert and the lessons Doris and Charles gave will be very stimulating, and they will talk more. But everyone seems to be interested in the dance there and interested in us.

So having been taken to the heights by these people and these surroundings and felt within me a new birth and an insight into my real intentions and capabilities, I look forward more than ever to my leave of absence in the spring, and forgive myself for my hatred of the kind of movement I have been forced to do, because I no longer hate it. I am free!

Dear Alice,

[Alice Marting, dancer and teacher in Cleveland.]

This letter must be primarily an apology. I can't think how it happened for I searched thoroughly several times, but in Los Angeles my jewel case popped up in just the place I remember putting it and remember searching for it.

The trip has been highly successful. We were received well everywhere, especially on the coast. Maxine Cushing did all the arranging in San Francisco, and we were invited to Tilly Losche's concert with the symphony orchestra and to Mills College for lunch where I saw Esther Williamson, the pianist composer. We saw Betty Ellfeldt at the University of California and she invited me over for breakfast the Sunday morning of the concert. She lives in a little house built by some Mexicans who were experimenting when they were drunk and added a new piece or gadget on every time they had a party. The house is on the highest hill in Berkeley and overlooks a constantly changing vista, and on clear days one can see the ocean too.

It was very changeful weather the day I went across the bay. I went alone, because no one else could face rising so early. It was much better alone, because I took the ferry and a sudden storm collected over the city while the bay and the hill on the other side were in sunlight. The storm followed us right across until the yellow smoke and yellow water with its white foam were bright against the battleship gray of the sky which blotted out the city completely, and yet the sun was still shining over the hills, and the sea gulls swerved about the boat. Finally the storm caught up with me as I waited at the Berkeley station, but during breakfast mists and sunlight played across the bay and the mountains until, when it was time to go, the whole harbor was green and clear again.

We received our best write-ups in history in San Francisco, five of them, and one was better than all the others. The program was *To the Dance*, *Happy Hypocrite*, and *New Dance*. We were almost a week there and, next to Salt Lake City, I enjoyed it the most. Los Angeles was a different matter. We gave our performances the first two days we were there, both concerts, and had the rest of the week off. Everyone wanted us to do things. We had tea with Carmelita Maracci. She explained why she had refused the Bennington fellowship. (She couldn't afford the trip.) She is very straightforward and outspoken and looks very much like Graham. Lester Horton invited us to his place to watch his group. And what marvelous studios all these people had, super colossal ones. If they could just see ours in New York! There were so many people and celebrities backstage in Los Angeles that I took it upon myself to pack costumes, so that I could stand and look at them all.

Well, Alice, let me know what you are doing and forgive me for suggesting the padlock, but I really thought my chain gone for good. Remember me to Eva, and Katie wishes to be remembered to you, too.

March 25, 1938
Houston, Tex.

Dear Bouchard,

The tour here has really been a huge success. We have had dandy receptions everywhere, especially in San Francisco where we received reviews that one might always wish for in a dream and never get. I'm sure Doris and Charles are terribly pleased. Los Angeles also was a success. We have had many little tiffs and disagreements on tour, about arrangements of programs mainly, and the general unconcern of the employers for their employees. But we have ended up with an unconcern ourselves, and despite the general triumph of the group everywhere and the general impression of everyone that we are one "great big happy family," we are all further away from Doris and Charles than ever.

I had a long talk with Doris on the train one day and asked her for a leave of absence, and we came really close in our old way again, but there is something so acid about the whole atmosphere that it is exceedingly difficult for me to remain moved by her. There seems to have come over me a psychological change in my attitude, for although I never believed her to be the greatest of all or the "ultimate ultimate," I was still able to accept what she had to offer and appreciate it and her, with a certain attitude of the admiring student. But now, having lost the latter, I find it difficult to accept anything. I recoil rather unnaturally from her every suggestion, just as the rest of the group seems to do. The situation is unnatural and bad; it ties me up in knots both emotionally and creatively. It seems that one must be on one side or the other, either with the group or with the artists. On this trip I have been with the group. They are warm, human, emotional but uncreative. I can see myself with the artists, creative but inhuman, and it is impossible to be on both sides at once, so the best way out is the leave of absence with an occasional artistic contact with Doris. I hope that will solve something. It is impossible to be alone on tour, for the group immediately resents it. What a strange thing society is! They sit and talk and discuss and argue and wrangle but do nothing, and as long as you are there with them they are also kind and considerate no matter how violent, but walk a few paces away, like Doris and Charles, and you walk away from humanity and are hated for it. What can you make out of that? It seems I am doomed to search for the middle path in everything I desire, a balance between the artist and the worker, that is a sympathetic, intelligent understanding for life. And in art I look for the middle between the dance and the drama the missing link of expression. However, I feel that although I look for balance it is really another search for another extreme.

I have met some very fine people on tour, Bouchard, people whom I love tremendously, people who are enthusiastic and artistic and who take great joy in finding us a noisy and a real group of people. They are always surprised to find us "human." One person in particular who has discovered us is the young man who sells our booklets. He is a toughie from Chicago and has been hanging around gambling joints and gangsters since high school days. He is thin and dissipated looking with big eyes and heavy lids and thick lashes, and his teeth are imperfect. The first week out he was a little surprised that we accepted him with the gang, for he thought we must be highbrow to be going around to colleges putting on that stuff. It was beneath his dignity to watch the program. But he became more and more impressed with us as people and soon began to give in a little on watching. Then he noticed how inadequate Pauline was with the baggage and offered to handle it himself. He started to offer to do favors. In fact, it was a thrill to see him so genuinely excited about us, in sort of a schoolboy way. He likes us as a bunch so much that he has nicknames for most and knows all our idiosyncrasies and wouldn't change any of them. He always goes to receptions with us, just to be around, although he hates them and had never met college professors before in his life. Even he, however, who makes no distinctions between us and who always tries to patch up our differences in the most jovial way, does make a distinction when it comes to the "big four and the little fifth" (Katie Manning) as he calls them. He is very sensitive to the reactions of people and feels definitely that they are concerned with no one but themselves and it hurts him. One day Jose went off in a car and left him to carry his heavy bag alone across campus, and it made him so ill at heart that he couldn't bear the thought of the University of Washington (it happened there) for days afterwards. No one of us would have left him and he knew it.

The scenery, however, has been my greatest joy. The West

is glorious. There are so many places I would like to settle down in for a while.

March 27, 1938
Fort Worth, Tex.

Dear Bouchard,

What do you think? I have a leave of absence from the group until Bennington. I shall work very hard and try to accomplish a great deal during that time. I have so many things to do that I hardly know where to begin. I have decided to get things in order now, so that I can start in immediately upon my return. The grasp of the group, which was so firm on me socially all during the tour with the exception of the first few days, is loosening now and I find I am taking pleasure in being my own master. It will really be marvelous to be living alone again, though I have enjoyed the companionship of the girls and boys these two months.

I have one dance that I shall work on, but especially I shall also work on technique of my own body and the notation system I told you about.

Salt Lake City thrilled me *most* I think, as it was the first and so unexpected. For some reason I had thought of it always as a barren, salty plain. But the white and blue mountains that encircle the city are superb with their green rolling foothills, and then there are seven canyons that one can explore, each different.

And so Bouchard, I shall be home soon, and I have thought much of my future and think I have decided pretty well the path I wish to take. I hope you have been well and happy all this time.

Affectionately,
Sybil

Dear Louise,

Forgive my neglect. And I have neglected everything. I haven't done anything you suggested except take it easy and really haven't done that if you consider the emotional tangents I have gone through because of Doris, etc. But still the trip has been delightful. I have met marvelous people and seen the most miraculous country and am happy about most things except that I have accomplished nothing.

But the great news is that I have a leave of absence from the group until Bennington! But I shall also, of course, have to have a vacation from the Theatre Dance Company, and that won't go over so well. However, I have made up my mind to be a hermitess in art and shall do it even if I'm disowned. In fact it is the only thing to do unless I wish to crack up completely.

I love you and shall do my best.
Sybil

Give my love to John, too, and tell him I haven't read the *NYT* since I left NY two centuries ago.

18

May 25, 1938
Three Arts Club

Dear Miss Humphrey,

In case Edith considers going to Bennington, I want to ask you again that you allow me to take my leave for the summer. You must know that it is a sacrifice for me in several ways not to go, but I consider the amount I can accomplish by not going worth it and hope so much that you will, too.

The question of technique I don't think I made quite clear. It is not that I might accomplish spectacular feats that I wish to work twice a day, but rather that I might gain control over my whole body to the point of being capable of any quality of movement which I would wish to use in the expression of an idea. It is control of these qualities of styles or emotional nuances that I think is lacking in most techniques, and it will take a long period of concentrated effort to accomplish this knowledge of my own body. Besides, as I said, I wish to study music and painting and sculpture as well as read philosophy and to correlate all the knowledge and feelings I have already on these subjects.

I realize quite well your position, but I really feel that your composition will be able to stand alone as something good, and that my absence will not mean nearly as much to you as it will to me.

Most sincerely,
Sybil

May 27, 1938
Three Arts Club

Dear Miss Humphrey,

I must not go to Bennington; surely you know that. Here, it is right in front of me or inside me or around me, and I can't ignore it. You are an artist and know that when it is here, you can't ignore it and let it diffuse into the people around, standing first on one foot and then on the other, all of them waiting. I must not wait. And as you march through these people who are all standing around waiting, please don't listen to what they are saying about me. Be glad that I'm marching behind.

Sybil

May 31, 1938
Three Arts Club

Dear Clair,

No need to tell you how I felt on Sunday. I only regret not having been alone with you more, as I have so many things to tell you about a marvelous person I am studying with.

But nevertheless it was amazing that we should have changed so little during these two years. The effect of your music on me is something indescribable, and it is about that I wish to speak to you, especially. Clair, you must compose more! You mustn't let people or desire for security take the time, the love, or the energy you would put into your composing, even if you are not satisfied with your creations when you hear them played. That is nothing but a good sign, Clair; if you are disappointed you will have to search for a better way of expressing what you wish to say. I don't think for a minute that you should give up your position at Vassar and the security it gives you. But, Clair, why do you work in the summer, too?

My love to you,
Sybil

June 5, 1938

Dear Miss Humphrey,

Your letter arrived and I have been thinking. The first violence of my state has passed, and I realize that I have taken advantage of your decision both by persistence and by my past behavior. And I desire more than anything else to be fair to you and to show you that I can cooperate with you, because this is a personal matter between us. I would feel very badly about not going to Bennington when you need me. To explain the last remark, I must tell you that my unpleasant behavior has usually been on account of the group or on account of other members of the group and seldom on account of myself. But from now on nothing can stir me, for I must be completely objective. There is nothing more useless or unpleasant than defending one's ideas in a negative way, aside from it being emotionally wearing to the point of exhaustion. I am through with it and would be glad for this experience to find it out, if I did not know that it had caused you anxiety and troubled thoughts.

Please accept me back on the terms as before, and let us hope that when we do part, it will be a fair as well as friendly parting.

Most sincerely,
Sybil

Dear Clair,

The potentialities in your improvisations are very exciting, and I can't help thinking how superb they would be completed. I have a feeling inside me that together we can someday create masterpieces. Seriously, are you interested in working with me? I don't know when I shall be ready, as again I have to delay my plans and go to Bennington. Possibly next summer I shall be ready, after a winter of concentration. Would you be willing to work with me then, I mean, give up the summer and really concentrate? Of course, it is looking ahead rather far, but if we continue to be a stimulation to each other, and I see no reason why it should not last forever, I know we can make real moving art for the world.

That joy so nearly akin to terror which you mentioned at Bennington, I have felt. It can do much to make our compositions emotionally complete, a trait very seldom found in musical and dance compositions today. Probably Isadora was the last to be really in sympathy with her music. Clair, it will be tremendous! I wish I could see you again soon, this month. Could you come down for the day, any day? Then we can really talk uninterrupted. I have so many things to tell you about discoveries I've made, and by the way how do you like Rudhyar?

My love to you,
Sybil

July 24, 1938
Bennington

Dear Bouchard,

Nothing exciting has happened! It is utterly dead, utterly sane! I tried to fall in love, perhaps I did, but everything is at a standstill now. There was one moment of excitement, however, when Barbara Morgan, the photographer, came up to see the lay of the land, and she has been engaged for the festival. However, when I spoke to Mary Jo about her and you, she said they weren't paying her a cent and that everyone not only liked her personally but also admired her technical skill and exactitude. She said, of course, she liked you very much, too, and admired your artistry, but that they hoped to get pictures suitable for publication from the festival this year by Miss Morgan. Frankly, Miss Morgan's group pictures are terrible, but as they were taken during a performance, there is some room for hope for the future. Mary Jo admitted that yours were better, but a variety of reasons have Morgan on top. Her portraits of Graham are quite startling and almost slick, but they do not have the nuances of shading of yours. Well, I was sort of wishing that I was important enough to announce that no one could photograph me but the great Bouchard, but still belonging to the future and my nerves never being too steady, I did my best to toss it off.

About the same time, to make things worse, Doris asked who of the group would like to step out and see the fugue in the new composition. I said, "I do" first, so I did. Oh, Bouchard, there must be something wrong with me, but I was so surprised and disappointed. I don't know exactly what I expected, but what I saw was a two-dimensional flat pattern of moving sticks in the form of arms and legs and torsos. They jerked and snapped in straight lines and "angles," and I was simply amazed at how little real heroism there was in the movement. Of course, that doesn't allow for smoothing off, of costumes, etc., nor for the rest of the dance, but nevertheless I was really ill after that experience. I must add that many others have seen it and were very thrilled so, as I say, there must be something wrong with me.

I have done some work since I have been here, but a good deal of the time I am aching physically and spiritually. However, that will pass. I have heard from both Rudhyar and

Louise Martin, and they were so encouraging. I know there is much to unearth and shall do it soon. I wish you were coming up. There have been several discussions at meals about the relative value of Bouchard and Morgan, and I found a kindred spirit in Mary Starks who said she had pictures taken by you this last year. She has also read much of Rudhyar and I am lending her what pamphlets I have of his. She is an exciting person and stands out in the technique classes which I watch from time to time. She says she will show me some of her dances before we leave.

Good luck to you, my good friend, and if you have time drop me a few words.

Most sincerely,
Sybil

July 24, 1938
Bennington

Dear Philip,
[A set designer at Bennington.]

You must forgive my seeming coldness, my avoiding manner when you mentioned your heart to me. I was suddenly struck with a real terror as the orbit of your psyche passed into mine, terror that I might have to face another change in my life now, when my artistic life is so completely upset, the change of being in love and of having someone really care for me as a person.

I believe all I said to you about work. I have always worked up to now, regardless of whether I was in love or not. If it were true that I were as objective as I talk, I would not have tried to know you better, for I knew you quite well the first minute I spoke to you. That would have been enough had I not also known that I could love you. But Philip, there is no reason to concern ourselves with being in love or not being in love as I did. The important thing is, rather, that we do love each other, and that is beautiful and should never be lost. Indeed, I don't believe it is possible to create without love, and that is one reason why I consider leaving Doris and Charles. As you say, life is tremendously complicated, but the only real complications, I think, are caused by fear and uncertainty, and those are only temporal things.

Sybil

August 17, 1938
Newark, NY

Dear Mr. Nadon,

Thank you for your letter and for extending to me an invitation to join the faculty of the Academy of Allied Arts. At some future date I would welcome such a suggestion, but right now I have just obtained a six-month leave of absence from both the Humphrey-Weidman group and the Theatre Dance Company, and I intend to study and experiment by myself. Consequently, I will not have time to plan or teach classes. Of course, I know you need someone right away to fill this vacancy, so I am sending on your letter to Leon A. Arkus, our manager, and he will get in touch with you as to the possibility of the Theatre Dance Company cooperating with the Academy.

I hope this all works out favorably.

Most sincerely,
Sybil Shearer

Dear Sybil,

How are you and what of the grand Bennington season? The campus must be teeming with limbs and tongues! Here the mountains are wondrously immovable and the desert so silent. And I am working as much as my as yet none too good health permits. I shall be here through August, but will presumably leave early in September for California. It looks now as if I might not be much in New York next season. I may lecture through the Southwest and South to extend my field and "public." This, anyway, is the prospect but reality may be very different! Do give my best to Doris and everybody. Keep strong and let the creative spirit possess you and free you through great dances!

Your friend,
Rudhyar

This statement, "my none too good health" reminds me that Rudhyar was always ailing, or seemed to be. I attributed this to the time he spent in India where I imagined all sorts of dark diseases lurked along with great wisdom.

I remember so well the time we sat in a New York restaurant having lunch, when he said to me, "You have a strong body. I have a strong mind," and suddenly a strong mind seemed definitely preferable!

Then several years ago I picked up a book of written portraits of interesting people, which the author said he was inspired to write because of the character of Dane Rudhyar. I was astonished to discover that he was past 90 when he died. Perhaps, it was mind over matter!

August 17, 1938
Newark, NY

Dear Mr. Rudhyar,

Thank you for your card. I was so very glad to receive it. So many things have happened to me, so many undulations in my mental, spiritual, and even physical well-being that I seem to have been bouncing up and down in mid-ocean for the past few months, just trying to anchor my inner being to something. I wanted to write to you, but could not offer you any real tangible hope that I would be possessed by the creative spirit, or that I would ever be freed through great dances. Then again for the nth time this summer, I decided that it is not possible for any creative spirit of any real worth to possess me, until I am prepared not only by complete knowledge of the capacity of my body and its physical possibilities, but also and especially by a control over myself, my spirit or whatever. This last seems more urgently important to me, because for quite a while I have not been able to control my physical actions, simply because my spirit seemed to be lost somewhere. I have known for so long that I must go within myself, must learn to meditate and to concentrate, without any result. Now at last, however, things have gotten to a state where it is do or die, and I can honestly feel a new thing happening to me.

Doris has given me a six-month leave of absence from the group and so has the Theatre Dance Company, so I am alone to think and work. They all think I can do great things, and the Martins wrote giving me encouragement and hope, and yet I can't help feeling that if all this encouragement and goodwill can exist when I am in a negative state of mind, what great things can happen when I have finally come onto the positive and truly creative state.

As to Bennington, it was most uneventful. Everyone was on his best behavior. Nothing was particularly glamorous or exciting. There were no real free-for-alls until the concerts.

But when Graham dared to do a love duet with her new partner, who was not up to her at the first performance, they shocked or embarrassed most of the audience. The boy pulled himself together for the 2nd performance, however, and the dance became superbly beautiful, I thought.

I did not work with Charles, fortunately, but understand from many sources that his was the only real temperament of the season. He made more people cry and get angry and swear that they would never work with him again than has ever gone down before in the annals of the modern dance, but strangely enough his was the most all-around successful performance of the whole festival according to the critics. I felt his work was very successful, too, for it mirrored him completely and was more finished than most of his works. But after Graham's performance, when I went backstage to see her, I was actually surprised to see Charles, and it took a bit of remembering back to realize that he too had been on the same program.

I met some really grand people this summer, and one of them, Mary Starks from Boston, has read your *Astrology of Personality*. I lent her the pamphlets, and we had several long talks. I noticed her the first week in the general course technique and admired her exciting work, leaping and jumping. I was rather surprised at myself for making her acquaintance for she seemed so completely extroverted that I was a bit afraid of her. I soon found out, however, that it was not because of any conceit that Mary was so bold, but because she is whole and real.

I do hope you will be in New York this fall. Please, even if you are there for only a short time, let me know. I shall be at the Three Arts Club on 85th St. as usual. I hope the time in Santa Fe has made you well.

August 17, 1938
Newark

Dear Martins,

I was so surprised and disappointed to find that you had suddenly left Bennington. I rather hoped to have a week with you or at least more time.

Our demonstration turned out to be a good show, and was enthusiastically received by all. The connecting forms quite stunned everyone, and I personally felt quite light and gay about them. The other two groups the following evening were characteristically good. Martha was so magnetic that even I, who have been a bit skeptical of late, was convinced that her power is a conscious force which she uses to enhance her art.

The audience was sitting waiting, chattering, laughing, moving around when Graham appeared in the door, stepping over people who were seated at the entrance. She had just run up the steps and was a bit breathless, but she wasn't coming in to start the demonstration. She was just coming in. The amazing thing that happened, however, was that the moment she appeared there was dead silence. After a few moments of picking her way through the crowd in silence she looked up as if surprised at the quietness and the number of people and said, "Oh, shall we begin?" and she began to speak. For a while, I did not hear what she said for I was wondering at her tremendous power over everyone, despite her slight embarrassment and her hesitancy over finding her proper words. Then, later on, after much talk about movement, she said just what I had been asking her about in my mind, so that when it came it was as though she were conscious of her power to answer my question, and was willing to impart the knowledge of it to whoever might be listening at the moment. I wonder now how many, other than myself, heard her when she said, "You don't go out to your dear public. You make of yourself a magnet and draw your public to you."

Then, unfortunately, some of her glory was dimmed as she brought out her acrobats who, no matter how wonderful some of them may be, are after all just girls.

Then Hanya came and her truly right conception of choreography, but I was so worn out by the preceding experience that I was unable to really appreciate the dramatic movement and the use of space that would have been so convincing had it come first.

But I want to thank John, especially, for the leave of absence idea. I am terribly glad that it has been settled so satisfactorily to all, especially to Doris who has been a truly good friend to me despite our differences. Of course, I had been told before just what you told me, by my parents and others, but that moment was just the right one to hear it, and you were the right person to tell me, I guess. In any case, I am convinced that things will really happen this time. I am possessed of many secrets, as I told you before, and I just have to make them blossom.

Much love to you both,
Sybil

Later I wrote my thoughts about John Martin after his death in an article for *Ballet Review*, printed Spring 1988. (See Addendum IV.)

19

Dear Agnes,

I was so happy to receive your letter, although it has caused me a bit of heavy calculating and thinking. Of course I wish to work with you. I always have, and as for taking the course at the YMHA, it is so generous of you and I thank you very very much.

The difficulty this time is not of distance. I shall be in New York, but strangely enough, of principle, because of time. For ages now (about a year and a half) I have been wanting to get off by myself and find out about myself and the dance, and I have been kept so busy flying about on subways and trains to keep appointments to lend myself out to other people that finally my mind almost stopped functioning because of lack of use, while my brain went around in circles. So after a great struggle and several attempts to get a leave of absence from all my duties both with the Humphrey-Weidman group and the Theatre Dance Company, as well as teaching, I have pooled all my resources and energies into a six-month period of hermitism and study. There is so little I know, and what I do know is not even organized, so it is for this that I am spending time by myself. I am composing too, of course, although I must find out about things before I even feel free to compose. The first question then is: how much time rehearsals for the concerts will take, as right now I am kept very busy just working by myself. However, I should be pretty well organized by December. But the other question in which more than my own likes are involved is whether or not Doris and the Theatre Dance Co will feel highly indignant at my plea for free time, only to attach myself to some new group venture! And if I am not able to be in your concerts I don't feel that it would be fair to accept your invitation to study. So you see what a strange predicament I am in. If we could only be conscious of at least one more dimension, then things could go on dozens at a time, and allegiances could be all the same allegiance and loves could be all the same love.

Thank you again for wanting me, and do let me know when you will be here so that we can at least talk. I am so glad your concerts were such a success and I am anxious to hear about them.

Most affectionately,
Sybil

Then I gave a lecture-demonstration in Virginia.

October 18, 1938
Three Arts Club

Dearest John Martin,

I am sending you my first review and the publicity which led up to it. George Harris is a music critic but is interested in the dance and has done composing for it. However, I was quite surprised when he told me after the performance that he liked my dancing without music so much that he felt now that music was not at all necessary, and that the dance was forceful enough without it. I was not conscious myself of any lack because of the absence of music. It seemed as though I was speaking directly to my audience, though I don't believe I would ever have thought that the music would not add a great deal if the proper kind in each case had been available.

One woman who had done a great deal of work in the theatre bemoaned the fact that my art would never allow me to speak and that was a pity, because she thought my voice pleasing. So I hastened to encourage her by our Theatre Dance vision.

But although the whole affair was most satisfactory as far as review, audience, and general compliments all around were concerned, I am quite aware that I am no better now than before I heard the good news. I know my technique is inadequate, that my ability to snap into a mood is still lagging, and most of all that although I have composed all my own studies, still they are only studies and not dances, and that my greatest concern is to make dances which will be as intelligible to my audience as my studies. The one thing I have learned and have in fairly good functioning order is my ability to love my audience, to want to give them the best I have at the moment. Without that, of course, there would be no reason to go on at all, and because of that I feel that I have a firm foundation on the bottom rung of the ladder, but I see the steps towering above in a blaze of light and love!

But now about you—Louise told me that she would be away for a month and that you would be alone and might perhaps get the urge to ask me to accompany you to one of the concerts. If you do, I shall be terribly, terribly pleased, but if for any reason you don't, but feel like seeing me at any other time, I shall be most pleased at that also. Perhaps you would like to go to the zoo? I haven't seen the panda yet.

Most affectionately,
Sybil

[See Addendum V, the George Harris review from the *Richmond Times-Dispatch*.]

Dear Bouchard,

This letter is a necessity, I feel, since I don't quite see how I could explain in conversation what I wish to say without this preparation. I am disturbed that you should think that I came back to you after so long because I felt the need of physical relaxation. Nothing could be further from the truth, for in the last two months I have felt less like lovemaking than ever before in my life, and when I did or did not feel the urge to see you, it was purely on the basis of telling you of my progress in my search for self-discipline or, to put it more mildly, self-knowledge.

And surely you could see today that I have found something when I said that I am in love with the world! Something that you could use, too, for you said you were depressed. Believe me when I say that I do not believe in abstinence for the sake of abstinence but merely as a preparation for a greater love. If in the past, as you said, I have always had some excuse or other, it was because I intuitively felt that there must be some meaning back of physical love which I would have to understand before really giving myself to it no matter how pleasant it might be in itself. I know now what the meaning is, Bouchard, and I am more than ever convinced because of it, that true love making can only be a result of divine understanding, each for each. So that the man who loves me and whom I love must share my vision of the inner light and feel it so strongly within him that forever after he will make the effort to banish despondence and hate and failure from his presence. Then natural desires will give way to divine desires. Of course, I speak in ideal terms, but because we are artists, I feel that we must live as closely to the ideal as possible. The terms natural and divine or spiritual are very well explained in Blake's *Jerusalem*. From my reading both contemporary and past and from meditation, I feel most strongly that the physical life is a manifestation of the inner light. And if many people seem frustrated or selfish, it is because they have not discovered themselves and therefore the meaning of their lives. They think it enough to have the physical necessities and when they have them, they are still not satisfied. And so many people are lonely, but there is no need for it, for once they have found themselves they have also found the world and nevermore will be alone.

This is, I feel, the only true salvation for the world, for every act takes on new meaning—now that the vision is beginning to become a reality to me—to conquer the world with love and forgiveness. It is the only salvation and a beautiful one, my dear friend Bouchard.

Sybil

November 30, 1938
Three Arts Club

Dear Doris,

I was so sorry to have to say what I did yesterday. I had hoped to say it to you in private, but it was really probably better for everyone to be there. I only wish everyone had been, Bea and Joan, I mean. I am sorry Jose was angry, though heaven knows he had a right to be. I just hope he doesn't think I was trying to be mean, for you know I wasn't. I said only what I really felt, and if I felt violently, it was because I was making a comparison between what I know the concert ought to and could be, and what it was.

All my talk about cooperation last month and especially what I said—if you don't have cooperation as people how can you expect to have cooperation as dancers—was so appallingly true that I was shocked at myself for having hit the nail so squarely on the head.

Consequently, when you ask me how I liked the dances, I

can truthfully say that I hardly saw them. I believe they are good dances. But without human vitality and warmth, they are nothing but pure, geometric, slightly inaccurate, design. The myth that *New Dance* can stand by itself no matter how bad the performance is a myth indeed. The dance was based on human relationships and is only good when the movements are done with conviction. And conviction is the keynote to the whole thing. We can't all have as good technique as Harriet, but we can dance with conviction; then our uneven abilities will not be so apparent and the shabbiness of the boxes and the costumes won't hit the audience in the face. We have a great deal of work to do to perfect the performance, but before we even begin to make improvements, we must be able to dance with conviction.

My idea of conviction is this. You *have* to love what you are doing, and I don't just mean you have to love to dance. No, it goes deeper than that. You have to love every move you make. If it is a sad movement or a happy one or an angry one it doesn't matter, you as a performer have to love it so much that you feel it in every part of your body. In that case you won't have to put your face into a pattern or a mask, it will just natively and sympathetically react to the feeling in the body. So many of the girls put on what they thought was a pretty or a becoming face and kept it there throughout the performance without regard for the rest of their body. That is just as bad as holding one arm straight up in the air throughout a whole dance for no apparent reason. Of course comedy results, but unintentional comedy is nothing but annoyance of a most trying sort.

But as you see, I can speak and feel with conviction. From now on, however, I hope to dance with conviction and have promised myself and the world that I shall do everything to further that end.

Most affectionately,
Sybil

Doris's brief reply to this letter was:

Dear Sybil,

Thank you for your letter—much of it seems true to me, although fortunately we have had letters and words from a great many who found the program, especially the *Passacaglia*, thrilling and inspiring.

Affectionately,
Doris

Christmas, 1938

Dear Bouchard,

How glorious it is here! We have everything. We live in a village yet are in the country. From my window I can see miles of winter farmlands covered with grey woodland patches and gold stubble coming up through the snow. There are red barns in the distance, and during the day the woods on the horizon are a deep blue. At sunset they become a dull red as though suddenly blood has begun to flow through the branches bringing them to life for a moment before dark. And when dark comes, it is still mysteriously light because of the snow and the stars, only the trees are black. I am now waiting for the moon. My ears and feet burn with the warmth of the house, for I have just come from a long walk in the winter air. I can see the village lights and the dark hills beyond, and I feel very temporary as though I never could settle down, never take for granted my neighbors and the landscape. I feel the constant possibility for change in every direction, and my whole body begins to throb with nostalgia. Yet I would not have constancy, there is no life in it. At this moment I think I understand universality. I know that I am not just I, and my neighbor my neighbor, but that I am he, and not only he, but everyone and everything; that I could not be more completely the earth if I were buried and distributed in it, for I have been that and will be again, and if I have been and will be then I am now as well. I know that all potentiality is in me and that I am the universe. And yet knowing and even feeling all this, my individuality still separates me from life, as it does for so many, especially those warring ones.

Going one step further, however, I feel that if one could reach absolute individuality, one would find universality miraculously and simultaneously. Is that not why Socrates said "know thyself," why the yogis say the individual is the microcosm and the universe the macrocosm and both really identical, so that you must look within to know the mystery, the enigma of life? Is that not why Christ said, "The kingdom of God is within you."?

We live on the surface of our lives, Bouchard, consequently there is terrible confusion everywhere. I want so much to dance the depths, but my time of apprenticeship is not yet up—the moon is out! The light in my window is staggeringly beautiful! And the country! How I wish *I* were the country covered with snow and trees and golden stubble! I would create a new dance in each millennium. Yes, the earth dances, too, a wild dance, but to us temporary fly-by-nights it seems impossibly slow. Oh! the great thunder and the noise when the Rocky Mountains shifted over to one side and shot up out of the Colorado plains. And the creaking and the squeaking of the lumbering glacier as it made ridges in the rocks and deposited tons of earth in wavy drumlins which now breathe fertility even in winter. Yet even the earth and the millenniums are microscopic in the universe.

Are you listening, Bouchard?

Sybil

20

Dear Champie,

I, as you know, intended to have a six-month leave of absence.
Well, I started off and then along about the last of November
the Theatre Dance Company decided it couldn't do without
me in its January concerts, so I just had to step back in. I am
glad I did, however, for it was quite an experience. George
Bockman was doing a new ballet, and he wanted me to do the
lead, which consisted of the part of a child who, during the
piece grows up, falls in love, marries and then just on the eve
of married life, her husband goes off to war amid much hero
worship. It was the first time I ever played a heroine, and the
part took quite a bit of acting, which I have not had a real
chance to do for a long time. I loved doing it and plus that it
was quite a success. On the same program, I was in three
other dances, one of them a solo which I created after the 16th-
century painter, Pieter Breughel. It was called the *Battle of
Carnival and Lent*, and was also interesting to do.

But the crowning joy of this last too short period has been
my work with Agnes de Mille, of whom I have been an ardent and constant admirer for the past four years. Well, for
the first time I had an opportunity to work with her when she
arrived from England in the fall to spend the winter in New
York. She is a born actress and a born dancer and an inspired
person in every way, both professionally and in real life. For

the first time since I left college I felt inspiration in my director, and have in consequence blossomed under her guidance. I was in four numbers in her concert, leading one of the group dances and doing a duet work with Agnes on the satiric theme of the New York hunger dancers. The whole first part of it was pantomime and only burst out into dancing near the end. The audience simply roared through the funny parts. [We wore black leotards and long black skirts, and I had a red girdle which probably had something to do with communism.] Agnes had the mad idea of having me conceal a bun filled with tomato, lettuce and mayonnaise in my girdle. I was supposed to be absolutely worn out from crawling around on my knees as all modern dancers do in rehearsal, and tried to eat my bun without being seen, but was of course caught in the act, etc. I wish you could have seen it. We played very well together as we are absolutely sympathetic. We are to repeat the concert again in February, before I go on tour with the Humphrey-Weidmans.

It is amazing to think that this is the first time Agnes has ever worked with a group in this country and that every one of us noticed immediately the difference in her direction as compared to all other groups we had ever been in. We were gathered from many sources and none of us knew any of the others. Some are ballet and some modern, but she was able in these six weeks or so to mold us into a harmonious whole both physically as dancers and spiritually as people. She is so generous and thoughtful and so honestly cares about what we think and do that it seems like the answer to my prayer.

One thing, however, that has moved me very much is that Doris was so impressed by Agnes and her marvelous magnetic performance that she wrote her a letter. It is most miraculous, because the last time they ever had anything to do with one another was a violent argument and a complete break over money some seven or eight years ago. It looks then as though Agnes were an angel of light, for she is able to make fun of the "hunger dancers" so prettily that they all love her for it. She is able to melt the icy heart of Doris Humphrey, and she is able to bring about my dream of a truly cooperative group (cooperative in spirit, at least), and that is the hardest but the most rewarding kind of cooperation. Dear Agnes, how I love her!

February 23, 1939

Here I am on tour now, fairly near you compared to where I have been—New York. We are on our way to Asheville, North Carolina and will go from there to Montevallo, Alabama.

Your letter of last year was very interesting and understanding of the situation in the dance field, and I wanted to write and tell you before, but time passed and I just tried to do something about the situation, which on the surface gets worse every year. Very unexpectedly, though, I feel sure it was a matter of fate, I unearthed someone [Yuri Bilstin] who will most surely be the savior of the situation, and through him I have been able to rip the top off of the tent that all these people are hiding and cavorting in. Most of them haven't seen me looking in yet, but it has all become clear to me what is wrong and what has to be done. The latter, however, is not easy, and the thing I have really found out in these six months past is that it can't be done in a leave of absence. It is a life work.

This man with whom I have been studying is a scientific genius besides being a cellist of incomparable technique and feeling, as well as a composer, a collector of antiques and a Russian to boot. I can't help feeling that one of the reasons why I was always so fascinated by Russians and always wondered if I would ever meet a real one was the fact that he was in my life so strongly.

I definitely feel new life surging up in me at this time, and I am sure that out of this, perhaps I should say of these new contacts, great things will come. Do write to me when you get a chance. I hope I shall see you soon.

Most affectionately,
Sybil

February 23, 1939
Asheville, N.C., on a train

Dear Agnes,

We have been out of New York a week and it seems like six, at least, for we have been so many places. For a while it was unbearable. However, I seem to have been able to take the first step toward clarity, and have given two performances which were really thrilling. I was absolutely lifted out of myself. Our audiences love it, or say they do. The critics give us good reviews. One this morning, however, said that it was an intellectual art with not much real warmth, but that the audience liked it nonetheless for all that. We are warmer than we were last year though. Charles has ceased to be petty. Doris acts very warm on most occasions, and although it is a little forced sometimes, still we are moved by her efforts. Last night, she had two corsages and offered the other one to the group, whereas last year, roses used to die by the dozens, and orchids, too, and she would never offer a single bud *to any of us.*

I almost knocked myself out again the other day breathing deeply, but just caught it in time. However, the process of breathing is having more power all the time, and I lay my control of my inspiration and decisions to that and meditation. It is marvelous to think that just the tremendous desire you have within you and any real effort you make to accomplish it will at once dissolve all the difficulties around. Of course, if you don't keep up the good work brambles grow in again. I do think, though, that the time has come when I will be strong enough to keep up the effort.

Let me quote to you a paragraph out of Rudhyar's book, which is constantly enlightening me. Probably you won't get the full significance of it without reading what comes before. Nevertheless, it is wonderful just as it stands.

> The positive conception of time sees time as the eternal birthing of wholes which do not necessarily die as such, but may keep combining with each other, forming in the process, even greater wholes through *participation in consciousness*. The individual may become an organic part of a greater whole, and thus achieve immortality within that whole as functional agent of the wholeness of the greater whole. This kind of immortality differs in meaning from strictly personal immortality, because it is not based on the overcoming of time, but on identification with the creative power of every moment. [*Art As Release Of Power* by Dane Rudhyar.]

Did you see Hanya's concert? And did you like it? Doris had the write up, and it was a fine one, indeed. Martin thinks she is on the right track, and so do I. Her dramatic movement is absolutely real, though sometimes it is very subtle, almost too subtle for one swallowing. She is an analytical composer, and fortunately has at her back the Wigman training in composition, which builds and grows on a theme. She is not a dancer, however, and neither are most of her girls, though they do move beautifully. I wish I could have seen the concert, for *Trend* last year was one of the most moving experiences I have ever had choreographically. Hanya is able to get drama into pure movement. I wonder just how far that can go, and wish I could have seen her new work just to see how far she has gone in the right direction.

I dream of you often, and keep thinking in the dreams that I have come back for the weekend, and am talking to you. I wish I knew what you are doing and planning. So you must write when you get this. It seems so strange for me to be sitting here looking over the city of Asheville in the mountain mist. There are no mountains, however, they are hidden. The four-sided roofs seem to be hewn out of the side of the hills, and the red earth with the trees seem to grow out of the houses, for the landscape is a solid mass with the rain filling in the space.

Several days ago it was warm and spring-like and the magnolia blossoms and the crocuses were out, and we went without coats. We were able to walk from our rooms to the theatre along a country street with green lawns. Last weekend we were entertained and dined and invited to hear Lotte Lehmann by Sweet Briar College. Everywhere the girls come out, greet us with open arms, give us their beds to sleep in, and their gymnasiums and studios to work in. It is all quite wonderful when you think of it, and quite as romantic as the lives of the old troubadours. Even the most skeptical of us begin to think that what we are doing is important. It is, too, for me, more now than ever before, and I'm glad I came, but I shall also be definitely glad to get back.

But about those letters (of introduction), I am not really sure what to do about them. Shall I mail them or present them in person or what? It's pretty dumb of me not to know, but I don't, and I don't want to end up by doing nothing. Agnes, I have enjoyed working with you tremendously and more than that, it has helped to broaden my scope. I feel we have a great deal to offer each other and look forward to the future when we can work together again. Also, thank you ever so much for the parting gifts. I am terribly proud and just adore to flash them in front of my companions.

My very best love to you, and please remember me to Joe and the others.

Sybil

Dear Agnes,

Here I am in one of the worst hotels of my experience, especially bad because the downstairs is quite respectable, with its windows down to the floor and its long, green, tied-back drapes and its antique mirrors. It even has a grand staircase which goes up the middle and divides at the first landing, giving an air of spaciousness that one doesn't often find. The first clue to the real state of affairs was a generous offer of as many single rooms as we needed, each for a dollar. But we accepted all in good faith and trundled up to expected luxury, but as we went higher up the grand staircase, the hall lights became fewer and the pleasant spaciousness of downstairs changed to nasty alleys and dark cubbyholes. Then as we opened our doors (each key fit all doors we found) we discovered new horrors. My room smelled distinctly of pea soup that had been standing for some time. There was a chipped slop basin under the sink. Only the edges of the sheets had been pressed. The towels had been put through the ironer so fast, that they were mashed into diagonal folds. The bureau was scarred with old burns from cigarettes. But the worst horror of all was Granny sitting in one corner of the room, smugly holding herself together. She is a tremendous overstuffed rocking chair covered with what used to be green and brown checked upholstery, but the green has faded away from all but the edges, leaving a red brown glow similar to the Georgia clay. There are three grease spots on her back, which make me think that she was originally constructed for a Siamese triplet. One person would be completely enveloped and lose all sense of his own personality if he were to enter into the middle of that bulk. I invited all my friends in to see Granny, and each one burst out laughing at first and then checked himself suddenly with, "but I wouldn't sit in it if I were you!" So here I am faced with the problem of going to sleep and perhaps finding in that condition that Granny is even bigger and browner than I thought. However, I must sleep and if I keep right in the middle of the bed, perhaps I can manage to keep out of pollution's way despite the overhanging cobwebs and the scrubby rug with no telling what's under it and what comes out in the dark.

March 10, 1939
Chicago

Necessity being the mother of invention, I finally mailed the letter to Katherine Dunham, not knowing what else to do with it. So I hope I meet her tomorrow night.

Well, I have been full of adventures, and have been riding up and down like a true manic-depressive. In Tallahassee where the weather was so depressing, and there were several people in the audience I knew, I actually had to lose my temper before I could dance. I stormed through *New Dance* and variations with such a vengeance that I didn't care, for the first time in my life, whether I was on or off the beat. I just got there when I could with a violence and a conviction that must have made everyone else look wrong. In the variations I suddenly hated every movement and just improvised wildly. The next morning when Bill (Bales) said, with his Uncle Dudley air, that I should learn to control my emotions, I picked up a glass of water and dashed its content in his face, feeling sure at the moment that only a physical action would keep him and his dictatorial manner to himself in the future. When he said, wiping himself off furiously, that he didn't think it a bit funny, I said I didn't intend to be funny and stalked off. We didn't speak for two days.

Now things are back to normal, and I have ceased to feel any violence toward *New Dance*. Last night I did exceedingly well, better than I ever could have if I hadn't had my little orgy, which affected no one seemingly except Bill. It is terrible when you have to choose between violence and death!

In Tuskegee the audience laughed itself sick during *To the Dance*. The laughter started in titters and then would mount in a crescendo to roaring then die down, then mount until we too were hysterical, and could hardly control our movements. Bill has a terrible snort when he laughs, and Lionel a high breathless honk, and we were all suffering for fear the two of them would lose control, and they were in agony trying to hold back.

[The laughing started before my entrance, so I looked out to see what was going on, and realized how funny it did look to see ladies in long dresses fall flat on their faces at unexpected moments. Suddenly, we all saw it—all but Doris and Charles and the president of the college and his wife who later, at the reception, hastened to blame this breach of manners on the townspeople!]

March 23rd
Grinnell, Iowa

Well, I have come to the conclusion that you have lost the itinerary I sent you. I saw Louis in Chicago, and he promised to call you up when he got home. He and Frances Hawkins and I met backstage at Martha's concert last Saturday and had a short talk. I was rather surprised that Hawkins could be so nice. She has never looked at me before, but I got the gist of things when Louis said, "This is the Agnes de Mille Company." Martha came up while I was talking to Louis, and took my arm and Bill's. I nearly fell dead. They were really glad to see us, I think. Then I was supposed to invite our group to Katherine Dunham's after the concert, so I asked her if she wanted the Grahams too, and she said yes, so we collected eight of them and took them to Katherine's. Most of them I had never spoken to before; it was quite a bit of fun meeting out of town, as we never would have in N.Y. I had dinner with Katherine at her apartment before the concert (formal) and met an Austrian doctor in whose car I left my one and only hat. I was frantic, of course, when I discovered it was gone, and me leaving the following day. I called him and found that he was miles out of Chicago, but would meet me in Englewood and wave the hat at me on the platform. I flew off the train, grabbed the hat while he thrust a bouquet of violets into my hand. I just had time to board the train and wave to him as we pulled out.

Chicago was one hectic rush of entertainment and dinner dates. One of the most outstanding of my experiences, however, was my visit to the Federal Theatre Ballet with that wizard of dance, Bentley Stone, performing. That was a real thrill. I met him later and that evening at the home of a friend of mine, and we had quite a talk. He is an ardent admirer of yours which made me love him all the more. Really, if you could have seen him as the rebel aviator in the Spanish ballet, you would have been spellbound. His technique is superb, but the thing which is really good about him is his manliness and his mastery of the role he played, mastery with the whole body.

Yes, things have been going very well since Tallahassee, and I sort of expect them to continue so, as a new sort of life and feeling is beginning to creep over me. You must wonder why I keep mentioning my mental state. But it is something I am really working on and experimenting with, because I believe that someday I can actually see the light if I try every day. I have really only been working constructively on it for about six months and a half, and of course it is a bit difficult to advance at a steady pace. I think, however, that I have had more opportunity to test myself on this trip, and, of course, I am conscious of every rise and fall in emotion and feeling.

I look forward to meeting your friends in Los Angeles. We will only be there a few days, however, maybe not even three, though I may go down again after San Francisco in order to see the Grand Canyon. Do let me know your plans about Europe, though, and the fall, etc. The following are good places to catch me . . .

March 24, 1939
Grinnell, Iowa

Dear Mr. Bilstin,
[Yuri Bilstin, a Russian musician-composer, who gave me extraordinary exercises.]

How are you? What are your plans for the summer? I am beginning to look forward now, as we only have one month left of our tour and Doris is beginning to talk of the summer plans.

I must tell you what's happened to me. Not a great deal, of course, but a steady improvement nevertheless—I try every morning to meditate, sometimes long, sometimes short, but I am positive it helps. On the days I don't do it, I get terribly caught up in myself and so depressed that it is almost impossible to get back into myself. These people, as you know are particularly disturbing to me, so it has been quite interesting experimenting on myself to find peace. The thought came over me that humanity is all one and a solid piece, while individuals, with their feet rooted in humanity, bubble out of the solid piece and dry up leaving a knob. Humanity then is covered with hard knobs, but the inside is liquid and flowing. If the individuals would only keep themselves moist, then instead of hard unyielding scale on the outside of humanity, there would be a constant alive pulse as if everyone were at a slow boil. My horror has always been that I would harden, and I think I actually did start to harden. My head was pretty solidly encased. But now I feel everything loosening, and I begin to feel alive, I begin to feel that I have some control over being alive, and at last, my brain arrives at moments when I can think clearly.

One thing I have discovered is that there is not only a circle of light around every object, but there is a circle around every sound, and touch, and taste, and smell. The last two I haven't actually experienced, but believe to be so. In movement it is different, however, I can't quite make out what the circle consists of there, unless it is the line in space which the movement has already traced and that which it will trace later. This circle, just as you said, seems to be vibrations. I notice it especially in sound. There is always a higher reverberation at the same time as the actual low sound. Also the beginning and end of each sound is higher. Those I suppose are the overtones.

When I was in Chicago I happened into a little bookstore to ask after an old dance magazine, and of course while there I browsed around among the art books and the occult literature, and much to my surprise ran across a book which I have wondered about for some years now. It is called *Personal Magnetism*. I first saw it on the shelf in the studio at Mme. Ouspenskaya's dramatic school when I was studying there and took it down one day before class to look in over. Mme. came in, however, before I had put it back and although she pretended not to see me with it, she must have, for when I went to look for it the next day it was gone, and I never saw it again. I learned afterwards that she is very secretive about those things. Of course that roused my interest more than ever, and I often thought of going back to ask her about it, but never did. In any case, I bought the book and have begun to read it. It is put out by the Personal Magnetism Club of America and seems to have sensible knowledge and advice in it. I haven't arrived at the exercises yet, but they are supposed to develop magnetism in anyone. In fact, the author contends that it is simpler to develop it than be born with it. The titles of the other books offered for sale on the flyleaf of this volume sound like so much hocus-pocus. They are called "home training courses." I would like to know, however, if you have ever heard of this organization, and of Edmund Shaftsbury who seems to be the leader. The book was printed (11th edition) in 1926. So it probably all went under with the crash in '29.

Well, please do answer soon, and remember me to Mrs. Bilstin.

Most sincerely,
Sybil

May 1, 1939
San Francisco to NY
Lovelocks, Nev.

Dear Agnes,

Well, I had a heap big conference with Doris and discussed the dance thoroughly, the point of it all being that I have resigned from the group. I became very sentimental after the last performance and almost wept on Pauline's shoulder when she wished me good luck. She is a real person. I could tell by the way she shook my hand. Of course, Doris expected it all along, especially since Tallahassee. They were all wonderful about it and Jose gave me a great big bear hug. But I breathed a sigh of relief, nevertheless, for I have felt a growing disintegration and certainly have not left too soon. I also feel, thank heaven, that it is not too late though I shall need a good deal of mental and spiritual nourishment in order to feel that I am really healthy again.

In our talk Doris and I discussed movement and composition and got pretty fundamental. I asked her point blank why she did a lot of things, and when she came out with it, I was forced to disagree most of the time. The whole thing was very stimulating and when we parted I was in gay spirits. The next time I saw her, however, all our intimacy caused by the discussion had disappeared, and she had become the schoolmarm again saying that in 15 or 20 years she expected I would come around to her way of thinking. I said, "Perhaps," to be polite, but to myself I said, "It's no use," and so I now dismiss the whole depressing business from my mind. Never again shall I discuss the Humphrey-Weidmans, pro or con. I float away leaving them on a little island by themselves.

But going over this again, my conclusion now is that Doris and I were both interested in philosophy and in the dance as a language to express ideas, but there was an essential difference between us.

Doris had an intellectual approach, and through this approach she carved out some of the most interesting choreography in this century. Some people are interested in technical ideas, not Doris. She thought in terms of movement—new movement—as the important part of this expression. She was a true modern of her day. For her the ballet was old-fashioned, as was the spirit, which she felt went out with Ruth St. Denis, whereas I was never a modern in the same sense. I went further back and at the same time further forward.

I relied on being guided through art as a doorway to fulfillment. I was therefore always preparing myself to be ready when the time came. I was interested in pursuing the *technique* of *expression*, because I thought of myself as an instrument for the spirit. Since this was an individual matter, it is probably the reason I was essentially a soloist.

The letter to Agnes continued:

What do you think? I visited your father and Mrs. de Mille while I was in Los Angeles. It was so nice of them to ask me and I just jumped at the opportunity. They have a perfectly lovely house and garden in full view of the ocean. Your father is terrifically proud of you, and says he likes you better than any dancer he's seen, not because you are his daughter but because he can understand what you're doing. I said as many nice things as I could without appearing exaggerated. The whole time was delightful and I liked them both very much. I have instructions to describe everything to you and to give you a kiss from your father. I didn't see any of your other friends, though I received a wire from Mary Meyer. I couldn't send the letter to Warren Leonard because I couldn't find his name or Carmelita's in the phone book.

I had a long and wonderful talk with Rudhyar, and saw my uncle from Australia off on the boat. I visited a friend in San Francisco and we drove down to Carmel and climbed about on the rocks at dizzy heights over the foamy waves. It was while I was on the beach looking at the wonderful landscape half oriental, half African that I decided it was time to go home.

I shall be at 53 Cherry St, Lyons, NY beginning Friday morning and I would like to know when you want to begin work, and if you want me in New York. I am free until the last of June and shall be busy July and August. If you want me right away, let me know and I shall go right down to NY on Monday. As for next year, I shall make my plans fit into yours. You set the dates. All I know is that I shall have to have some kind of a job.

I look forward to New York. It seems funny to think that outside the train, California is slipping by.

My love to you,
Sybil

Dear Carolyn,

[Carolyn Bilderback, a talented friend whom I met at the Three Arts Club.]

There is much to say of many things, especially that I enjoyed my stay with you tremendously, and thank you ever so much for giving me such a good time.

The country here is just beginning to turn spring, and I think I must have known that I would miss the blossoms if I stayed any longer.

I had quite an interesting trip home in a coach marked "Exclusively for Women." The first rub was that the lady did not wish to give up her seat, but as I had to sit with someone, I sat down where the porter put me, though unwillingly enough with all the to-do about seats, and who was there first, etc. Unfortunately, I placed—very gently—my hat upon hers, there not being another inch of room in the car. It was discovered all too soon, and more fuss started. The lady complained to her friend in a loud voice adding, "I'm always so careful of other folks' things, aren't you?" etc. etc. These wailings went on all day with many variations, while I tried to bury myself in *A Pot of Gold*. Toward evening, when I was out having supper, someone left the train making an empty seat across the way, and when I came back, I found that all my belongings had been deposited across the aisle.

This gave me a new outlook, because up to that time I had been convinced that there were nothing but the old crones in the car. Now I looked across the aisle on a new set in a double chair. For a long time the second day I tried to read but could not help noticing a jolly woman with white hair and a round face, and I kept hearing what she was saying. She said she had spent 14 years in Alaska—from age 10 to 24. She had a good wit, and more than once I laughed at her jokes. Finally, the woman with her asked how I liked the Stephen book, and then started a conversation. Eventually, I found out that they were followers of Krishnamurti, and the woman who attracted me first gave me a pamphlet of his lectures from Camp Omman, Holland, where she had been a year or so ago. She seems to have traveled everywhere, and it seems that three of them are on their way to Detroit to buy a car and travel around the East. They are from Berkeley, and Mrs. Kennedy asked me to stay with her the next time I am on the coast. I had lunch with them in Chicago, and then we went to the museum. I can't tell you how surprised and pleased I was to find out more about Krishnamurti, and Mrs. Kennedy is a living example of his success in his teachings. They were both theosophists before they became acquainted with his work and ideas.

Then upon entering the train for home from Chicago, I tried to settle myself for as comfortable a night as possible on the coach, for I was unwilling to spend $3 for the Pullman. Well, I was sitting reading Krishnamurti and eating a Cotlet [a candy bar] when someone rapped heartily on the back of the seat in front of me. I looked up and was surprised and rather embarrassed to see before me a Catholic priest, for as I said, I was most comfortably arranged, and took my shoes off, too. He was the "take you by storm" type, and I could hardly believe my ears when he said, "Have you been reading my mail?" I said, "What?" He explained, "Well, I left my mail on this seat in front and wondered if you had bothered to read it." I was still bewildered, but finally decided that he was joking, so I did my best to reply in like manner. He said, "I'll be right with you," so I made ready for his presence by putting my shoes on and hiding my candy and making space in the seat for him. He tossed an Irish postcard at me, and we began a jovial conversation about Ireland and the Irish. Then he sat down and he asked me what I was reading. I showed him *A Pot of Gold*, and before I knew it, he had borrowed it from me, promising to send it back shortly. I put my name and address in it, and away it went, for he got off at South Bend, Indiana. He was a professor at Notre Dame. Since then I have received a letter asking me if he might annotate it and keep it a bit longer, and he has also sent me two books, one precious little volume given to him by his mother, no less, and another volume explaining the Catholic religion, and especially, why people become nuns and priests. It was interesting, because I remember mentioning in Carmel that I couldn't understand what those nuns were really in that convent for. It was all rather unbelievable.

My guess is that he saw me with the Krishnamurti literature, and thought I might as well have more of another variety. He certainly is zealous, and it is quite an experience. I don't think I have ever talked to a priest before.

Well, Carolyn, now I come to the unpleasant part. I left my brush as you probably know by now, and I want it back. Enclosed five stamps for postage, and thanks for the trouble.

May 31, 1939

Since I wrote last, I have spent two wonderfully hectic weeks in New York working with Agnes, and am now home again. Papa has been inspired to give me a studio. That is, he is having a floor put in the top of the barn, and I am genuinely thrilled. After the floor is laid, I am to paint the walls a beautiful yellow, so that the sunlight will be diffused into all corners of the room.

Well, much love to you, Carolyn.
Sybil

21

Dear Clair,

It is with great joy that I think of September, when at last we will be together to create as we always wished, but I shall spend the summer learning the technique of composition, so that when we come together our emotional outpourings will flow into form.

We can do colossal things, Clair. Krishnamurti, the Hindu philosopher, says, "One can be oneself at all times only if one is doing something that one really loves, and if one loves completely," and Krishnamurti also says that to be oneself is to have peace. But to have peace it is not necessary to cut out, or try to cut out, all other moods and emotions. It is simply to have an understanding of them. I know we ring true, because when we create together I forget to be intellectual and give way to emotion, and that is the only alive state.

My love to you,
Sybil

June 2, 1939
Lyons, NY

My Dear Mr. Nadon,

Last year, you offered me the opportunity to teach at the Academy, but I was unwilling to do so since I was just starting my six-month leave of absence from the Humphrey-Weidman group, and wished to spend that time on myself. Also, I did not wish to teach only Humphrey-Weidman technique, but preferred to have something of my own to offer upon starting out by myself.

I have worked considerably during the winter, and feel finally that I have something definite to offer my students, both in the line of bodybuilding for the layman, and variety of expression for those who wish to be dancers. The beauty of it is that both types of student can come into the same class with perhaps one exception, in that later those who progress more rapidly would prefer to start a class of their own.

I have left the Humphrey-Weidman Company, although I did go on tour with them this past winter and I have joined Agnes de Mille on whose programs I shall do my own solos next season.

My idea is this—I have five free hours a week which I could give you, and I feel that each student should take as many lessons each week as he or she is able in order to show some progress, both to himself and to me throughout the season. (And I am confident that there will be improvement!)

What do you think of this plan, Mr. Nadon? I am sending you some clippings which may interest you. And I hope to hear from you soon.

Sybil Shearer

So my field of operations for teaching became the Academy of Allied Arts with good old Mr. Nadon. What I remember about this period is not the classes but the Thursday afternoon teas.

At that time in New York, there were many émigré White Russians of the aristocracy, and on Thursdays they would gather, wearing their furs and jewels, drinking their tea from the samovar (one drop of potentized tea to one cup of hot water), and nibbling on the best cookies I had ever tasted. Since they all spoke Russian, my interest was mainly watching them move and gesticulate, although the sounds that issued from them were a marvelous accompaniment.

On several occasions—there being always some concert or other in the intimate space to climax the afternoon—I offered my talents as a performer with the idea that Rudhyar and I would do improvisations together. He thought this would be interesting. So each time we would plan four different ideas which would balance each other in mood, then make transmutations in music and dance, improvised on the spot. This was very exhilarating.

Rudhyar was tall and thin with very large hands and long fingers that seemed to take the grand piano by storm. He was dark with a long face and short beard. He looked like a Mexican saint. Actually, he was French, and had been secretary to Rodin in his youth. His music, no matter what the mood, was powerful, and I responded in kind.

I have no idea how those Russians, living in the past, responded to our immediacy, but we were asked back. After one performance, a turbaned Hindu approached me and said, "When were you born?" Without hesitation I said "Which time?" He nodded and smiled, and that was the end of our conversation.

Dearest A.,

Forgive me for not answering your letter. Of course, I am very glad that we are giving a performance for an audition. I think that is much more satisfactory, but honestly, I hate to leave my studio. It's done now, and I am doing such work. It is beautiful and inspiring, too.

After you left I fell into a lethargy such as I haven't experienced in an age. I couldn't do a thing but lie on the bed, and I made up my mind that I would try the Krishnamurti method of nonresistance. So I just let myself lie and decided not to move until I spontaneously wanted to do something. That lasted several days, and then as though someone had put dynamite under me, I got up one morning and started to clean the barn—that is, my section of it. Well, I got all the instruments out and swept down the ceiling and the walls and the floor, knocking down cobwebs and wasp nests and bird droppings, all of which had been up there for the past dozen years. There were nails and sawdust and shavings and barrels and broken antiques, and I worked from 9 in the morning until 7 at night, with a few minutes out for lunch. At the end of this time, my hands were covered with blisters and my hair filled with dust. Also, it was devilish hot up there, and the dirt had plastered itself over every uncovered part of my body. When I finally was clean enough to go to bed, my legs were just throbbing under me, and my shoulders wouldn't rotate.

Then the next day I arose bright and early and gave myself a good workout.

I worked out on the lawn because, after this clean up, Papa put down a new maple floor on the second story of our barn, and for the next few years, until my parents' deaths, I spent my summers in Lyons, New York, on Cherry Hill overlooking the rolling country and the drumlins of Wayne County, creating solo dances and holding summer courses for special students.

Papa and I were not exactly kindred spirits. He did not understand what all the excitement about dance on my part was worth. And on every possible occasion he played the balky horse by saying, "No." However, I began to realize that this was simply a stopgap to give him time to think.

So the studio was an enormous concession, and I shall be forever grateful for that "giving in" (which I learned through Mama, who said to me, "Your father has decided to put a floor on the second story of the barn.")

Papa did think I was funny, but I was not conscious of it until he volunteered in an offhand way, "I think if you stuck to comedy you might be a success." Of course, this was not what I wanted to hear, but he meant well!

The letter to Agnes continued:

> Here's one thing to report anyway. I've started on the Bach. Last Sunday I went to church and the minister so infuriated me by his manner in delivering his sermon—his voice was positively rancid with boredom—that I came home with every intention of writing him a letter to put him on the right track and suggest where and how he might find interest in his work. After about an hour of mental letter composing, I went for a walk, which led me out through the fields and right back into my studio where I composed most of the first half of the Bach. Something magical happened in the meantime, just as Mr. Bilstin said it would. He said Bach whipped his children in order to stir him to composition. Something told me to go to church. I shall go again and see what happens.
>
> That's all now. My love to you. See you soon.
>
> Sybil

August 25, 1939
Lyons, NY

Dear Mr. Rudhyar,

Thank you so much for your letter, and for letting me know about *Art As Release Of Power*. I hope to heavens that I have not put it off so long that I can't get three copies.

I had a feeling that you knew Krishnamurti, for you both speak with equal enthusiasm about spontaneity of expression. There is a difference, however, between your philosophies when it comes to organization of thought as material for creation, as a steppingstone to more creation and creative living. Krishnamurti does not believe in any kind of organization. One might even say he doesn't believe in thinking as a means to anything. He feels that creative living comes only out of feeling and any check to the feelings comes as a barrier of thoughts!—am I right so far?—whereas you go so far as to attempt the organization of a whole life at birth. Also your musical compositions are in repeatable form, etc. (I just get a bright idea here. Can it be that Krishnamurti means that the universe or whole has certain fixed laws to run by that cause or produce change of which we are almost totally ignorant, so that when we try to work things out in our own limited way, we simply clog up the line of progress by substituting our own invented theories for laws that will go on no matter what we do or think; therefore, it is better to feel out the universal laws by developing our instincts or intuition instead of our brains?)

I have a feeling that Krishnamurti would think that my improvised dancing on the spur of the moment is much finer than anything I could put into form and repeat. Mr. Bilstin says that a work of art is a combination of many moments, and not just one as an improvisation is. But on the other hand, you might say that an improvisation is a combination of moments, because all of the moments you spent training your body and your mind and your feelings as well as your contact with the infinite or the fourth dimension, or whatever, is combined into a whole at one moment and is set on fire by the music.

This afternoon I improvised on the stage of the local theatre for my former dancing teacher and a few of her pupils and relatives. I was quite aware that I had no control over what my body was doing. I had simply set it in motion by my will and then allowed myself to react emotionally to the movements my body was doing. And I was amazed at what I could do and with what fleetness I could run and turn and jump, with what strength I could sustain a movement. The floor was full of slivers, and yet I had none in my feet. I forgot to warm up, but there seemed to be no need of it. When it was over, my teacher said, "My! You have complete control of your body." I could have said, "You are wrong, my body has control of itself. I simply react to its movements." But I said nothing, for I knew it was not the right moment, and I've reserved it for you. They were all amazed that I could create dances on the spur of the moment, and each one different. They informed me that what I had done was much more difficult than making a "routine" and following it. I couldn't help telling them that they were wrong there. But they wouldn't believe me. The afternoon was so successful that I have made up my mind to give an evening of improvisations, *but* only after I have been able to give an evening of dances that I have composed and can repeat. [See Addendum VI.]

All summer, I have been working on a Bach Chorale which I shall do on Agnes' programs next year. It is so difficult that it will take me a while to get it under control. But it is the first dance I have ever created which is not furry around the edges, that is partly improvised, and I'm right proud of it.

My father has put a floor in the barn, and I have been working there all this month. Last month, I spent in the Berkshires with Mr. Bilstin. We studied interior development, composition, yoga philosophy, relaxation and orchestration, all of them fascinating. I wish that I could always keep all of those studies up at the same pitch as I did while there. Next year, if there is any form of livelihood forthcoming, I shall start harmony. I want to be a thorough musician. That's a big order, for right now I am as ignorant as possible. Mr. B. says that if I practice an hour a day on the piano, I will be good enough in two years to play anything reasonably well, and to compose anything I wish or have inspiration for. This summer I composed a little piece of music which Mr. B. laughingly said must have been dictated to me by a 16th-century Italian, for it sounded like ricercare music. In any case, the future looks very full, and my ankles are at least swinging into line with my knees, so that I am beginning to jump like Nijinsky, and I am quite hopeful and happy despite the European situation, which, by the way, must have been a tremendous shock to my many Jewish communist friends in New York. I am anxious to hear their explanation. Perhaps they are all Trotskyites by now.

I wish you the best happiness, and look forward to hearing from you and seeing you in the future.

Most sincerely to you both,
Sybil

All that autumn, 1939, I worked closely with Agnes, and it was another learning process. I found again that my world was different. One might say I was unworldly, but incidents like the following one made me wonder about other people's thinking. I saw that Agnes had two sides—the imaginative, enthusiastic, loyal side, and the worldly, "practical" but, to me, completely unreal side—the need to follow customary thinking about relationships.

Lubitsch, the director of Garbo's *Ninotchka*, was in town. Agnes knew him through her father, William, and her uncle, Cecil B. de Mille. She thought it was important not to miss this opportunity to audition for him.

I offered the Theatre Dance Company studio for the audition. It was a five-flight walk-up on 19th Street! We were to do the *Hunger Dance* duo, and then Agnes would perform a series of her solos.

Lubitsch arrived and was politely placed on a folding chair in this vast, gloomy space covered with a floor cloth. We retired to the dressing room to change, and suddenly Agnes panicked. Perhaps she realized this was crazy. I became the duenna telling her he would love her dances. (There was no possibility of backing out.)

Agnes's naive side always amazed me. What possible use could Lubitsch find for her dance? I don't think she had thought that far. She simply felt it was important not to miss an "audition"—a chance to show a great movie director her work, whether or not it made sense.

Here she had chosen concert dance as a career, but she had it mixed up in her mind with show business. This was the dilemma. This was her hard business side, and it did not fit with her soft inspirational side.

After our demonstration, Lubitsch thanked us and walked down the five flights. As far as I know, neither of them gained anything. I was probably the one who benefited just by being there.

Later, Walter Terry accused me, in a review, of seeing people as "shallow, aimless, and close to bordering on insanity," though two weeks later he reduced this to "the foibles of man." (See Addendum VII.)

If the finger I pointed at people through my dances was more sword-like in those days, whereas now I have perhaps more sympathy, it is not because I am more tolerant of the crazy things people do, rather I have learned I can do nothing but state my opinion, because each of us is a solo contributor to life, and the whole of life is a learning process.

Of course, in those days I thought people would heed my warnings and shape up!

January 22, 1940
Three Arts Club

My Dear Mrs. Hammond,

[Mrs. John Henry Hammond, president of the Three Arts Club, and mother of John Hammond, who launched Benny Goodman.]

Mrs. Markloff has very graciously offered me the theatre at the Club for Thursday evening, February 8th, so that I might present a program I have composed on the Art of Movement. It consists of a talk and demonstration of dance studies and is suitable as an educational program for women's clubs and schools. I hope by this preview performance, as it were, to interest program chairmen of the various clubs in and around New York in bookings for next season.

Since the art of the dance is rising in popularity everywhere in the country and is one of the most recent additions as a major course in the college curriculum, it seems imperative to me that people know more about this inevitable influence on our culture.

I do hope you will be able to come to the Club that night. I might add from past experience that the program is entertaining as well as instructive. I am being assisted by Miss Katherine Litz, professional dancer and nonresident member of the Club.

Most sincerely,
Sybil L. Shearer

About this time there was also a talent night at the Three Arts Club, and I was asked to contribute a dance. The singers would present arias, the pianists Chopin, Brahms, etc., the actresses scenes from Ibsen and Shakespeare, and there was a flutist and a poet—with Mrs. Hammond in the audience.

I don't know what they expected of me. I had been creating for several years on the second floor landing in front of a huge mirror, and those using the stairway had long since decided they did not have to greet me each time as they passed by to their various rooms. I was a fixture, if mostly a moving one, in my long black skirt and black leotard, hair flying, arms waving, though sometimes I was meditatively thinking about the next move.

What actually happened was that I was inspired to create a satire based on the personality of one of the girls at the Club. She was a fascinating creature, young but definitely an old-maidish type with her horn-rim glasses, tight skirt, hair pulled up on top of her head, full of conversation about herself, her family, and home. I did not know it at the time, but she was in therapy, writing a journal every day regarding her thoughts and reactions to everything.

Her last name sounded like *failing* which was a perfect picture of what she seemed to be. Actually I did not think of her as pathetic, rather as a very interesting character, entirely different from everyone else, struggling to get into the mainstream.

Secretly I made her the subject of my satire called, *African Skrontch by Mail*, with music by Chauncy Moorehouse. This was the portrait of a middle-aged spinster practicing in the privacy of her room, having subscribed to a correspondence course in *African Skrontch*. The script, which unfolded out of a business-size envelope, covered the floor as she checked for last-minute instructions before starting the phonograph; then diving into the dance, she kicked the script aside. The music carried her everywhere, including down on her knees as best her tight skirt would allow, until at the end, exhausted, she grabbed for the chair and sat panting and fanning herself, till suddenly she realized that she was not alone, that there was an audience out there. Then getting apologetically behind the chair, she decided to bolt for the door.

272

It was a success. The audience screamed with laughter and applause. Pleased with myself I headed back into the dressing room. I could hear the next performer singing away as I changed. Then, suddenly, the door from the hall opened, and standing there was the subject of my dance! I didn't mean to hurt her. It never occurred to me that she would be in the audience (until the door opened, and there she was facing me). I was horrified. There was no escape. As I held my breath, the words came from her—"That was wonderful! Where *do* you get your ideas?"

Then it dawned, along with a huge amount of relief, that people do not see themselves as others see them! It was something to ponder on for the rest of my life. Actually, these satires that I was doing, though funny, were not comedies at all. They were tragicomedies on the human dilemma—Who am I? Why am I here? Where am I going?—and on the seriousness with which people were so often picking the wrong road for ludicrous reasons.

Then I wrote this very formal letter to John Martin, critic:

May 4, 1940
Three Arts Club

Dear Mr. Martin,

I was very much interested in your last week's article, and quite amused by the picture you drew of all those thick-shanked modern dancers sweating at ballet barres. However, I differ with you on one point, and that is your interpretation of the reason for this new wave of enthusiasm for the ballet. These people, I am convinced, have not the desire to be blithesome butterflies as you suggest. They have found, rather, that here is a technique that goes beyond their experience. Here is a way of learning to point one's toe, straighten one's knees, jump, do adagio, and turn, etc., and a dozen other things that the personalized techniques of the various modern dancers cannot, or at least, do not give them. So having exhausted the Graham and Humphrey and Holm techniques, they are looking for new fields to conquer technically. It is just here that I feel them to be absolutely wrong, for if they would go within themselves and learn their own bodies, muscle by muscle and joint by joint, they would find the basis for movement for which they are looking. I believe that if you are a creative dancer by profession, there is absolutely no reason to study ballet, unless you wish to become a ballet dancer, and I feel that these people you speak of are simply collecting surface knowledge, which they intend sooner or later to apply to "The Scotsboro Boys" or "Hurrah for Stalin."

I am studying ballet myself now, and I am doing it purely and simply in order to become a ballet dancer. My basic technique was such before even starting ballet that in a class of experienced dancers, I have more endurance and control of balance and line, more in an adagio than anyone else in the room. Everyone remarks on my elevation and the flexibility of my feet. The things I have to learn are the new coordinations of the ballet style, but I have enough knowledge of my body, so that it should not take more than a few months of concentrated effort.

Don't mistake me, however, I do not wish to become a ballet dancer to the exclusion of all other styles. Rather, it has always been my desire to make myself as complete an instrument of the theatre as possible, so that no matter whom the choreographer, I would be able to express his ideas with emotional conviction if they were there to be expressed. I believe that within a dance, there should be one style only, but within a dancer there should be many, just as there should be many qualities in order to have as great a range of expression as possible.

Also, to get back to your article, I am not sure exactly what you meant when you said, "the modern dance and the ballet— are complementary divisions of a common art which overlap at no point. The former is devoted to the communication of emotional convictions; the latter to the presentation of esthetic beauty." Do you mean that the above is the present state of affairs only? Or do you mean that it is a fact now and for always? If you mean the latter, then I must disagree with you again, because it seems to me that only by a combination of these two entities, emotional conviction and esthetic beauty, can we arrive at the real and the highest form of the dance art. If we don't have it now, at least we can work toward it. And no matter how much we may fall by the wayside in single performances, sometimes stressing one side and sometimes another, still it is the ultimate coordination of the outer and the inner, the science and the religion of art, which makes the really moving experience both for the artist and the audience.

Most sincerely,
Sybil L. Shearer

22

By 1940 I knew I had arrived at the place where I was ready to try my dances on the public. However, I did not have a full program, so, needing a good pianist, I decided to ask one to collaborate with me, sharing half the evening.

Louise Martin suggested someone she knew who played well but had not made a formal debut. She agreed to work with me and came up to Lyons to rehearse. Temperamentally she was rather bland, but I was thankful to have a collaborator for this first adventure.

On looking back, it surprises me that I was so practical in deciding to try out my dances in my hometown where I knew my mother's friends, my high school teachers, and acquaintances would support me. Mama had been president of every club and church bazaar, and from the beginning of my career had notified all her friends of my successes in New York, on the road, etc., on every possible occasion putting little news items in the local paper.

So I was, in a way, a small celebrity and everyone rallied round. Of course, there were others, too, because I had arranged with the manager of the local movie theatre to do my program between shows. I remember being very fussy about who and what was on the screen sharing my program with me. I did not want war pictures or Betty Boop things, and finally decided on a wholesome comedy with Judy Canova—not perfect but possible.

Probably nothing but the senior plays had been experienced live in our town for years, so the power of live performance, between two showings on the silver screen, was a novelty. The audience laughed and clapped at the unexpected experience of viewing "art," and they found it palatable. (See Addendum VIII, the local reviews.)

I knew a solo program had to have variety, lyricism, drama, and comedy, so among this array was *African Skrontch by Mail*. I had two things in mind in giving this program—a trial away from critical New York and an opportunity to show my work to the head of the high-school assembly programs who was stationed in Rochester, New York, only thirty miles away. He came. He liked it, and he arranged for me to audition in Chicago when I went on tour with Agnes. But he insisted that I do *African Skrontch*, because he said I could not miss with that piece—"the rest of the program can be as instructive as you like."

As it turned out, there were 6,000 students in the school auditorium in East Chicago at that audition. The authorities had supplied me with a huge orthophonic Victrola, the needle of which would not stay on the record. It was a nightmare, but I kept in character and made the most of it while the whole place rocked with laughter, and I was in—twenty weeks on tour in the Midwest and East; two to three performances a day in high schools and colleges, dashing in our little car from place to place, finding the "stage door," and setting up before the principal could delay us with welcomes and instructions.

One time, as we were warming up on stage, the principal arrived and started talking to me. I was jumping up and down, so he jumped with me asking questions in midair!

It was a wonderfully successful tour, lots of fun, and very educational for me. Despite hollow stages and splinters on the floor in many places, the only really bad time was in a coal-mining town in

Pennsylvania when we had to perform in front of a huge American flag as a backdrop—our costumes were rust and green! It was for me an artistic disaster, but the audience seemed not to notice, and the applause was thunderous.

The intellectual aim of this huge effort was to instruct, but my initial aim was to inspire. I hope it did both, but feel that probably we, Allison Choate and myself, received the real benefits by being able to share our enthusiasms—talking, illustrating different kinds and qualities of movement, and dancing. (See Addendum IX, letters from fans.)

But this experience was still a year away. In the meantime, I was on tour with Agnes through the Midwest, ending in Chicago, where I had my audition. This tour with Agnes, doing her choreography, was a great experience. Her dances were really crowd pleasers. The other members of the group were Katherine Litz, Joseph Anthony, and Louis Horst, who was our accompanist. Louis, on the other hand, was accompanied by a large stack of murder mysteries which, one by one, appeared on the piano while we rehearsed. Even during performances, he would be playing and reading simultaneously, having learned the music by heart.

We traveled in two cars and switched around so that we could visit with each other. Louis and I did a lot of talking, and he was heard to say in his booming voice between numbers at one of my later solo performances in New York, "We argued halfway across Kansas." These adventures were fun and I also became friends with Joe Anthony, an actor-dancer, who occasionally partnered Agnes.

After this success in my hometown, the tour with Agnes, the audition, and the contract for future performances on tour, I felt it was a necessity, in fact it was my greatest desire, to make my debut as a soloist in New York. So the whole next winter I was preparing for this event while I worked and performed with Agnes.

December 26, 1940
Lyons, NY

Dear Joe,

Your very nice card arrived this morning while I was eating my wheat cereal and discussing the mechanical problems of my invention with Papa whose interest is slowly being aroused. [I had some idea for a rhythm machine.] On Christmas Eve we went over the whole thing, until my eyes felt as though they were on long poles extending painfully out of my head, and finally Papa pronounced that it was possible but would take at least $1000. At that point, I kissed him good night and trounced upstairs in rather a huff, because after all the only thing necessary is a little careful planning, some patience, the ability to measure correctly and handle a saw. But Papa, being a perfectionist, looked on me a bit scornfully when I rejected the idea of precision tools in making a first model. But, as I say, Christmas dinner and two days at home, a walk in the fresh air after huge quantities of turkey and pudding, and a new green sweater, etc., have mellowed his point of view and now I think we may get something done.

By the way, did you see that Jose Limon has been drafted in California? He's been playing soldier so long now, it will be interesting to see how he comes out of the real thing. I had a Christmas card from "Bent" Stone.

Mama knitted me a new yellow sweater which you will just love.

Best of luck to you, Joe. Get that part if you want it, and write me if you have a moment. I liked your Christmas card best of all.

Most Sincerely,
Sybil

Dear Joe,

You can't know how I miss you. Tonight during rehearsal, I suddenly knew that all the juice had run out of *Night Scene*. Hugh [Hugh Lang, dancer and co-worker with Antony Tudor] will improve, of course, but it will never be the same. And at this point I would almost rather not go on, because I feel more strongly than ever that there is really no need for me on the program, especially if I can't muster up any feeling. I guess I'll just have to do a Stanislavsky and substitute you in my mind. The worst of it is that Hugh is like cast iron one minute and lukewarm pulp the next. There is no in between give as yet.

The fall, which came so easily and naturally to us, has now become a difficult technical feat. Either Hugh throws me around too fast, or I come up on the wrong foot. In any case it never feels right. [This fall—the swirl around to the floor and up again—was designed by myself at the revival of *Night Scene* in which I took over Agnes' part. When I saw her do it earlier, it had been mostly acting. In my version, the acting was transformed into flowing lyrical movement that came out of the idea of a lover's tryst.]

I feel perhaps you are right about us, except Joe, I can't believe that the sympathy between us and its expression was in any way unfair to the dance. On the contrary, it enhanced it, making it something alive. *Night Scene* is now just a dance, part of an evening's entertainment. I believe, probably because I am an idealist, that all dancing should be sacred, just as life is, but perhaps I want the impossible. In any case, you know you were never a "stooge" in *Night Scene* even though I had all the swoops and falls. It was you, your movements and positions and emotions which caused everything, and I never once felt that I wanted to take the dance into my own hands and excite myself merely by my own movements. Always, I felt uncertain and expectant about what would happen next.

With Hugh it is quite the opposite. I see him lift his shoulders and relax his chest at given moments, as though Agnes had pushed a button. And I have now taken the dance into my own hands.

Agnes thinks the whole thing is much better, despite Hugh; that my dancing has improved, and she has also made some changes in the choreography.

But Joe, it is just the difference between aesthetical and sacred art. Have you read any of Rudhyar's book? Have you come to the place where he talks about this? "Aesthetical means extra, that is, not absolutely necessary to life, a sort of luxury, perhaps an entertainment. Sacred means a part of life, an action with a purpose, an idea or an emotion which, because it is important to the performer as a human being, it is also important to the audience."

This "fall" has excited Hugh so much that he had Antony [Antony Tudor, great English choreographer] look at it, and has begun most enthusiastically to give me private coaching in ballet with the idea that I should get into Ballet Theatre and be first in Antony's things and later work up to the purely classical . . . ! He was a bit disappointed, however, when he found I couldn't do pirouettes.

This afternoon after Hugh and I had rehearsed, we were invited to have tea at one of the boys' apartments, and about eight or ten ballet dancers were there including Gene [Eugene Loring, dancer and choreographer of *Billy the Kid*]. I somehow started to read palms, and when I came to Hugh's hand I was really shocked. It was such a violent hand, absolutely misshapen as though he had been madly clutching at something, because all the muscles on one side were very developed, but the most noticeable thing is that the head and heart lines are combined in one deep gash across his palm. The rest of his hand is cluttered up with triangles and stars, etc. And he is a fantastic fellow, quite childish and full of moods.

Write me, Joe, if you have a moment this week, and let me know how you are.

Sybil

I was very interested in Tudor, and he was interested in me. Hugh confided that Tudor wanted me for Hagar. (He was currently and secretly at work composing *Pillar Of Fire*.) But I had to be in Ballet Theatre to do it. Agnes also wanted me in Ballet Theatre, because she was composing *Three Virgins and a Devil* for them that season, and I had created the part of the Devil, which Eugene Loring was scheduled to perform.

It was a kind of conspiracy to which I was impervious, because I had plans. I was working on my own solo debut, but this was not public knowledge. I kept it inside me. I simply said to Hugh, "What's the point of being on point?" I had done point work in high school, and now it was a thing of the past. The whole style seemed too stiffish, unless you were going to say something with or about these techniques.

Of course, if I were ever going to be in another company, this would have been the right one, because Tudor was using all this in a new way, and I admired him tremendously. But I really did not want to be caught in a company where I would have to do all these other ballets and ballet things at the same time, including pirouettes. That did not interest me. I was wary of the temperament of Hugh and the Svengali attraction of Tudor. I felt he would devour me. I was strong, but not like Nora (Nora Kaye, the Hagar whom Tudor picked out of the company and with whom he closely worked for many years). My soft side would have given him everything.

But all through the years there was a bond between myself and Tudor. I could always feel it in his presence, on the stage and off.

He told Hugh that he could watch me dance forever. In 1983 when *A Sheaf of Dreams* was shown at the Dance Library in New York, Tudor was there, and it meant a great deal to me to have this last contact.

January 12, 1941

Dear Joe,

Sunday, as you know, I went to see the H-W group, expecting the worst as usual, and what should I find but a simply delightful theatre and a really nice performance. I wish you had been there. Charles was absolutely on top and gave a performance that I didn't expect possible from him. His movement was beautiful both in its flow and its rhythm, and I was really moved by his emotional power. Believe it or not, I refer to *On My Mother's Side*. They have a perfect dance theatre, and it is especially good for solo and duet work, although the whole group looks much better than it does on a regular stage. I long to dance on it.

Although I know you were fooling when you said that Doris and Charles were hurt that I hadn't been to any of the performances, you were right I was quite surprised that everyone was so glad to see me. I must say I was happy to see them, all in such good spirits and performing so well.

I suppose Agnes told you that I won't be able to go on tour with you next year, since you will probably go in March. I am disappointed. However, it will probably be much less exhausting for me to stick at the one job.

Joe, write to me soon. Time flies by so quickly.

My love to you,
Sybil

January 23, 1941
158 W 13th St, NYC

Dear Joe,

I dare say you will be happy to be back in New York, since from your letter and from what Agnes says, it was pretty unpleasant in the show. The performances in Hartford were most exhilarating, despite the fact that I had a sore heel, that I was quite hurt and annoyed by something Agnes did before the performances—she was quite unaware of it—and that I missed you. I really enjoyed meeting all those people. Also, Mr. Kleiner's [Arthur Kleiner, pianist for many of Agnes' concerts] reserve gradually broke down, collapsing completely after he had burst into the dressing room unheralded to find me in a state bordering on nudity. He apologized profusely, of course, giggling a good bit the while, and the next day talked to me for five minutes straight over the telephone—so you see.

I am working with Agnes on the new ballet and I like it. Also, I got my scholarship at the Club, so I expect to apply myself to study for the rest of the year.

See you soon,
Sybil

March 21, 1941
Three Arts Club

Dear Joe,

I like my rose. In fact, I think I like flowers more than I like people. That's rather an anemic thing to say to be sure. But in this hot-blooded age where you have to bayonet the other fellow with joyful cursings before he bayonets you, I feel very limp and bloodless. In fact, things have really come to such a pass that I find I must take a stand. It is necessary either to bury myself in a rose bed and rest peacefully ever after, or to die fighting. Actually, I'm in the position of a commissioned officer who is without any talent for, or knowledge of, the use of arms. It's not that I don't hate enough. I hate people who cry into their soup as much as I hate the little Hitlers that infest the world; as much as I hate you for being around when I should be weeping by myself in a corner because all this talk won't make a soldier of me. Only "voices" can do that and mine have deserted me.

Sybil

April 24, 1941
Lyons, NY

Dear Joe,

The air is so good here, so sweet and the wind blows over the hill in soft, strong breaths, and I feel the urge to buy a gun and go out shooting in the woods. Not that I want to shoot anything alive—just targets, some special leaf or maybe a swinging tin can hitched over a limb. It was so much fun shooting at the Palisades with you. I never thought I'd like it. In fact, I had a very good time all week with you, and that reminds me I owe you a dollar out of the five, and also something for the Rainbow Room. It was most embarrassing that you should pay for Mary Hunter [Director of the American Actors Company and Agnes' best friend] and me, too. The only thing I really wanted was to dance with you, and there you were with that horrid girl. I was about to ask her husband to cut in on her when he said, "She dances the waltz so perfectly, and I can't do it at all." So I was forced to relax.

At any rate, here is $3. Please do something special with it.

April 27, 1941
Lyons, NY

Dearest Joe,

Today is the screen test, and I wish for everything that you wish. Please let me know what happens. I am busily putting bookshelves in my studio, sawing and measuring, etc. There is such an accumulation of things from N.Y. that I sent home and no room for them in the house, and anyway I've always wanted to start in with a saw and hammer and secretly envied you making those flats.

Mama is much better, and I don't think she was worrying about me at all. It was just my conscience.

My piano is in fine shape after a hard winter. I gave her a good rub down and she sparkles. My beautiful black kitten of last summer has three babies of her own now, and I am to have two of them.

S.

June 1, 1941

Dear Joe,

It just crossed my mind, as I was looking at the houses on our street, especially our white one surrounded by trees of all varieties, that trees are to houses what domestic animals are to people. This week sometime I shall have my kittens. Then the house and I shall be in better balance. Mr. Johnson does not like the idea of the kittens, because he is a bird lover and has two bird sanctuaries—one in the valley across the street and the other in back of his house in the form of an old apple orchard. I like especially the latter, because I can go from our garden way down in back and over the fence right into it, and from there can have a view of my favorite hill. I often go to the Johnson's that way because, well, it's as though I melt or fade into their presence. When I go by the street I have to walk. But when I leave I always leap down the road in great bounds. They are wonderful magical people and make me feel gay and beautiful.

But Joe, although the above may sound to you fantastic, possibly "creative" and probably quaint, you know as well as I that the essence of truth is there. The fault merely lies in my method of saying what I have to say. Now I shall try to be as matter of fact as possible, to tell you that I have thought all week pretty steadily about what you said to me last Saturday at lunch. You did hit the nail on the head almost squarely. And the blow knocked me almost completely out of myself, so that when you said that "I might as well be carrying a calla lily on my arm," it was quite true, for I was off trying to survey the new territory that you had suddenly opened up.

Yes, it is probably true that in the minds of most people who know me, I am just an idea, and if I were to vanish into thin air, their only comment would be, "isn't it too bad, she was so talented," and most of them would not even have experienced my talent. The funny part of it all is that for the last four or five years, I have directed all my thinking and what I thought were my efforts toward being a human being because I thoroughly believed that it was impossible to be a great artist without that.

What I have tried to do was to feel myself in everyone, and everyone in myself, both past and present. It is not an easy job. But sometimes things click, and I suddenly become one with someone else, like the first time I saw you perform at the McMillian. Moments like that live forever and, given a chance, should accumulate and would have, I suppose, if suddenly all the juice hadn't gone out of me—if I hadn't become utterly frustrated mentally and emotionally. I was definitely not myself. You said, how can anyone be other than herself? The thing is I was not anyone else. I was simply in abeyance—nothing, and throwing out a smoke screen of fantastic remarks didn't help.

You said, "What makes you unhappy. I feel happy, although things are not going just as I would like them." How could I say, "You make me unhappy?" I couldn't, unless I could supplement it with a reason why. And now suddenly I understand. . . .

One of your accomplishments of your 28th year was finding me out. Why, I don't know. But I was playing guinea pig. And all I added up to at the end of the year was less than a human being. No wonder I always felt uneasy with you.

Yes, I am angry, even more angry and hurt than I was the time you came up to dinner when you should have stayed home and washed your hair. I don't know why I let myself think that you just wanted to see me, but when you finally came out with it and asked me if I would reconsider working with the American Actors Company, I saw your reason for coming, and I could hear Agnes in the background saying, "You speak to her Joe, she'll probably do it for you." Oh, I hated Agnes, but I tried to be reasonable, to put myself in her place, to tell myself I shouldn't let it influence me personally, etc. etc., until I couldn't stand it another minute. It was disgusting, just as you said. It's disgusting that people should have emotions at all. But people don't, I suppose—only weak-minded artists.

As for my preferring to be an artist, well there is no choice; I am an artist. I know that, because only at moments when I am creating, or giving or receiving creations am I really happy and alive. Actually, I can't imagine life without those moments. Perhaps, the difference is that artists are more intense, so that when they are not creating they feel as miserable emotionally as they would physically if some organ were not functioning properly.

There I was all winter long, just like my father's power mower, which he has to crank and crank until she gets flooded, and then he has to wait and then he cranks again for a long time, and then she floods again, and then just as Mama calls, "Dinner's ready," the darn thing starts to chug and has to be turned off.

But I would like to be a person, too—a real live one. In any case, I am glad that you said what you did and in the tone of voice that you did, because I knew immediately that you were not fooling or pretending, that it was the real you speaking, and I have been set thinking very hard about everything.

With love,
Sybil

June 12, 1941
Lyons, NY

Dear Joe,

How are you? Well and happy I hope and getting ready to fly to Hollywood or motor to Connecticut. I am very gay, full of spirits and ambition. But please think of me in the rock garden with the moss and coral-bells and violas and yarrow, feeling as though I couldn't bear it another minute if I didn't do something about the beauty of the patterns and the color of it all. It's like the green and red and yellow fields outside Chickashee; like the thought of you and the American Actors Company; you in the cellar making scenery; you dancing the Pavane, the Parvenues, the Hornpipe. In fact just you, it's like the fertile black earth and the lush green fields of Egypt that I have been reading of. The fellah hating war and loving life, like the papyrus and the lotus and all marshes with bull rushes and frogs, like the girl I heard playing Lizst's Valse Oublie. I am in love, Joe, but you are quite right, I'm in love with an idea, many ideas. In fact, no matter how violent at the actual happening, the idea or memory of a thing is always more vivid, and my whole past, instead of fading, becomes more brilliant as time passes. And when I am practicing, I am living in the future. Each movement I perform is a step toward a vision which keeps extending ahead. In fact, the whole world is now turned upside down because of memories and visions. We are living in a world of ideas which affect us physically, emotionally, and spiritually to a terrific degree, and who knows perhaps we shall some day be in a universe of ideas. Nevertheless, it is not possible to dispense with experiences, and if I do not enjoy them as much at the moment of happening as I do before or after, they are still a necessary part of life and very often revitalizing. I find that people sometimes cause me to be confused, because it is hard to be objective, and especially with someone you like, and yet if you don't lose yourself you can never find yourself, and so it's a vicious circle.

Anyway, best of luck, Joe, and my love to you,
Sybil

From this time on I was concentrating on my solo career only. I wrote my thoughts to John Martin.

23

June 24, 1941
Lyons, NY

Dear John,

First of all, please remember me to Louise, and tell her I actually made the 12 noon train the day I saw her in N.Y., but with the most hysterically funny consequences, e.g., we got to the train ahead of the porter, and Eleanor Lauer [the pianist] was running up and down inside the train, and I outside looking for him, not being able to believe that he wouldn't come, while Katy was standing splitting her sides laughing. He wasn't even a speck in the distance when the train started pulling out (he had all my costumes). But miraculously, out of nowhere, the baggage master appeared and took my name, address, etc. (he ran along the platform shouting) and said he'd send everything up, which he did.

Our demonstration concert was a success, though I think we really put on a better show on the station platform. Mary Starks from Boston and Allison Choate, my next year's partner, were there, and they were very enthusiastic.

But what I really want to tell you is that I have interesting plans for the fall. Mari Harding, an excellent pianist and a friend of mine from five years back, and I have decided to give a joint recital at Carnegie Chamber Music Hall in October, before I go on the tour through the schools. I wanted to talk to you about it when I first got the idea, but you were never in N.Y. Of course, I like the H-W Theatre better for my purposes, but they have no grand piano, and anyway it is not as good for a musician as the C.M.H. Since I will get the bulk of the reviews because I have composed my dances, I want her to have some advantages. I would like to know, though, if you will review the performance as a whole, that is mention whether you consider it a good program besides criticizing the dances.

I had a long talk with Helen Adams of the C.M.H., and she was very nice and very helpful. She went over the costs, etc., and she also advised me to try to get Fern Helscher [manager for Ted Shawn] to help me put the concert on. She said Miss Helscher was very efficient and could save me money, time and energy. I then got in touch with Miss Helscher and went over costs with her. She assured me that the whole can be done without loss but advised performing two nights, which frightened me at first a bit. However, she was so certain and so business-like that I took her advice, and now we plan to perform October 21st and 22nd.

My chief reason for wanting to give a recital at this time is to interest managers for the following season. I know from my experience last November when I tried for the school assembly service, that you have to do things a year in advance, and if I wait until the following year, 1942–43, when I feel that I will be more ready to appear as a soloist, another year will be lost without performing experience. I want very much to get around and give concerts and try things out so that I can grow as an artist and really reach people.

Working with Agnes is fun, but it by no means satisfies me, because I don't think that my dances or my ideas are suitable on her programs, not even my so-called dramatic dances, and besides, I want to stand on my own feet; I believe the old advice that you and Louise gave George and me years ago, that we would never get anywhere until we made names for ourselves, is perfectly true.

Speaking of George, his program over at Adelphi College last month was one of the best I've ever seen put on by a college group. He also has a group of students who have been out of college a year, and they work with him in New York, and they did some excellent dancing. I think it certainly speaks well for George that these girls are interested enough to continue to dance, after they are working in other fields. Also his choreographic ability is improving, and he has a great deal of enthusiasm about his work.

But back to the N.Y. debut. I feel that a joint recital is a very good idea, in fact indispensable to my performing at this time, for several reasons. One important reason being that I couldn't afford to give a recital if I had to pay a pianist to rehearse with me, and besides I like someone who feels artistically responsible for an excellent performance, someone who works with me instead of for me, as most of the music I use is quite difficult. Also I feel that two personalities are much more interesting than one for a concert manager or a booking agent, and I am terribly anxious to make a try for a tour in 1942–43. I have spoken to Columbia Concerts and even had an interview with the Great God Hurok, and both seemed to be interested. I just thought I might as well give them some advance knowledge, so that when they receive notices of the recital later, they will at least have heard of it.

I read your account of Eleanor's recital on Sunday. [Eleanor King, dancer & choreographer; formerly with Humphrey-Weidman and Theatre Dance Co.] It sounded very fine. If Mama had not been ill, I would have stayed an extra few days to see it. Katy wrote me a description of the whole last week. Her reports were good, too. I hope you will have an enjoyable summer in the country. If you ever pass this way, do stop in and see my studio. I shall be here toiling.

My best wishes to you both,
Sybil

After this description of what I planned for the future, the next three-and-a-half months were fraught with problems: I had asked my teacher, Mr. Bilstin, to compose the music for my three new dances, never dreaming that his odd theories of composition would not work for me. It seems he left most of the actual music, between suggestions, to my pianist, and as she was not a composer, rather a very capable performer, she was completely bewildered. I was shocked and worried, and took the situation in hand, as best I could, by writing Bilstin a letter for which he never forgave me. He thought I simply wanted famous names on my program, which could not have been farther from the truth. I had to have music which complemented what I wished to say, and my loyalty to him stopped before disaster.

August 22, 1941
Lyons, NY

Dear Mr. Bilstin,

Mari arrived last Sunday with your music, and we have been working together all week. However, after repeated tries and hearing the music again and again, I finally have definitely decided that it won't do. The trouble is mainly that the music does not have the quality that I intended. It simply does not *do enough* for the dances, no matter how we play it. I don't mind rearranging the dances. I would have to do that anyway. I feel rather that we should have had more time together, and since that was impossible, it is too bad we attempted it.

I have collected quite a few records over the past ten years, off and on, and when I finally made up my mind that I would have to try other music, I went through them all and found three pieces—by Ravel, Villa-Lobos and Moussorgsky— which are exactly what I meant in quality, feeling and humor. It means arranging and a lot of work, but more successful dances in the last analysis, I am convinced. We could probably argue that point for days, in fact for the rest of our lives, but I hope we won't.

Believe me, I feel very badly, and I hope you will understand. It never occurred to me that I might not be able to use the music.

I hope you keep well. I shall see you in N.Y.

Most sincerely,
Sybil

Also, I had to tell Eleanor Lauer, my first pianist, that I was going to do a Carnegie Chamber Music Hall performance with an old friend who was studying with Egon Petri at Cornell. This was hard to do, because although I had not promised Eleanor anything, I knew she would be disappointed. Mari Harding was a better pianist, and a very much more interesting personality.

Then I wrote to Hurok.

September 26, 1941
Lyons, NY

Dear Mr. Hurok,

Last spring, I had the pleasure of an interview with you, and we discussed the possibility of my giving a debut recital under your management. Since I am a dancer you felt it necessary for me to make my debut at the Guild Theatre. The figures you quoted, however, were beyond my budget, so I have decided rather to have the Carnegie Chamber Music Hall, which has been remodeled especially for dancers.

Although I do not have the money for a big spectacular debut, I assure you that I have the talent and something definitely good to offer the public at large as audience and you as manager. And I can say the same for my collaborator, Miss

Mari Harding who is a fine and moving pianist. Please let me know how many tickets you would like and on which evening. I look forward to your presence in the audience.

Most sincerely,
Sybil Shearer

Hurok did not answer, so I sent tickets. He returned them.

But the final blow came later, nearer the concert, in fact almost too near. Fern Helscher found she was too busy to handle my debut personally, so she turned me over to her assistant. The circulars, the stamps, the mailing list were delivered to her. (Agnes gave me her list and it consisted of every name worth having in New York. I only realized this years later after my career was over and I was burning the whole card file. Every name was a personality.)

Then I found that none of my friends knew about this event. No one had received notices. I began calling. It was a blank. I called the assistant. Everything seemed fine, but nothing had happened.

I called John Martin. I had not communicated with him since June. He had received no recent official notice and no press tickets. I called Walter Terry, of the Tribune—same. I began to be frantic, and finally ended up calling everyone I knew.

Then something interesting happened. I was sitting at a drugstore counter after a rehearsal, wondering how I had ever gotten myself into such a pickle. As I turned around and slipped off the stool, there was a rack of paperback books, and my eye fell on the *New Testament*. I thought if I ever needed this, it is now. I took it off the shelf. It opened, seemingly by itself, to Matthew, chapter 7, verse 7: "Ask and it shall be given you; seek, and ye shall find; knock, and it shall be opened unto you."

It was an absolute revelation! And it worked. I was assured that it would work in verse 8: "For every one that asketh receiveth; and he that seeketh findeth; and to him that knocketh it shall be opened." Although I always knew I was being mysteriously helped, this time I consciously asked and the first night was filled with interested people! Agnes de Mille rushed backstage and said, "Did you hear that huge guffaw during *In A Vacuum*? That was the *Herald Tribune*!" And I was certainly pleased to receive a note from Ruth St. Denis, whom I had not met, but about whom I had heard so much. (See Addendum X.)

And the second night was filled with those who had read the reviews of the two outstanding critics of the day: John Martin of the *New York Times* and Walter Terry of the *New York Herald Tribune*. This was the big event and the real turning point in my career. I became an acknowledged soloist, no longer a follower. (See Addenda XI (a), (b), (c), (d).)

The negative, which turned out to be this really astonishing positive, was that the assistant manager was on drugs and quite unconscious of what she was doing, although she did appear at the performance. Taking one look at her at the reception, I realized that there was something wrong physically, but I did not know what it was until I saw someone else in the same condition years later.

Armed with these wonderful reviews, I went on the twenty-week tour of schools with Allison Choate and met again Edward J. Sparling, president of Roosevelt College in Chicago. He had offered me a position when on tour with Agnes, but until I made my solo debut, I could not think of leaving New York. Here was the offer again.

January 18, 1942
Lyons, NY

Dear Mr. Sparling,

Since talking with you in December, I have done a great deal of serious thinking about the future.

In the first place, I have been considering the gigantic problem of trying to teach the dance to people who consider it either a luxury or a passing fancy but certainly not in any way a necessity of life. My natural place up to now has been in the theatre as a performer, because there is the place that will pay for my talents. And into the theatre I would most probably have gone if I had not been a rather mad idealist.

Now, however, since the declaration of war, the natural place for me is the idealist one. Suddenly, the dance and its basic principles of body movement have become a life necessity for everyone. We must have strong, vigorous bodies in order to resist death and destruction. We must use action in order not to be destroyed by our enemies. Of course, this has always been true, but only now will people feel the pinch of immediateness. And I hope they will turn, consciously or unconsciously, to the dance as the primitive expression for power that it really is. If this is the case, the dance then becomes a functional art and no longer a luxury.

This new situation is important to me, because it makes it possible for me to face the problem of teaching the untalented pupils who ordinarily are as appalling to me as the idea of lifting a leg is appalling to them. Now, even though they move in anguish instead of in joy, it will be a blessing because they will at least know that they are alive. The talented that you dream of will really be able to get something from me. I know that, but how long will I have to wait before they come?

And have you talked to your board about a guarantee for me? I am most anxious to hear about this, because I would like to come to Chicago, and feel that I can make a success of a school. However, I would have to give many demonstrations, and also it would be very wise for me to make a Chicago debut as a concert dancer, either in the late fall or in January.

Dean Smith, with whom I talked at your suggestion, felt as I do that it would be essential to continue as a concert dancer, and even to use that as publicity for the school. Before leaving

Chicago I spoke to Walter Larson of the National Concert Bureau on South Michigan. At first he was not at all interested in dancers, but after saying that he could only give me ten minutes of his time, and eventually giving me two hours and the admission that he did not have a closed mind on the subject, I asked him to see my work, and we arranged for an audition. He was definitely interested and impressed by the press notices that I showed him, and I think he liked my dances but would probably not book me until he saw a performance.

So, my teaching would be based on the desire for and the method of abstracting creative movement from natural movement with emphasis on a knowledge of natural movement as the only possible point of departure for creation.

Under separate cover, I am sending you some literature of my former activities.

Sincerely yours,
Sybil Shearer

During the winter break, I also wrote to Hurok.

January 23, 1942
Lyons, NY

Dear Mr. Hurok,

Last spring I had an interview with you when you told me that you were interested in young American dancers and said you would come to my concert. Much to my dismay you returned the tickets I sent you and, consequently, since I am on tour this whole year building an audience through educational programs in schools and clubs, and will not be able to give another concert this season, you won't be able to see my work. I am disappointed because I had hoped you would be interested in me. The next best thing to do is send my reviews, and here they are. Please note especially the one where I am compared to the ballet.

I shall be in and out of N.Y. on weekends through February and March, and in case you wish to get in touch with me, any letters will be forwarded from the above address. Congratulations on your success with Amaya.

Most sincerely,
Sybil L. Shearer

He sent me congratulations too, and a number of years later, on two separate occasions, he made me offers. But by that time I was no longer interested in being managed or going on long traditional tours.

Then on Sunday morning, June 14, 1942, when I was at home in Lyons the phone rang. Papa answered, "Oh, is that so. Well, thank you very much." He turned to me and said, "The station master says your name is in the paper—*The New York Times*." I leapt to my feet, but he had already picked up his hat on the way to the door. "I'll get it."

Papa brought home three papers, but we did not know till later that actually he had bought every paper in Lyons. Mama was indeed upset when she found that no one knew about this important event, because no one else in town had a chance to read it.

But I didn't care. My heart thumped wildly—the year's Dance Award by John Martin—"to her unhesitatingly the laurels"—in the same article with Antony Tudor! (See Addendum XII.)

On the strength of this, and probably also because of Walter Terry's articles, I was invited to do my solos in August on a program with young dancers called "Stars of Tomorrow." This was at Ted Shawn's summer theatre, Jacob's Pillow.

I informed Mr. Shawn that my dances had to be done in sequence, because I composed them to follow one another. He paid no attention to instructions, and made a program to suit himself, mixing us all up, because he did not like spaces between numbers for costume changes.

My dresser was so nervous, because "Mr. Shawn doesn't like waits," that she fumbled and didn't get me properly hooked, so in my first leap onto the stage, my skirt fell off and the curtain man was so shocked that he pulled the curtain closed on my second leap.

Well, I went back to the dressing room, took my time, returned well anchored, and the audience clapped as I landed from that first leap.

Later in the program, I did *In A Vacuum*. The applause afterwards called me back on stage again and again. So I kept bowing. Then someone called out, "Encore!" There was silence. Stunned, I shook my head and said, "I don't want to." Everybody laughed. But I was *serious*. It did not make sense to me to repeat a dance. More would be less. But it seemed Shawn always did encores.

I was pleased, of course, that they wanted to see it again, and I hoped they would some other time—in some other place. This place was not for me. Later, in my solo programs, I never took bows between dances. Nevertheless I remained on good terms with Shawn though I never accepted to dance there again. (See Addendum XIII.)

While I was at the Pillow, Margaret D'Houbler arrived. She was guest teaching. I was about to teach in Chicago and remembered how inspiring I thought she was several seasons back, so I watched her classes. She was a great teacher. This was her performance, and she was terrific. When I returned home, I wrote to her.

August 19, 1942
Lyons, NY

Dear Miss D'Houbler,

The longer that circumstances make me put off writing to you, the more material piles up until I feel as though it would be an imposition to ask you to sit down and read all I want to say. I don't know when I have ever been drawn to a person so vitally and in such a short time as I have been to you. And I am so happy that I shall be near enough to see you sometime during the winter.

My pupils are here for a two-week intensive course, and really I am wearing myself down to a rag, because I want so much to give them things and I can't seem to accomplish enough. The way I felt about you when you were teaching was that somehow you were fulfilled by it, whereas I seemed to be drained. However, I have no pianist, and I do think that it makes a great deal of difference not to have music. It is as though I were an illegitimate mother having to take care of my brood all by myself. Whereas a pianist would round out the picture, so that we would be one happy family.

In choreography, I am working from two different angles—rhythms as organic wholes, and emotional situations as organic wholes, and have gotten some very nice results from both. The girls seem to be enthusiastic. Only, I hope there will be a good pianist in Chicago.

Actually I wish I could study with you a year before teaching. I certainly wish I could.

My love to you and do have a very fine vacation.

Sybil

Dear Miss D'Houbler,

No doubt you will be surprised to hear from me again so soon, but I just had to tell you about the marvelous discoveries that I've made this week. I have gone so far as to be actually jealous of myself. That is, I find it so much easier to teach choreography than to do it. In the six days that I have been teaching, I have hit on at least one, often two, new ways of creating each day, and I amaze myself in that very few of these were actually thought out in advance. Ideas seem to come out of nowhere, and I find I can vary a theme or develop a design of one of my pupils for illustrative purposes in a split second, almost without thinking. And the pupils have turned some interesting things out of all this, too.

There is Anne, for instance, a mad helter-skelter girl with long thick straight tresses always falling in front of her face as she dances, but as she usually closes her eyes anyway (she is short-sighted) it doesn't seem to bother her. Her body is soft but not light, and she seems to splash through space. She is slightly deaf, and if you do not push her before you begin to speak—unless of course, she is already looking at you—she just goes on dancing, throwing her body about without hearing a word. But behind all this madness are a brain and a group of very active and sensitive emotional reflexes. All I have to say is "fear" or "timidity" or "joy" and the most expressive movements burst forth from her. No one but a dancer would recognize them, however, because there is so much extraneous matter which would, to an ordinary onlooker, present a combination of mouse, sofa cushion, and wet spaghetti all tossed about simultaneously and in counterpoint by a strong wind. But to me she is one of the most exciting choreographic experiences I've had, and without any effort I can surmise her intention and weed it out in a second, so that she screams with delight—"Yes, that's what I mean, exactly," and we are all delighted. She would be a tremendous boon to a choreographer—whether she could ever actually pull herself together to be one, I don't know. But before this week, neither of us ever knew that she was creative at all, and I've known her for five or six years in and out of the H-W studio.

Carolyn is a beautiful animal and moves in solid blocks—strong and muscular, yet not on tonic chords, rather in diminished or augmented intervals. And she hits into space with intensity. Jane is a ballet dancer, soft and beautiful, pale and ethereal. She makes long lines with her arms and legs and thinks of herself as a person in a vacuum, so that when she tries to compose it is always an arm against a leg or an arm against an arm, in opposition or unison. Finally, creating becomes impossible to her, because it was so mechanical. Then I told her to think that she was in space, and that in order to go anywhere or do anything, she must go through space so that she could cut it or push it or kick it or melt into it, but she must no longer think of herself as alone. None of us are alone. We are with space and unless we love it, it is impossible to really dance. She was surprised and so was I. I had honestly never thought of it that way before.

So we do learn by teaching. I must take it all back about being drained.

Very best,
Sybil

In the fall of 1942, I moved to Chicago where a whole new life awaited me. Suddenly I was in a different atmosphere, an atmosphere of infinite possibilities. The light in New York had been brilliant, reflected off the cold hard streets—the rock below and the buildings above, which cast sharp shadows against the cool sun. Even blinded for a day by rain it shone back the next day as brilliantly cool as ever. There was no fog or mist in the city, and the country was distant and difficult to achieve.

So a new wind blew in my face as I stepped onto the plains where the sky begins with the earth. A mysterious mist rose from the landscape as Chicago seeped into the country and blended with it. This was not just a move from one city to another. It was a move from one world to the next.

At the age of thirty I found myself in a magical place—long vistas, groves of oaks in savannas and forests preserved by Jens Jensen, the great landscape architect. I became aware of the rising and setting sun, and the rising and setting of the changing moons. This was the Midwest, the place that the philosopher Alfred North Whitehead had said was the seedbed of creativity out of which so many artists had come. The stage was set. Everything called for me to create in a new way.

But every artist has to have a helper. Louis Horst had once said to Katy and me as we stood there in costume for one of Agnes's ballets, "You two will never amount to anything—you have no Louis Horst!" I drew myself up and looked at him rather defiantly, smiled and said, "How do you know I have no Louis Horst?" Well, this was something that flashed to me from the future. I was positive I would be taken care of. And I was. I met my "Louis Horst" within a month of coming to the Windy City. After a lecture demonstration for the Dance Council of Chicago, I was introduced to Helen Balfour Morrison, the portrait photographer. Her remark was, "Well, the sample was good. When are we going to see the real thing?"

Addendum I
"My Hanya Holm"
Ballet Review 21:4. Winter 1993, pages 4–7.

Hanya Holm stood high in my thoughts about modern dance and its meaning in the arts, right from the beginning of my career, although I never studied with her, except for a week the first year of the Bennington College Summer School of the Dance, and one private lesson she gave me in lieu of flowers after a concert much later. That first summer at Bennington I wrote many letters to friends, and the following are some excerpts about Hanya.

I must tell you about Hanya! She sends you her love. That sounds as though we were well acquainted but really I have only spoken to her three times. I reminded her of the introduction last February, which she remembered after 'walking back' in her thoughts. Then I spoke to her after receiving your letter. Tonight she was sitting on a bench in front of the Commons with a woman she knows. I sauntered out, and after me came several others. A conversation began and we had a really jolly time. I started on dancing and other things came up quite nicely. . . .

Everyone feels filled with joy near Hanya, her classes are just bubbling with fun. We leap or run or skip or wiggle across the floor with the pure delight of cutting space. She herself is the most attractive person I have ever seen. Her skin is tan, her hair yellow, and her legs marvelous although she wears a long, circular skirt to cover them. Her eyes twinkle and she makes faces at everyone who misses a step. She sings to the music in her soft, high voice 'up—down—right—left' as we go through the exercises. . . .

You asked if I was convinced of the virtues of the modern dance. I can frankly say—not until yesterday. The Wigman technique is so satisfying because it has a reason for every movement and believes in the possibility of every movement, so that as Hanya said this evening you can go for years and never repeat yourself. . . .

It is a day later and I have not had time to send this letter. I want to add the things that happened today. Of course, Hanya's class was marvelous, but tonight was even better because there was an open discussion on dancing. Hanya insisted on sitting outdoors on the grass which was a much better idea, and so we went to the quadrangle at the barn and talked for about an hour and a half. There I learned (I am almost sure) that it is the Wigman technique that I want. Hanya spoke in terms positively exciting about dancing being a constant discovery. Of course, all of life is, but it seems so new to me in terms of dancing.

To another person I wrote:

Hanya Holm was at Bennington for a week. She was simply perfect!—both as a person and as a dancer. I was just swept off my feet in admiration along with the entire school. One morning two girls and myself determined to ask her to go for a walk with us or have a picnic lunch somewhere. We arrived in the living room just outside her apartment at nine in the morning. She was not up, so we waited talking and laughing until ten, when Hanya's assistant, Nancy McKnight, arrived on the scene to ask her about breakfast. Coffee was desired, so the three of us made some in the kitchenette, found some fruit which we sliced and served the great Hanya in state. She was perfectly darling to us and drank the coffee appreciatively though she volunteered that it was a little stale; she winked when she said it.

When the coffee was gone she talked to us and told us the most delightful story about the way she found an island off the coast of France that she had made up her mind to go to after putting her finger on it on the map when she was blindfolded. She acted out the complete story in her delightful, slightly broken, but very literary English. By literary I do not mean it was correct but that it was beautiful because of her splendid choice of words and vivid similes.

She told us of going out in a fishing smack on an 'unluckily stormy day' and of her tremendous seasickness. Unfortunately she had sat on a barrel of bait which she described as being 'mackerel which were mashed to soup, all the fish being completely disturbed.' Her story was so convincing and so interesting that two hours passed before we knew it, so we felt that we had monopolized her long enough. She was so perfectly darling that we all felt very adolescent, but quite smug at the same time for having put one over on the rest of the college who would have given anything to have thought of it first. . . . The latest development is that I am going to apply for a scholarship at the Wigman School and take a chance on the future. In order to get one you have to dance before a committee and present a composition of your own. It sounds rather scary. . . .

Well the Bennington episode is over and as far as I am concerned it was a great success. Perhaps you will be surprised to hear that my whole attitude toward life has changed during the summer at Bennington. Everything seems to be much more worthwhile now than it was at school, and I have developed a profound respect for the modern movement in every art, especially dancing. . . . Yesterday I received a letter from the Wigman School answering my inquiry about tryouts. It was a short little note asking me to call at the studio any day this week, so I wrote back frantically that I was 300 miles away from New York! I am now waiting results. . . .

Since arriving in New York on Thursday morning life has been one continuous upset. In the first place I must tell you that as far as I know now the Wigman School and scholarship is out. I am quite disappointed. The explanation follows: Miss Forchemer, the secretary, talked of the dance in high flung phrases. I understood her, but my parents thought it was a farce because everything she said she announced immediately afterwards was as yet unsettled. Then she said that the course was for three years, and everyone trying for the scholarship would be expected to sign a petition saying she would stay the full time. I like what she said, and would gladly work and dance and create for three years, but I cannot for both Mama and Papa say that it will be impossible to support me for that length of time without any prospect of earning money ever. That is true, I probably would not have any money, but I really do not care for it. . . .

Then later:

I'm beginning to wish I had tried out anyway just to have Hanya once more. Of course, I do not know whether I could have won the scholarship. A friend of mine who tried said it was much worse than she had expected, and the other people who tried were marvelous dancers, some of them already concert dancers! ...I am thoroughly convinced that I should take some work with Hanya for I feel that the Wigman technique is the only actually individual technique, and many of the girls I have met who are studying feel the same. . . .

But it wasn't to be. My parents enrolled me at the Academy of Allied Arts, and the only money available belonged to them. This was a wise move financially on my parents' part, since the Germans are very thorough, and I received a quickie education and was teaching and *almost* earning a living within a year with the Humphrey-Weidmans, who were only interested in dancers for their company. They used dance studies, which I memorized, to train people to do their choreography. So I was forced to find for myself what Hanya talked about: "Dance is a constant discovery," and "You can go years and never repeat yourself." These were the themes of my career as a dancer and choreographer, which stimulated my imagination and kept me searching in the art of movement. I owe much to that first summer at Bennington, with its overview of opinions and techniques.

Later, after I had made my debut as a soloist and moved to Chicago, I again made contact with Hanya through Helen Morrison who had photographed her earlier. This began a series of meetings in New York and Chicago, which Hanya had to pass through to go to Colorado Springs for her summer teaching. It was the train in those days, and she would break the trip and stay over. Once we invited a large group of people for supper and she talked afterwards from the porch about the dance while we sat on the lawn. Hanya was always a charmer with her accent and her creative use of the English language.

On one of these trips during the war (World War II), when all Germans were suspect and sabotage was a household word, Hanya found that the conductor had not given back her return trip ticket, and she was frantic because he had left the train. Bob Morrison, who was a pepper pot, took the case in hand. There was some talk of searching Hanya, at which point she remembered a Pullman towel which she had "borrowed" to be "returned later." She whispered to me her predicament, and since she knew exactly where it was (she was very organized) I shielded her while she whipped it out and stuffed it under my sweater. We were ready for the search. But it was not necessary. The ticket was found on the conductor, and the towel was not found on me. Hanya, chastened, mailed it back "anonymously" to the company.

Although Bob used to claim that he was all 'dancer-ed' out (most of the talk around here was about this strenuous art) he never felt that way about Hanya, and when he went to New York on business trips he would always take her to dinner and the theater with clients or alone, and they would have jolly times. They were great friends. When I visited her at age 98 she wanted all the news about Bob.

As things usually go full circle, I was able, in a round about way, to pay back Hanya on a material level at the end of her life what she had given me in inspiration at the beginning of my career. It happened like this. On one of my trips to New York to give a solo concert, Annabelle Lyon came to see me at the Plaza Hotel. I had known Annabelle since early Ballet Theatre days when we did *Three Virgins and a Devil* with Agnes de Mille, and later in Chicago, and now she was doing a bit part in a musical with Agnes because she was recuperating from a foot operation. During the conversation, she said with a sigh, "I don't know what is the matter. I used to love dancing, but I don't seem to like it any more." Thinking of all the limitations that always seem to me to exist in the ballet where she had been brought up, I replied, "Annabelle, maybe you have never really danced. Why don't you study with Hanya?"

She did. They became great friends. She came under the spell of this wonderful free movement and Hanya's enthusiasm for it. She told everyone in the show, encouraged them to come and try. They did. They told others, in other shows. Word spread, and in two years 250 dancers from Broadway were pouring through the doors of the Hanya Holm Studio. Then came the cry, "Hanya, why don't you do a show?" "Ach, no, I have my school, I have my company." But her son Klaus wanted to go to Yale Drama School. That took money. So Hanya finally decided to accept an offer, and a new career began.

She was a huge success on Broadway because she understood the requirements. She did not mix it up with the concert stage. She planned in advance. She was positive and strong, but not temperamental. She had stamina and real love for the job, the dancers, and everyone concerned. But she would not give up teaching; that for her was the seedbed of the future. As far as her concert work was concerned, *Trend* was one of the greatest works I ever saw. Her use of levels of space in movement was not only masterful in conception and execution, but it was emotionally compelling on a grand scale as well. So Hanya was able to make money and save money and live well up to almost 100 years, with round-the-clock help when she needed it.

Actually, I heard from John Martin when he was 90 that Hanya was five years older than he, but had taken that five off her age some time ago, and didn't feel she could put it back with any grace in her nineties, when it would have been so useful. There it is: the records will say almost 100; the actuality may be almost 105. So the two little white lies in Hanya's life, the Pullman towel and the lost five years, have been revealed to prove my mother's maxim: "Be sure your sins will find you out." But the real truth of Hanya's life expressed itself in the joy of waggling her finger at me in our last meeting and the strength in her eyes when she said, "It is will power!"

Addendum II
"A Salute to Agnes de Mille"
Ballet Review 22:4. Winter 1994, pages 10–12.

Agnes had an acerbic wit and a telling humor. This was her weapon against solid block followers of other persuasions. She was a loner, not associated with any group, but using everything that came her way. And because she was observing and quick, she also saw her own limitations and voiced them, giving those who feared her tongue, or envied her success, a handle on their own weapons with which to fight back.

Nevertheless, she did not stint in praise when someone touched her heart or her head, and she was loyal to friends and co-workers over the years.

That first year in New York when I was studying dance with Doris Humphrey and Charles Weidman and drama with Maria Ouspenskaya, I went to the Guild Theatre every Sunday evening, sat in the last row in the balcony, and watched what the dance world had to offer. There were other places where dance was shown, and I went there too. Much of it was bleak, but I wanted to know everything.

One Sunday night in February at the Guild it was Agnes de Mille. She was entirely different from everyone else. She had variety in her dances, she could act, had costumes of all sorts. She had a sense of humor and wit, fun and pathos. I loved her. I wrote her a letter. She wrote back! I wrote again, and asked if I might call on her.

Before she could answer, I was thrilled to see her walking out after a dance performance at Columbia with two people, one of whom was my singing teacher, Miss Marion Rich.

I was sure it was Agnes de Mille, and I followed them to the subway and sat opposite. They were in animated conversation. The seat next to Miss Rich was vacated, and I slipped into it, and whispered loudly, "Is that Agnes de Mille next to you?" She nodded and I said, "Will you introduce me?" She did, and Miss de Mille said, "Oh, you are the girl from the Three Arts Club who wrote to me." I nodded enthusiastically, and she said, "Will you have lunch with me on Tuesday?" Almost fainting with joy, in my mind I said how can I, I have rehearsal with Miss Humphrey, and we are not allowed to miss. But out loud I said, "I would love to." And it was arranged.

I wrote to a friend—if you have never seen her you will be anxious to hear what her appearance is. She is small and dainty with light complexion and curly hair, a darling smile with rather crooked teeth, which is disarming because when she is not smiling she looks rather stern, but when she is, she looks not a day over 12. Her clothes are quite dolly and she wears bonnets, but it suits her perfectly.

That was the beginning of a friendship and a correspondence, documented elsewhere, which lasted, up and down and in and out, through the years.

Agnes was passionate about wrongs, and blew them up to enormous proportions to the point where we would call her "Agonies" de Mille. But she spoke up against the wrongs of the union system in the theatre, stagehands in particular, when no one else would mention it—not that she was able to do anything about it. But if more people had backed her up, something might have happened. As it is, there is constant talk about the financial plight of the dancer. Committees, panels have been formed to discuss this, completely avoiding mention of the biggest financial hurdle. Agnes dared to speak about the unions openly from the platform, not once, but every chance she got. And she was right. I went through it with the Schuberts in New York and Carnegie Hall, and in every theatre in Chicago, including the Arie Crown and Ravinia. That is where the money went, and on top of that, one had to put up with absolute incompetence. In my solo concerts, I had to run around between numbers and check gel changes, so often wrong through sloppy thinking and a don't-care attitude. If you wanted it right you had to have your own crew and pay double for the stand-ins who went with the theatre.

My best years were spent bypassing the unions in becoming artist-in-residence at a college in Evanston, Illinois, where I had stagehands that were creative people who loved the theatre. They became our friends and part of the team.

One time when Agnes was in Chicago rehearsing an opening with Ballet Theatre she called and asked me to come down for dinner. I said, "I can't. Why don't you come out here?" She said, "Way out there?" But she decided to come, and when she saw my studio and my theatre, after having thought for years that I had simply been out in the country 'smelling the daisies,' she said, "Why don't I have a place like this?" Then she, too, became artist-in-residence at a college in North Carolina.

From a movement point of view Agnes was not a creator. She was a researcher, a student of different styles. The ballet, ballroom, folk, tap and court dance were forms of dance in the public domain. But what was disturbing to choreographers and dancers who developed their own personal styles was that Agnes was consciously and unconsciously predatory. The movement was not copyrighted, and it appealed to her, or was useful at a certain time or place. No one thought anything of all the dancers who borrowed heavily from Martha Graham. But they were followers, so it was all right. Agnes was not a follower, and this upset everyone.

In fact Agnes was always controversial. When she wrote *The Book of the Dance* she was bitterly accused of leaving certain people out. Her reply was, "This is *my* book. It is not a scholarly listing of everyone who has ever danced. These are the people who interested *me*," which, of course, made perfect sense. In actuality her creativity was centered in language, out of which developed visual form on the stage and in books.

So she was an excellent director, because she could express herself so picturesquely in words. She would pique the imagination of the performer. Agnes and I worked together choreographically like Gilbert and Sullivan. She would say something interesting and I would say, "Like this?" and do a movement which her words suggested. She would say, "Yes, exactly." Then she would gradually build up the dramatic form out of my movement. This would have been an ideal situation if I had been willing to go on and we had become a team. But I had other ideas, many things I wanted to say through movement, and my work with Agnes, although I loved it, was simply in passing. But we were the best of friends and would often stop to talk over tea. It was much more fun working with Agnes than with Doris and Charles because I too was creating, and I admired her attention to detail of expression and meaning as well as her interesting conversation.

Agnes was enormously surprised when I stepped out on my own, as she related in her first book. But she was generous. She did not try to hold me back. Later she told Helen Morrison in my presence, "Don't think I don't know where I leave off and Sybil begins." She evidently thought creating the movement was more important than arranging it.

If she had accepted the offer of the Guild Theatre to establish a company of her own within their ranks, I might have stayed with her, because she had a wonderful sense of theatre, and I could see great creative possibilities because I was interested in theatre, too.

But it was inevitable that we would part. The difference between us was that Agnes was interested in making money (after all her background was the commercial theatre), and I was not. Art was the only thing that interested me. As far back as that first luncheon in her mother's apartment on Park Avenue I was amazed to hear her say that she was "starving." My idea was that the artist pays back for the privilege of being an artist by sacrificing. But I loved her anyway; she was so passionate about everything.

So later I did not believe it when she said, "You can make money in the commercial theatre, and then you will be able to do what you like." I feel I was right, because when Agnes got her own company, she could not rise above the habits she had developed in her Broadway shows, whereas her first solos and her first ballet, *Rodeo,* were masterpieces. She did a tremendous amount for Broadway and for all the dancers who wanted to earn a living dancing. But Broadway only gave her fame, not even fortune.

For all our differences and disagreements I value tremendously the warmth of our friendship and our experiences together. Her words to me on our last visit, May 1993, were, "I am interested in love." This meant to me that through this life she had grown. Agnes de Mille had great personal courage.

Addendum III

Today, in choreography (1995), connecting forms have almost disappeared. It is one body against another, or several bodies grouped with running or walking in between designs. This method of choreography almost erases dance, and the meaningful qualities of movement. Now most choreography remains in the mind as shapes rather than action. 'Dance' has become more strenuous physically, and more barren choreographically. The skilled performer, with nothing to say except "look at me," dominates the scene. And there is very little difference between choreographers. The style is a general style as the performers slip from one dance company into another. This describes the modern dance.

In the ballet world the flow of movement is more evident, for example, in the choreography of Kudelka's *Cruel World*, which bodes some hope for the future.

When I go to the theatre I look for three things. What I hope to see is innate wisdom, inspired movement, and form that has content worth thinking about. So, after a lifetime of working in and looking at dance, it is my view that the *artist* is the one who has to train the "world's people," not the other way around. We have to have guides, even though we choose to ignore them. Hopefully, each generation will see further through these guides. Anyone who stands at the podium or the pulpit or on the stage has to be a leader with a goal, has to be willing to take the responsibility for his or her acts and thoughts. And the listeners and followers should be conscious of the message.

Addendum IV
"John Martin: A Tribute by Sybil Shearer"
Ballet Review 16:1. Spring 1988, pages 49–52.

Fifty years ago and for many years after that, John Martin was a very important part of our community. Without a voice, our American modern dance would never have been heard of; and his was a strong voice. He said he believed that art was compensation; but "Is it art?" was what interested him. He told me that he always went to the theater in a state of expectancy and excitement, and as he sat there waiting for the curtain to rise, this feeling dominated his senses. He based his evaluation of the performance on whether this feeling continued and grew or diminished after the curtain rose and why.

I have always been grateful to John for recognizing me as an unusual talent, not a follower. I could so easily have been crushed by a less imaginative critic. So we remained friends through the years, and right up through his ninety-first year our phone conversations, full of wit and humor and creativity of thought, were a delight to me, and I hope to him. I shall miss John Martin.

He and I spoke the same language, and that language was movement. When I use the word "movement," I mean the stuff of which dance is made—all of it, from complete tension to complete relaxation and all the universal qualities in between: sustained, swaying, suspended, swinging, bouncing, staccato, jerky, vibrating, pulsing, and shaking, plus all the specific variations in the animal world, the plant world, the mechanical world, and the human world with all its subtle and involuntary emotional gestures as well as physical techniques, and finally the flow into and out of the special depths of the universe with the trillions of shapes these qualities can assume in the process of becoming a whole, moving form. Everyone is moving if they are alive, so since dance is heightened or elevated movement, those who dance and create dances are free to use anything or everything in their chosen medium—and they do, from the wild flailings of a Lar Lubovitch to the static punctuation of a Merce Cunningham. The dancer's preparation, however, must deal with this teeming medium not just physically, but mentally and intuitively as well.

John followed my designs and body gestures and understood, although he did not interpret, because that was impossible. Words could only give the general direction. His talk about dance was to some degree mysterious to me, just as my dancing was to some degree mysterious to him. This was our attraction to each other. But because I was an actress as well as a dancer, and he had been in the theater first, he understood subtleties of meaning through movement, even when they were abstracted beyond verbal identification. In the end, the clutter of dancers and choreography upon the scene, both emotional and mechanical, repelled him to the point where only the abstract purity of an aesthete like Balanchine was bearable. But he said to me at one time, "Balanchine is an aesthete. You are more than that."

At first choreography was the only thing he looked for in criticizing a performance—a new work by Graham, a new work by Humphrey or Holm or, as time went on, by dozens of others. Even when Ballet Theatre opened, it was the works and the marvelous array of diverse creations that attracted him. In the second year of Ballet Theatre, when dancers began to emerge and different dancers would do the same role, he completely ignored the individual performers. I was backstage a great deal; because Agnes de Mille and I were rehearsing *Three Virgins and a Devil*, I became aware of the dancers' plight—all that work and effort and artistry going unrecognized by the *Times*. And so I went to John and asked him why he never mentioned the individual performers. After that, he did.

But his real appreciation of the individual performer was when the dancer was also the creator of the movement. This he understood as language, lyric poetry transformed into movement—strange gestures, unexpected twists and turns suggesting but not illustrating inner meanings.

I have always felt that, ideally speaking, the critic should be the ideal audience—"ideally" meaning that the critic must be responsive to the language of movement and "ideal audience" because he or she is always there following the development of the dancer and the creation, making continuity on both sides of the footlights. So many times general audiences base their judgment on one performance only, whereas the professional audience, the critic, sees the whole process and the artist, as a complete entity.

I had many wonderful reviews, but John Martin was my barometer, because he was my "ideal audience." He was always there approving or disapproving. He saw all my solo work. Through him I felt myself to be a part of the dance community, because he saw everyone else, too.

When I decided to work permanently in Chicago, I left New York. At first he was angry with me. When I returned for a recital, he wrote, "She came from Chicago for a one-hour program which was provocative, engrossing and infuriating—but it cannot be gainsaid that she has a touch of genius." He said to me, "You should get back here and rub elbows with the rest of us." But after he had been to Chicago and seen the results of some of my company choreography that I never took to New York, he said, "Remember this one thing, young lady, you are living just this side of heaven and we are living just this side of hell."

In Chicago, during the intermission of an evening-long work called *Wherever the Web and the Tendril*, John turned to the person next to him (she happened to be one of my dancers) and said, "I'm leaving—anything this good can't possibly continue." She begged him to stay, and afterwards he said to me, "I'm coming back. I'm going to spend a week. I'll just be a little mouse in the corner. You'll never notice me. I want to know what makes you tick."

He expected the outcome of the visit would be a magazine article. I was quite terrified at the beginning, because I had no formula, no theory; and he was no mouse in the corner. He was fascinated by the "creative process," as he called it, so I just let it flow. The results of each rehearsal, each creative session, were what he enjoyed, and he finally settled for "Nature Mystic." But after the week was up he claimed to be as mystified as ever, and there was not enough material for an article. However, it was a memorable week for me, and we didn't like each other any less for all our discussions and differences of opinion.

My first encounter with John Martin was at Bennington. He was, of course, a revered figure around the campus, but a distant one. It was my third summer, and I had graduated from being a beginner the first year, to being a Humphrey-Weidman company member the second, to being a faculty member the third, but I was still full of awe and wonder at my good fortune.

One evening after dinner I walked out of the Commons building, and as I glanced at the deck chairs on the terrace, I saw John sitting all by himself, not a soul around. I was flooded by a great excitement and, after a moment's hesitation, headed for the chair next to him. He turned to look at me as I sat down, and we nodded to each other and then sat there looking over the Green Mountains together in silence. I had a terrible urge to say something, so I turned to him and said, "How would you like to go to the secret garden?" His answer, after a quick look, was, "I don't believe in secret gardens." At that moment a wave of people came out of the Commons building from the dining room, and we were saved any further conversation.

My next encounter was a few days later in the dining room. I was sitting at lunch at a large round table with six or seven others. I think Doris and Charles were there, but I only really remember vividly John Martin, because suddenly he announced to the table, "Well, I saw Sybil talking to the trees again today." I suppose I flushed, but I was just a little indignant when I replied, "Mister Martin, you are mistaken. I was simply testing the rebound of various branches." Contact had been made, and he seemed interested in everything I had to say after that, especially if it differed from his own opinion.

Then I met John's wife, Louise Martin, who was a very dear person, and we became good friends. George Bockman and I were interested in improving not only our performance but that of other members in the company. We felt we needed acting, and because our leaders—Doris and Charles—seemed to be interested only in choreography, we felt we could help if we learned to be better performers by ourselves.

Louise had been an actress and had studied the Stanislavsky technique. I had also studied with Maria Ouspenskaya of the Moscow Art Theater. The Martins, however, did not approve of the Russian method for Americans, and Louise had theories of her own. George and I gathered a group together to study with Louise, and as the experiment progressed, she became interested not only in the performance, but in the progression from performance, which she said should be "organic," to "organic form" itself. No doubt she and John discussed this a great deal, and we began to make compositions out of dramatic studies. Before anything really developed, however, most of the dancers became impatient. They wanted faster results. We had formed the Theatre Dance Company, and the dancers wanted to get on the stage with their own works. Their chief concern, it seemed to me, was raising money to make this possible. So we hung on for a while longer with depleted numbers and then disbanded our studies.

Later, when I had returned from Chicago to New York for a performance, Louise said to me, "When we stopped we had never reached the work of art. There was a big gap from the study to the finished product, but now you have done it. John and I wonder how you did it and what happened in the meantime." Well, I didn't know. I couldn't tell her. That is one of the mysteries. When the urgency comes, it rides over everything and expresses itself whole. As I see it now theories and studies in depth are a part of postulancy. I think this is necessary, and I am grateful for every bit of information and experience I was given because the seed has to be real in order for the plant to emerge.

In the meantime, I had made my debut at Carnegie Chamber Music Hall, and John Martin not only had approved, he named me the most promising debutante of the season. I was very happy. At the time I didn't think of it, but as I look back, I suppose some people thought John Martin gave me good reviews because we were friends. I know, however, that we would never have been friends if I had not been an artist. Our relationship was always controversial. I learned from him and he learned from me, just as he did from all the other dancers and choreographers, as well as from such writers as Louis Horst and Lincoln Kirstein.

John took me seriously, but our seriousness often had a humorous twist. One time after a performance he said, "Why did you put the *Prologue* at the end of the performance?" and I replied, "Prologue to next year." He slapped his hand to his forehead and said, "Do you expect me to remember everyone's work for a whole year?" And I said, "You don't have to remember the others, just remember me."

So in the end, in one of our last talks, since both of our minds were roaming over territory that was not just of the moment but close, Heaven and Hell emerged into the conversation, and John said, "Oh, not Heaven, please—all those feathers!"

In my garden all the Astilbe is dedicated to John Martin, who turned from red to pink to white in his lifetime and retained his grace and refinement right through Sunday, the ninth of December, 1984, which was the last day I saw him.

Richmond Times-Dispatch

Sybil Shearer Demonstrates ModernDance

By George Harris

The ambitious and energetic Junior Woman's Club of Ginter Park presented last night Sybil Shearer in a lecture-demonstration of modern art dancing. Miss Shearer's explanation of the ideals and mentality that every dancer should have. which coincided exactly with those of the musician. revealed much of this newer and higher point of view.

Although this discussion and demonstration emphasized the educational and technical side, the esthetic rose powerfully through it. as every technical process revealed beauty of movement and of the thought behind it. in both of which phases Miss Shearer is the real artist. Falls with tension and relaxation, sustained movement. broken movement with strange angles of elbows, knees and head. and vibration, were all imbued with beauty.

Symbols of dramatic thought were brought in to transform these movements into something more living. and then all this was brought to bear on the delineation of character. It was an unusual exhibition of the building up of an artistic thought. All but one number at the end was without music, and was so forceful in beauty and in individuality that each thing was a complete artistic entity and was of absorbing esthetic interest.

Addendum VI
From a letter to Katy Matheson who asked me about improvisation, written February 1, 1985.

I suppose anyone can put things together on the spur of the moment, and there will be reasons why the result will be good or bad. But improvisation, as I know it, means giving one's self up much like being in love.

Of course, I *realize* that you would like to make a scientific study, but I have never had too much respect for rules where creation is concerned, because if I don't tune in, it is as dry as dust for me, and I find much dance to be either as dry as dust or boring athleticism. Baryshnikov is one exception, because movement flows through him as I feel it flows through me; Astaire is another and Cagney—the last, perhaps the most moving because of what might have been. Any really fine performance is an improvisation, because you are giving yourself up anew.

People can see this, but they don't know why it happens. I think it happens because you have faith that you are loved. It is the gift to *understand* that movement is a language that is being *spoken* to you. It is *not* some kind of a *translation* of thoughts into another medium. And it doesn't have to be abstract or dance for dance sake or any of the other theories. It is talent—given. If you have it you use it. The fact that you can remember and repeat is like remembering a dream. It is not the everyday, cut-and-dry, rules and regulation world, but rather the direct mystical line to the source world. That is why a person who can improvise seems to be original, because the creative source is a never-ending fountain of movement for him.

The fact that my dances looked like improvisations, and my improvisations looked like dances was not just easy for me. I had to work to be in tune. All my technical facility and experimentation with movement was geared to the moment when I was able to be in touch with whatever it is that makes everything right.

Addendum VII
From "The Dance" by Walter Terry
New York Herald Tribune, **May 4, 1946.**

In nature, Sybil Shearer seems to find serenity, beauty, grandeur and normalcy, but in her probings of man, she has apparently found him shallow, aimless and close to the border of insanity. Her dance program yesterday afternoon at Times Hall indicated such findings, and she expressed them sometimes brilliantly, sometimes obscurely but never ineptly."

From:
"Four Recitals Here Called Indicative of Future of Dance"
by Walter Terry
New York Herald Tribune, **Sunday, May 19, 1946**

. . . Her program, almost equally divided between the foibles of man and the beauties of nature, already gives evidence of a trend of thought apparent in few dance programs. . . . Miss Shearer, in her dances, makes man petty and wasteful of his gifts, and in other dances exalts the order, the beauty and the richness of nature. . . . [She] is heading for a dance not concerned with homely events of perhaps passing interest, but dedicated to the pursuance and reve-lation of beauty and perfection in a mankind which recognizes the laws of nature.

THE LYONS REPUBLICAN & CLYDE TIMES.

LYONS, N. Y., THURSDAY, SEPTEMBER 12, 1940.

800 APPLAUDED SYBIL SHEARER IN FIRST CONCERT

Lyons Girl Sponsors Her Own Debut As Dancer; Originates Dances And Costumes

With very few exceptions the 800 people who saw Sybil Shearer dance at the Newark Theatre on Friday evening got their first introduction to what is known as esthetic or classical dancing.

Miss Shearer, personally, is lovely to look at. She is beautifully proportioned and appeared on the stage to have been moulded by an artist.

To the eye of the novice she cleverly and distinctly interpreted through body movements alone with only the aid of the piano accompaniments and intermissions played by Miss Eleanor Lawry, New York Concert pianist, the following program:

1. (a) Sarabande, Bach; a slow pre-classic dance form. The lady grows impatient waiting the arrival of her partner. (b) Passepie, they dance gaily together.

2. (*) "O Sleeper of the Land of Shadows, Wake! Expand!", William Blake, Bach.

3. (*) In Thee is Joy, Bach.

4. Intermezzo in B flat Major, Brahms; Intermezzo in C Major, Brahms; Eleanor Lawry.

5. (*) Nocturne, Chopin; "Beyond the bounds of their own self their senses cannot penetrate. As the tree knows not what is outside of its leaves and bark, And yet it drinks the summer joy, and fears the winter sorrow;" William Blake.

6. (*) Prophesy, Chopin. "A universe of fiery constellations in their brain; An earth of wintry woe beneath their feet;" William Blake.

7. Scherzo from the B Minor Sonata, Chopin; Etude in A flat Major, Chopin; Eleanor Lawry.

8. The Battle between Carnival and Lent, Old Flemish; A suite of dances suggested by the painting of Peiter Breugel, the elder, Flemish master of the 16th century. (a) Games at the fair. (b) In the Cathedral. (c) Street Dancing.

9. African Skrontch by Mail, Chauncey Morehouse; This creature aspires to be a jitterbug, but not wishing to appear in public before being perfect she has enrolled in a correspondence course. We discover her hard at work in the sanctuary of her own living room.

10. Flossy a Soubrette, Chopin, (*) These four dances attempt to express in movement, without the aid of pantomine, the idea indicated by the title and accompanying quotations.

Miss Shearer is not only a beautiful dancer who seemingly without effort is able to control every muscle of her body as she wishes and always most gracefully, but she is also an excellent actress as was borne out perhaps most markedly in her presentation of the African Skrontch dance. This number was so different from the entire program presenting as it did "The Jitterbug" as learned through a correspondence course with the aid of a victrola. Jitterbugging is a dance that we are all very familiar with and the entire audience enjoyed her humorous interpretation of it.

Miss Shearer created her own dances for the entire program and personally designed the costumes (and they were beautiful) for the first seven numbers.

Addendum VIII (b)

THE NEWARK, N. Y., NEWARK UNION-GAZETTE

COURIER, SEPTEMBER 12, 1940

SEPTEMBER 12, 1940

Miss Shearer Scores Hit

An appreciative Newark audience was given a rare treat, Friday night, in the dance recital by Sybil Shearer at the Capitol Theatre.

Miss Shearer's repertoire of original dances was a most ambitious one. Taking her themes from the classics in music, poetry and painting, she has created completely new dance forms and patterns.

Like Picasso and Matisse in their medium, Miss Shearer strikes out boldly in her initial concepts and in the technique of developing the study in movement. Showing complete understanding and mastery of the underlying art of the dance, and its more common sequences, Miss Shearer's talent has a quality of its own, making up in the element of surprise what it seems to lack in "continuity" to use the movie phrase.

This reviewer got the same reaction from several of the numbers as that given by the best German and British cinemas — a series of highly dramatic "stills" each a masterpiece in its own right, but somehow not completely integrated with the flow of the theme.

Miss Shearer's costumes, of her own design, demonstrated a broad versatility in this related art.

The presentation was graced by Miss Eleanor Lawry at the piano, who played an important part in making the recital an altogether delightful and memorable event.

Dancer Captures Acclaim of Crowd In Newark Recital

Returning to her former home town, Sybil Shearer, well known concert dancer won the acclaim of a Newark audience in an interpretive dance recital at the Capitol Theater last Friday.

Carrying the entire program alone, the former Newark girl demonstrated her skill as a consummate artist by holding the interest of the spectators throughout the recital.

Miss Shearer's poise and control, her suppleness and grace, are remarkable. In her presentations, all of which were original, she interpreted various themes with amazing perception of feeling and artistry. In addition, her cleverness in pantomime numbers demonstrated that she is outstanding as an actress as well as being talented as a dancer.

Designs for the dance costumes were also created by Miss Shearer and exquisitely reflected the theme interpreted.

Miss Eleanor Lawry, concert pianist of New York City, added to the enjoyment of the program with her piano accompaniment, and with several delightful piano interludes from Brahms and Chopin.

Addendum IX

April 22, 1942
50 Chestnut Street
Rochester, New York

Dear Miss Shearer,

The program given by you and Miss Choate at Franklin High School this morning was so thoroughly enjoyable that I feel impelled to tell you about it. Apart from the grace and remarkable technical ability shown by both of you, your voices and diction were delightful and you exercised good showmanship in the handling of high school pupils. You did not tell too much, you did not talk down to them, and you used plenty of humor without impairing the dignity of your work.

Many older members of your audience felt that they had learned something, too. Your program is very much worthwhile.

With best wishes,
Blanche S. Thompson

Dear Mrs. Johnson,

Sybil Shearer and Miss Choate gave us a beautiful demonstration. It was stirring to see how quickly and completely their "lesson" was grasped and shared by these little country children to whom the dance as an art is indeed a closed book. These two "pioneers," as Miss Choate called them, are indeed doing a superb educational job. I was only sorry we were unable to do more for them. They did so much for us. . . .

Addendum X
Letter from Ruth St. Denis

Dear truly, lovely Dancer!

I never have seen more exquisite movement in the human body—than your spirit-lifted gestures and your quite matterless runs! You seem to *think* yourself from one side of the stage to the other!

Deep gratitude for a revelation of apparently effortless dance!

Affectionately,
Ruth St. Denis

Sybil Shearer Seen in Debut As Solo Dancer

Young Artist's Program at Carnegie Chamber Hall Is One of Varied Moods

By Walter Terry

An exciting debut took place last evening at the Carnegie Chamber Music Hall when young Sybil Shearer danced her way into the top-notch rank of American dance artists. Miss Shearer has been seen in the Humphrey-Weidman programs and also with the Agnes de Mille company, but this marked her bow as a solo dancer, and the tremendous difficulties of varrying a dance performance single-handed bothered her not at all. She has a style of movement unlike that of any other dancer, and this freshness of articulation makes her a constantly absorbing artist. Her technical equipment enables her to reach the heights of virtuosity, for her balance alone would make a Russian ballerina assoluta green with envy. This virtuosity, however, is not used to create applause-getting tricks, but is made to serve as a dramatic accent on the theme at hand.

The opening "Sarabande and Passepied" were presented in the traditional style, but flavored with a slight personal characterization and the "O Sleeper of the Land of Shadows, Wake! Expand!" was a beautiful exposition of the quality of reverence. Quick of motion and released in spirit was "In Thee Is Joy," a dance which brought to the fore Miss Shearer's breadth and ease of movement. The quality of "Nocturne" is difficult to desribe, for it is a dance of quiet exploration, of subdued self-appraisal. And "Prophesy" on the other hand, was stirringly dramatic. Miss Shearer's body was flooded with dynamic energy, to the point of explosion. Here again the wealth of newly designed movement and of unbelievable body control made for stimulating dance.

For her closing solos, the dancer offered "In the Cool of the Garden," "In the Field" and "In a Vacuum." "In the Field" was a dance of rare beauty, a stylization of the labor rhythms of sowing seed. In the center of the dance was an interlude which seemed to be an incantation for fruitfulness, an almost forgotten ceremony to celebrate the magic of growth. The closing dance "In a Vacuum" was one of the funniest things I have ever seen. The dancer's arms, legs and body flew about in split-second rhythm, running the gamut of impossible positions. This dance of intense aimlessness with no theme nor characterization, was an example of pure kinetic slap-stick, and there is nothing funnier in this world than a giggling musculature.

Sybil Shearer's choreography, as well as her dancing, was splendid. There were occasional flaws as far as dance structures were concerned and moments that could have done with more dramatic accent, but these are inconsequential in the face of Miss Shearer's dance achievements, for she is an exciting dancer and an artist who is surely destined to contribute richly to American dance. Mari Harding, pianist, shared the program with Miss Shearer and also played the dancer's accompaniments. The program will be repeated this evening.

THE NEW YORK TIMES,
WEDNESDAY, OCTOBER 22, 1941.

SYBIL SHEARER SEEN IN A DANCE RECITAL

She Makes Local Solo Debut at Carnegie Chamber Music Hall

By JOHN MARTIN

There is no question that Sybil Shearer, who made her local solo debut last night at the Carnegie Chamber Music Hall, is a talented dancer. In advance her performance was perhaps of more interest than the average debut recital, for she was for several seasons a prominent member of the Humphrey-Weidman company and for the last two seasons has been appearing with Agnes de Mille.

Even those who have watched her closely for the last five or six years, however, must have found things in her work last night that surprised them, as well as a few that disappointed them. Her technique is of a high order and besides mere facility she has a beautiful quality of sustained movement on those rare occasions when she makes use of it. She also has a flair for costuming that is most unusual among the young recitalists, and she can extract comedy out of movement with ease when she turns her attention in that direction.

But more important than any of these things is the unconventionality of her approach, which is unstrained and obviously altogether native to her way of thinking. Sometimes, as in her opening "Sarabande" and "Passepied," she works outside her own medium and is, truth to tell, not particularly interesting, but when she is entirely herself she has real quality. (in spite of inappropriate music), called "And Prophesy," her movement achieves a tinge of creative madness that promises the existence of a realm of her talent which, though filled with danger, is capable of genuine power.

Sentimentality constitutes Miss Shearer's greatest peril. She creates too much in the over-lyrical vein of the recital dancing of fifteen years ago to be considered a mature artist at the moment. Quite the weakest number of the evening attempted to couple Chopin with William Blake (not to mention a jeweled necklace) in a mystical "Nocturne." Nevertheless, through it all gleams the light of a definite and an original talent, and there is every reason to watch and wait with interest for the time when it really finds itself.

The program last night was a joint one with Mari Harding, pianist, who played solos by Bach-Siloti, Bach-Busoni, Beethoven, Brahms and Scriabine. The two young artists will repeat the performance this evening.

Addendum XI (c)

NEW YORK HERALD TRIBUNE,
SUNDAY, OCTOBER 26, 1941

THE WEEK'S DEBUTS

By WALTER TERRY

A pretentious premiere flopped. An unpretentious debut rang the bell. These two events occurred last week when the Ballet Russe de Monte Carlo proved with "Saratoga" that a bad ballet is still bad no matter how lavish the production, and when Sybil Shearer bowed in as a solo artist at the Carnegie Chamber Music Hall and proved that really fine dancing, simply presented, can be theatrically exciting.

Without benefit of elaborate staging, Sybil Shearer offered her debut program at the Carnegie Chamber Music Hall last week and, all by herself made her evening of dance far more exciting than the opulent "Saratoga." Miss Shearer has been seen about in the companies of Agnes de Mille and of Doris Humphrey and Charles Weidman. Now, as a solo artist, she has climbed to a position of prominence along with the very few young American dancers of major importance. Her dance style is distinctly her own, and this serves to highlight her particular personality and to give freshness and strength to the themes she dances. Her technical equipment is something to marvel at, and her balance alone, with its quality of suspended action, will make you gasp. This virtuosity is dramatic rather than acrobatic, for Miss Shearer uses it to give special accent to a phrase, added significance to a dance characterization.

A Dancer's Range of Action

Essentially a lyric dancer, Sybil Shearer can, nevertheless, win effect in highly dramatic and comic dances. Her "And Prophesy" is almost maniacal in its savage display of physical and emotional outbursts, and in contrast "Nocturne" reveals through serene movement, the quiet analysis of a girl who seeks to explore her own emotions. There is nothing particularly profound about "In Thee Is Joy," but the breadth of the movements, the sense of the spirit's release in joy are strongly communicable, leaving an audience refreshed. Miss Shearer is also a comedian of great ability. She doesn't mug and she doesn't pantomime, but she makes her quips with her muscles. "In a Vacuum" is one of the funniest things I have ever seen. It is pure kinetic humor; it is "Hellzapoppin" distilled into a single dance.

Sybil Shearer has launched her career in splendid fashion, and few of her contemporaries can match her skill, but that does not mean that she can be content. As she develops, her themes should develop in scope, and I think that her movements could be filled with greater dynamic shading without becoming exaggerated. She must guard against an overuse of her beautifully expressive hands. A dancer relies on breath control for innumerable dramatic effects, and Miss Shearer could make fuller use of breath-timing to give pulse to a phrase of action. Even including these minor and temporary flaws, Sybil Shearer's program of last week was exciting dance and far more exciting theater than the gala prestige premiere of the wealthy Russian ballet's "Saratoga."

Addendum XI (d)

THE AMERICAN DANCER

NOVEMBER, 1941

SYBIL SHEARER, *Carnegie Chamber Music Hall*, October 21.

Sybil Shearer has already appeared hereabouts in various group concerts but this performance was actually her formal debut. She has impressed previously, as a very capable dancer possessing that all too rare asset, a big sense of humour. On this occasion, however, and regrettably, she chose to be more formal and stressed the serious side of her work. She moves fluidly and is both strong and lyrical, using her hands especially well. She has creative ability both in her dances and in her costumes which were effective and suitable. One number, *In Thee Is Joy*, was a joy to watch because of the great vitality in the movement. But *And Prophesy* was one of the most thrilling solo dances I have ever seen. The originality of the expressive movement and its whole dramatic conception, to say nothing of its magnificent execution, marks Miss Shearer as a very talented young artist.

Addendum XII

The New York Times
SUNDAY, JUNE 14, 1942.

THE DANCE: YEAR'S AWARDS

Season's Laurels to Antony Tudor and Sybil Shearer

By JOHN MARTIN

THIS annual period of selecting the best this and that in various fields of art has brought grief in several worlds of creative endeavor, but certainly not in the dance. The Drama Critic's Circle decided to forego any award in the theatre, and the Pulitzer committee followed suit. The newly formed Music Critic's Circle made one award and decided not to make a second one which it had hoped to make. But in the dance things have been up and doing, and the season, besides being one of the fullest on record, has also been of unusual seriousness of purpose and distinction of accomplishment. This one-man committee of awards, accordingly, has an embarrassment of riches to choose from.

"Pillar of Fire"

The selection of the finest composition of the season is an obvious one—Antony Tudor's "Pillar of Fire," produced by the Ballet Theatre in its Spring season. The work has been reviewed and re-reviewed in these columns so recently that further detailed discussion of it would only be repetitious. It is nevertheless, an important work that may well be discussed as of historic moment in the development of the ballet as time goes on It marks not only the maturity of Tudor's talents, but his unmistakable position as a leader of the art from now on.

Whether he stands on any self-conscious platform of reform or not, he has enunciated a policy as radical as that of Fokine some thirty-five years ago, and has just as ably proved its tenableness.

To "Pillar of Fire," then, the season's award, for whatever it is worth.

Season's No. 1 Debutante

The other annual award which traditionally is made in these columns is for the most promising debutante. In a season with more than the usual number of debutantes, Sybil Shearer seems to fit that designation to a nicety. For those who have watched Miss Shearer for the past seven years or so—with Doris Humphrey and Charles Weidman, with Agnes de Mille, with the short-lived Theatre Dance Company—it is not a surprise that she is a talented dancer, but now that she has actually stepped out on her own, the idea takes on new and concrete form.

Technically she is beautifully equipped, well beyond most dancers of her experience. Not only is her body under admirable control and capable of handling difficult problems with ease, but there is also an inherent beauty in her movement, and that is a thing that most young dancers never manage to achieve. Movement for itself apparently has value for Miss Shearer, for she is able to create in its terms along wholly original lines and in response to inner direction. Since she is gifted with imagination almost to a fault, she is able sometimes to touch upon a kind of creative madness that, whatever its dangers for her, contains elements of great power and communicative vision. She has enormous concentration, characterizes well, and can play comedy to the hilt. For good measure, she has also an excellent sense of costume, which is by no means a common gift in the dance world.

In her first New York recital she had manifestly not reached her potential level, and, indeed, it would have been unnatural if she had. Much of her work was still experimental and missed fire; occasionally she was vague and once in a while oversentimental. Nevertheless, the total impression was a positive one, an assuring one. With that clear fanaticism that belongs to artists, accompanied, as it not always is, by the saving grace of a capacity for hard work, Miss Shearer should certainly be heard from. To her, unhesitatingly, the laurels.

Addendum XIII

P. O. Box 147
LEE, MASSACHUSETTS

August 22nd, 1942.

Dear Sybil:

Your letter and check is deeply appreciated—in fact I was genuinely touched by both the expressions in the letter and by the gift.

No, it's not as perfect as it seems, but thank God, most of the headaches are mine, and the pupils and the public are getting fully what I wanted them to have. And in undertaking this project, I knew that I was taking on many ordeals—and I am having them!

From my side, it was a privilege, in my small way, to be associated with you at the beginning of what <u>has</u> to be a very great career. You have the unmistakable marks of true greatness, and I salute you.

Cordially and gratefully,

Shawn

Notes on Dances in the DVD

In this first volume of her autobiography, Sybil Shearer writes of her early years in New York and ends with her move to Chicago in the fall of 1942. Only one of the dances Ms. Shearer chose for the DVD dates from this period. *In a Vacuum* was performed in her 1941 debut at Carnegie Music Hall, but *O Lost* first appears in her program in 1943. *No Peace on Earth* appears in 1947.

The suite of four jazz dances (titled elsewhere as *Salute to Old Friends*) was made in 1948 when, as Shearer noted, "Jazz first entered my consciousness." However, it honors four people who were already important in her life by 1942: Doris Humphrey, Agnes de Mille, Walter Terry, and John Martin.

The untitled opening dance, to selections from Moussorgsky's *Pictures from an Exhibition,* did not appear on Ms. Shearer's programs until 1949.

All of the dances on the DVD were filmed later in Ms. Shearer's studio at Northbrook, Illinois, by Helen Balfour Morrison, who was Shearer's artistic collaborator from 1943 to 1984. Two pianists, Jeanne Panot and Marion Hall, accompanied Ms. Shearer's programs in the 1940s and 1950s, and it is not clear which tape recordings were used for these films.

James Cunningham, who handled all the technical work for Ms. Shearer, has stated:

> "Most of the dances were filmed in the last half of the 1950s at the Studio. Robert Oakes Jordan and I recorded the sound from records as Sybil danced, using the Oricon System to record on a magnetic stripe on the film, in sync as she danced. Some, like the Brubeck number [*Salute to Old Friends:* Agnes de Mille], were filmed first without sound, and later Sybil had

somebody lay the sound to the mag stripe on the film. They did this several times until she felt that it 'worked.'"

This explains why the film or music occasionally seems to "jump" to get back in sync, even though each dance was filmed in a single "take" from start to finish.

Fortunately, Ms. Shearer was able to complete the production of this DVD before her death in November 2005.

Dances:
1. Untitled (Moussorgsky)
2. *O Lost* (Chopin)
3. *In a Vacuum* (Moussorgsky)
4. *No Peace on Earth* (Scriabin)
5. *Salute to Old Friends,* Doris Humphrey
   ("I Don't Wanna Be Kissed By Anyone But You,"
   performed by Miles Davis)
6. *Salute to Old Friends,* Walter Terry
   ("St. Louis Blues," performed by Count Basie group)
7. *Salute to Old Friends,* Agnes de Mille
   ("Stompin' for Mili," performed by Dave Brubeck Quartet)
8. *Salute to Old Friends,* John Martin
   ("I Cried for You," performed by Benny Goodman Quintet)

Permissions for music and photographs appear in the DVD itself.